The Tempest *as Mystery Play*

The Tempest
as Mystery Play

UNCOVERING RELIGIOUS
SOURCES OF SHAKESPEARE'S
MOST SPIRITUAL WORK

by
GRACE R.W. HALL

McFarland & Company, Inc., Publishers
Jefferson, North Carolina, and London

Library of Congress Cataloguing-in-Publication Data

Hall, Grace R. W., 1921–
 The tempest as mystery play : uncovering religious sources of
Shakespeare's most spiritual work / by Grace R. W. Hall.
  p. cm.
 Includes bibliographical references and index.
 ISBN 0-7864-0631-3 (library binding : 50# alkaline paper) ∞
 1. Shakespeare, William, 1564–1616 — Tempest. 2. Shakespeare,
William, 1564–1616 — Religion. 3. Shakespeare, William,
1564–1616 — Tempest — Sources. 4. Christian drama, English —
History and criticism. 5. Christianity and literature — England —
History — 17th century. 6. Spiritual life in literature. 7. Bible —
In literature. 8. Mysteries and miracle plays, English — History
and criticism. I. Title.
PR2833H28 1999
822.3'3 — dc21   99-39100
                                                                          CIP

British Library Cataloguing-in-Publication data are available

Manufactured in the United States of America

McFarland & Company, Inc., Publishers
 Box 611, Jefferson, North Carolina 28640
  www.mcfarlandpub.com

For
my wonderful children,
Brent, Pamela, Craig, Gordon
and their Dad, Eldon;
they have greatly enriched my life.

Acknowledgments

The author is indebted to her mother, Grace Gleason White, who enhanced her childhood experiences with à propos quotations from Shakespeare and who handed her a Bible when she was ten, advising her to read it every morning. Dean Bertha Munro, a college dean and literature professor, offered Shakespeare summer courses for high school students and later inspired the author as a college chemistry major, taking world, English, and Bible literature courses, who later became a physics graduate student. Great appreciation is also due Dr. Wylie Sypher, my literature graduate school professor, for sharing his encyclopedic knowledge and scholarship through his teaching and his books.

Appreciation is due Heather Dubrow, who graciously read and evaluated an early version of a chapter, and to Glenn White, who was the first to read the entire manuscript. Particular appreciation is due Dr. R. Chris Hassel, who wrote extensive notes on an early version of my manuscript and suggested a direction for further research.

I was privileged to have the services of the director of the group who developed the Apollo Guidance Computer — my spouse, Eldon — in setting up a computer and printer in my office. He also responded promptly to calls for programming, backup services, and drop-off transportation at Boston University's Mugar Library, where parking is impossible.

Contents

Preface

Other critical writings on *The Tempest* have focused on sources, structure, themes, meaning, mood, and hidden parts waiting for discovery; all have provided an inspiration, a challenge and a sure foundation on which to build my own study.

All quotations of the play are taken from *The Tempest*, edited by Frank Kermode, Arden Shakespeare Series, 6th edition (Cambridge, Massachusetts: Harvard University Press, 1958). Quotations from Shakespeare's other plays are taken from *The Complete Works of William Shakespeare*, edited by W. J. Craig, The Oxford Shakespeare (London: Oxford University Press, n.d.). All biblical quotations are taken from the King James Bible, except where otherwise indicated or where they occur as parts of quotations from other sources. All OED quotations are taken from *The Oxford English Dictionary*, 2d edition, James A. H. Murray et al., editors (Oxford University Press, reprinted with corrections, 1991).

Introduction

As intricately woven as a medieval tapestry, *The Tempest* portrays humanity in a fabric that encompasses both the heavens and the earth. A great variety of thematic threads contribute to the complexity of its fabric and make it sparkle. Its airiness, overarching beneficence, and peaceful resolution qualify it as a vision. In harmony and organic unity it is the equal of any great symphony; its tempestuous and cacophonic sounds are stilled as its airy songs and solemn music prevail in a harmonious close. Whether viewed as a tapestry or heard as a great symphony, *The Tempest* is wonderful — and the qualities that make it so wonderful have been hard to find in any work so far considered as a possible source.

The Tempest's interpreters have searched far and wide for sources, unearthing literary bits and pieces in earlier works and cultural proclivities in historical documents. In marginal readings critics have claimed correspondences between certain sources and a variety of elements in the play, but those correspondences fail to produce evidence that any source provided a basic fabric or a plot-line. Like other marginal readings they do not establish meaning or unite the whole. Nor has any document yet been identified which is comprehensive, harmonious, or visionary enough to be claimed as a basic source for the play. As late as 1995 in his discussion of work in Shakespeare's plays Maurice Hunt wrote:

> [A]n irony of *The Tempest* is that a short play of remarkable lyrical ease should be so focused on industry. The symmetrical craftsmanship of the play, and most notably, its apparently *sourceless status* belie Greenblatt's portrait of an opportunistic Shakespeare stealing the labor of others [emphasis added].[1]

In his Preface (prefixed to an octavo edition in 10 volumes, 1790) of Shakespeare's plays, Malone advised the continuation of a search for source, setting forth a goal that has not been fulfilled to this day:

When our poet's entire library shall have been discovered, and the fables of all his plays traced to their *original source*, when every contemporary allusion shall have been pointed out, and every obscurity elucidated, then, and not till then, let the accumulation of notes be complained of [emphasis added].[2]

Since a better understanding of Shakespeare's emphases and meanings in many of his other plays have evolved from comparison with their obvious sources, further searches for sources of *The Tempest* are justified. However, this study did not begin as a search for a particular source, but as a response to the impressions made by the play's sounds, particular words, emotional cruxes, ("ye elves" and dissolution speeches), and characters. From the beginning, the study proceeded in the modes suggested by Bethell, Coleridge, and John Russell Brown. Bethell pointed out that the "literary critic ... reads a poem to reach the poet's mind, not by formal logic or the regular inductive method, but by a general sensitiveness to impressions, catching a hint here and there, allowing his emotions to be stirred and directed."[3] Coleridge claimed, "The power of poetry is, by a single word perhaps, to instill that energy into the mind, which compels the imagination to produce the picture."[4] Brown, concerned with performance, asserted that Shakespeare's plays "are recreated in our imaginations, drawing on whatever we have experienced or dreamed before that time of performance."[5] As Samuel Johnson asserted, "Every reader should be his own commentator, which is merely another way of saying that everyone should be able to form an independent judgment as to characters and events."[6] This study is the kind of independent evaluation that Johnson recommended. As suggested by Malone in 1790, it investigates some contemporary allusions and elucidates some obscurities.

In this study discovery came in part through resonances. As I read *The Tempest* "to reach the poet's mind,"[7] echoes resounded from great depths, suggesting what Righter called "hidden dimensions" and likened to "an iceberg," which "conceals most of its bulk beneath the surface."[8] The resonances set up sympathetic vibrations which intoned another text, the Bible. They accord with what Bethell calls "the audience's ability to respond spontaneously and unconsciously on more than one plane of attention at the same time," the "principle of multiconsciousness."[9] Although *The Tempest* may be classified as a romance, multiconsciously it is much, much more.

This book, then, is an attempt to record my impressions and the pictures my imagination has created from the energy instilled by the many words, numbers, and phrases in *The Tempest* and to describe the associations of characters with space and time, associations evoked by a structure that various words suggested. However, lest the fabric of my vision be criticized as baseless, I have attempted to identify both the notes that are sounded and the origins of the echoes. I have also made an effort (to use another metaphor) to follow the thematic threads running through the fabric to show how they contribute to the unity and meaning of the play. As Bethell suggested, "There is a good deal of disentangling to be done in order to see what is really there."[10] Some reweaving will be attempted.

The response to resonances involved close readings, engaging particulars to clarify senses, unearth new dimensions, resolve some enigmas, and justify this interpretation. Consciousness of a relationship among the particulars effected an integrated vision of the play. My pursuit of a vision of *The Tempest* complies with the method recommended by Bethel: "The critic's task of abstraction, is not the isolating of a playwright's 'message,' but a purely clinical analysis, only to be justified by the fuller response to the play as a whole, which should follow a close and leisured examination of its constituent parts."[11]

To validate my sometimes subconscious impressions I examined words for their double, treble, and obsolete senses, particularly those meanings which were extant in the Elizabethan and Jamesian reigns. The awarenesses induced in early readings were heightened as I discovered these older word senses. I also explored resonance that was induced by similar word sounds, paronomasia. (An unusual example will be discussed at length in Chapter VII.)

Some words and phrases appeared luminous, and in the pages of another text they retained that glow, almost as if they had been highlighted for easy location. The lucent words suggested a particular harmony with the Bible. Although more prosaic, the numerics and nomenclature also pointed to Shakespeare's use of the Bible as fabric and its story as plot. Shakespeare's language in *The Tempest* not only intones a source, but a source which provides both a plot and similar characters.

Although no one has identified the Bible as a basic source for *The Tempest*, a considerable number of critics have identified biblical elements in his drama. Amongst them are Battenhouse, Bethell, Bryant, Burgess, Coleman, Hirsch, Knight, Milward, Morris, Noble, Paulson, Rosten, Shaheen, Sims, Warburton, and Wilson. Warner wrote that Bishop Warburton "was the first of the long line of clergymen who made Shakespeare the companion of the Old and New Testaments."[12] Noble compared several biblical passages with Shakespeare's text, but he found that "scriptural interest is small." He identified Ariel as a "Biblical name," but found Ariel "independent of any Biblical model."[13] Coleman identified Shakespeare as a Christian philosopher and claimed

> that Shakespeare was certainly not only a thinker and a Godly man in the broadest, truest sense, but a discerner and purveyor of heavenly light, of something far above ecclesiasticism, clericalism, creed, dogma, or doctrine. In his day, the Scriptures had been for the first time, over the objection of the established church, made available to the people. ... Shakespeare in fact brought the Bible to the theater.[14]

Coleman was less concerned with exact biblical quotations than with the biblical sense of specific Shakespearean passages.[15]

Although Wilson did not point to the Bible as source, he acknowledged Shakespeare's use of its themes. Citing *Cymbeline, The Winter's Tale*, and *Pericles*, he wrote, "Reconciliation and forgiveness formed the theme of all four plays, but in *The Tempest* above all they formed the atmosphere of serenity, grave benignity, peace."[16]

In an insightful book with abundant documentation from various plays, Burgess proved Shakespeare's use and knowledge of the Bible. He cited parallel passages and common themes. He compared biblical and Shakespearean tragedy, and pointed to the numerous references to divinity as well as Shakespeare's use of biblical names and character types. However, his findings in and references to *The Tempest* are very limited. He recognized the word "Providence" as a reference to God and acknowledged the similarities between the account of Paul's shipwreck and the first scene of *The Tempest*. He associated the "cloud-capped towers" speech with I Peter 3:10–11. His references to the history plays are far more numerous. Nevertheless, he showed that throughout his plays Shakespeare was not only aware of Scripture, but had so absorbed it, that he "breathed" it into his work.[17]

Responding to resonances in the initial stages of this study, I focused on the Bible as source. However, I soon began another search to find one or more intermediary sources from which Shakespeare might have drawn his imagery and vocabulary and in which he would have found a selectivity and condensation of Scripture, one that also would have been familiar to a seventeenth century audience. The sources resurrected, the Mystery Plays, will be noted in Chapter II and discussed at length in Chapter V.

The Tempest harmonizes with the Bible and its derivatives, the Mystery Plays. This study will attempt to show that the title, introductory scene, characters, time references, nomenclature, the emphasis on hearing, and dénouement of *The Tempest* suggest a biblical source. The play has elicited from its evaluators such comments as "mystical"; yet its use of biblical imagery, characterization, and time and its condensation of biblical history with its concept of a "split" in the human race and a means to reconciliation, often as they were interpreted and acted in the Mystery Plays, have not been fully explored. To conclude that the *The Tempest* is influenced by biblical writ and the Mystery Plays is consistent with Northrop Frye's affirmation:

> As a reflection of its own time, a play may reflect many things, including the general framework of assumptions and values and moral standards that Shakespeare's audience could be assumed to have brought into the theatre with them. This framework at the time would have had a general Christian shape.[18]

Shakespeare's use of magical elements and mythological gods and goddesses and his apparently mortal dénouement have provided some uncertainties for critics and interpreters. Focusing on these features distracts from the deeply spiritual nature of the play so evident in its resonances, and from the part a spirit, Ariel, performs in awakening the minds and consciousness of the play's characters, and in the process, no doubt, awakening the minds of Shakespeare's audiences. This interpretation admits nonbiblical elements in the play but finds them peripheral, parallel, or transient, rather than central. However, once Shakespeare's sources and his plots have been identified, their relationship to the magical elements and the gods and goddesses can be established.

In "Recovering Elizabethan Staging: A Reconsideration of the Evidence," Dessen's attempt to establish what "original playgoers actually saw when they watched a given scene,"[19] was disappointing. We know, however, what they *heard*; the words are before us. Thus the images the words might conjure up and the memories they might resurrect should afford more evidence of the early playgoers' experience than less determinate visual impressions.

This book reexamines the language of the play and the resonances it induces. Primarily concerned with the play's purpose and meaning, it attempts to uncover imagistic, thematic, and structural links and character likenesses with the Bible and its derivatives, the Mystery Plays and the 1559 *Book of Common Prayer*. It proposes to show that words, phrases, imagery, character portrayals, and time concepts used in sixteenth century and early seventeenth century popular drama and rituals are so pervasive in *The Tempest* that Shakespeare's play was intended to "mean" what *they* meant.

Recently, along with the questioning of critics' ability to determine Shakespeare's meaning, a shift in critical perspective (which affects meaning) has taken place. Hawkes proposed a different perspective on meaning, "meaning by." In "That Shakespearean Rag" (1986) Hawkes "questioned whether we could have any genuine access to final, authoritative or essential meanings in respect of Shakespeare's plays. Implicitly and explicitly, it put the case, that, like it or not, all we can ever do is use Shakespeare as a powerful element in specific ideological strategies."[20] Hawkes' later essays "aim to probe some further implications of that position.... Traditionally, critics, producers, actors and audiences of Shakespeare have assumed, with Ophelia, that the 'meaning' of each play is bequeathed to it *ab initio* and lies — artfully concealed perhaps — within its text. Each account, or production of the play, then offers to discover and lay hold of this meaning, hoisting it triumphantly like buried treasure, into view."[21] The validity of Hawkes' "discovered" meanings "dramatically presented" depends on how carefully they have been researched and how closely they follow the text.

In his description of the shift in perspective, Dessen essentially opposed Hawkes' denial of *ab initio* meaning. Focusing on the history of the adaptation of Shakespeare's texts and the beginning of criticism, Dessen emphasized the importance of Shakespeare's words as the locale of meanings. He described the way in which meanings have been reconstructed by recent Shakespeareans who

> conceptualize both the object and the activity of their work in rhetorical and cultural terms. From their perspective, the interpretation of Shakespeare consists not so much in uncovering the meanings already embedded in a more or less stable and self-explanatory text, but in constructing meanings which have themselves been provisionally constructed and reconstructed in socially specific and ideologically motivated ways.[22]

By placing "embedded" meanings in opposition to critical "provisionally constructed" meanings, Dessen questions the latter's viability. With his concept of embedded meanings, he also contradicts Hawkes' refutation of *ab initio* meanings. The attribution of meaning should rest on the textual evidence supporting it; the presentation should rest on both the textual evidence and the play's artistic unity. This study relies heavily on Shakespeare's words and the multiple senses available to him as the carriers of his meaning. It uses the societal, cultural, and religious climate to validate meanings embedded in the text.

To further confirm my impressions and to discover the play's organic unity and its meaning, I undertook considerable research in both sixteenth and seventeenth century documents and critical studies of the play. Some of the images woven into the fabric, familiar enough to sixteenth and seventeenth century playgoers, are not likely to readily divulge their significance to audiences of today. As Wilson suggested, they, too, invest the play with more meaning then we are consciously aware of.[23] Like Caliban, we are wondrously affected by the sounds, but we do not perceive all that they mean because much is lost to us, not only through changes in word sense, but through unfamiliarity with sixteenth and seventeenth century culture. The experience of listeners and readers attests to the wholeness, beauty, and effectiveness of the play's fabric and its symphonic tone, and one may enjoy the playing of *The Tempest* without apprehending the mystery concealed in it or comprehending its meaning. But without an analysis of the intricacies of the play and an examination of its imagery, time references, themes, characters, and structure and comparison with its probable sources, twentieth century readers and audiences may miss the values inherent in the play and the excellence and comprehensiveness of Shakespeare's artistry. Therefore, a thorough analysis has been undertaken in this book. No interpretation can include every element of the play, but the discoveries I made in examining obsolete word senses, identifying Shakespeare's use of Mystery Play modalities and character types, tracing continuities, identifying plots and a structure, and incorporating clues in Shakespeare's introductory scene and dénouement led me to a unified vision of the play and a sense of its meaning.

In an historical review of adaptations and eighteenth century theory Marsden concluded, "Critics and playwrights define his [Shakespeare's] genius in terms of his words, focusing on characters in relation to his diction, language, and imagery. Such a change indicates a stress on text rather than performance, on defining the literary work in terms of its language rather than its plot."[24] Meaning depends on text, which involves all the aspects Marsden defines, as well as on structure and plot, which are not related only to performance. All aspects of the play are part of its artistic unity, which surpasses dramatic rules of any kind including those of time and place. Meaning is the gift from an inspired poet, who, seeing whole, has a vision, and uses language and presents characters who offer humankind socially useful knowledge and a picture of life that makes other living meaningful.

This study proposes that Shakespeare appealed not only to his era's knowledge of the Bible and its derivatives, but also to its exposure to old and new concepts of the heavens. The spatial effects and the atmosphere which Shakespeare seeks to "set ... in the mind" are accomplished in part through his adaptation and transposition of a cosmic model, the Ptolemaic, which was very familiar to Renaissance persons. Many references in the text, taken together, produce a picture of that model. The model provides a real framework for a spatial array of characters with whom Shakespearean characters share qualities. It also provides a structure, unique to this play, by means of which plot, time, characters, and themes can be integrated. Knight's claim for the tragedies that an atmosphere is created by a "set of correspondences which relate to each other independently of the time sequence of the story"[25] must be expanded in dealing with *The Tempest*. In *The Tempest* Shakespeare integrated atmosphere *and* time *and* characters, creating a unified inclusive vision.

While some words and phrases suggest a real space model, others bring to remembrance biblical characters. After a close reading of the play it became apparent to me that some of Shakespeare's characters figure biblical persons even though Shakespeare does not use biblical names. *The Tempest* is unified temporally and spatially because Shakespeare's figurative characters belong to different time periods. The spatial-temporal array of figurative characters along with the action and key words and phrases invoke the comparable texts, creating an atmosphere of an all-engulfing time in which all other times and representatives of the play's contemporary society move. Chapter IV in this book is devoted to disclosing textual references which helped uncover multiple character identities. Chapter VII is devoted to describing the space-time continuum and the position of the characters in it.

What has been missed in critiques of the play is not the unity and spatial sense, but the source texts which provide continuity, themes, and imagery, and the real model which Shakespeare transposed and used to arrange time and persons in an ordered space-time pattern. Thus I have attempted to show how Shakespeare intertwined his many concerns to create a fabric whose many scenes reveal the greatest mystery of all time and man's proper place in the universe.

This study is concerned with the complexity and meaning of the play, whereas, according to Greenblatt, Cultural Poetics deals with the peripheral or marginal.[26] Nevertheless, this study involves contextual works which validate the findings. Contemporaneous events from which its audience would have derived meaning were investigated. Rituals and festivals of the sixteenth and seventeenth centuries, the English Church and the 1559 *Book of Common Prayer* were found to have a significant influence on both text and timing of performance. Word usages in those documents were found to concur with the senses evolving from the overtones.

After examining the play's constituent parts, identifying multiple word meanings, comparing religious documents and practices, and studying thematic continuities, I made an extensive examination of critical scholarship. The playing of *The Tempest* with its many variations has evoked a multiplicity of responses from audiences and critics. But there is something missing in much of the criticism — something that can be understood in terms again, of resonance. Since the quality of a sound is determined by the number of overtones present and their respective intensities, the complexity is in part determined by the induced resonances. In order for such sympathetic vibrations to augment or enhance the words of Shakespeare's text, a proper resounding medium is necessary. More importantly, the fundamental must be heard and its source recognized, since if it is not, it cannot effect the overtones that were intended and thus expand the text. Some fundamentals and their overtones have been unheard or unremarked in critiques of the play. Shakespeare's juxtaposition of the noise of a tempest, sometimes base, and the sound of music, sometimes airy, in *The Tempest* has inspired a host of critics with as much diversity in interpretation of the play as there are sounds in that romance. Some critics (see e.g. Coleridge, Knight, Sypher, and Wilson) note the play's unity and emphasize mood and wonder, avoiding an in-depth analysis of its components. They have been satisfied with the mystical aspects and intuitive sense of the play and leave the details to the more practical minded. On the other hand, some critics (see e.g. Breight, Still, Wagner), responding to the individual notes which Shakespeare struck in the play, have offered particularized interpretations which vary widely since the echoes in their minds have been induced by different notes.

Critical scholarship provided a basis for comparison and for testing my vision of *The Tempest*. In some cases this study shows specifically how Shakespeare achieved the effects experienced by other critics. In some cases it amplifies or extends the criticism and evaluations of the play. In some cases it differentiates between other critics' focuses and interpretations and those in this study. Particularly relevant to this interpretation are the suggestions of critics like Chambers and Clark who have attempted to identify the emphases of the plays with seasons in Shakespeare's life or a developing vision. Thus, several of these critics find in the late plays a changed, more subdued Shakespeare and use such words as "spiritual" or "conversion," "faith" and "joy." Chambers found that a "profound change in spiritual mood ... underlies the transition from tragedy to romance."[27]

Clark wrote:

> Studying Shakespeare's history from the supernatural plays alone, we surmise that he embarked upon life with all the easy optimism of youth; that he soon came face to face with obstacles, temptations, and difficulties which sobered his lightheartedness; that, as he battled with all the disillusionment and disappointment which seem to be the inevitable concomitants of human life he found himself the prey of cynicism and despair; and finally, that he passed through the valley, and came once more to the peace and calm of a new faith and a new confidence in a benign Providence.[28]

Of *The Tempest* Clark wrote, "The last drama itself is suggestively allegorical of the experience of his closing period." He finds Shakespeare's imagination "under the control of belief, in the reins of a steadfast faith and a mature joy."[29]

Whether changes in the plays can be associated with actual events in Shakespeare's life is debatable. The plays may instead form a broad pattern investigating the follies of humankind and earthly government in the comedy, tragedy, and history plays, with the late plays recovering, reweaving and strengthening "The bonds of heaven" which were "slipp'd, dissolv'd, and loos'd" (*Troilus and Cressida* 5.2.153). The differences and emphases remain apparent.

Some critics see correspondences between Shakespeare and Prospero and believe Shakespeare played the part of Prospero in *The Tempest*. They associate Prospero's rejection of magic and his return to Milan as Duke with Shakespeare's departure for Stratford. However, those who equate Shakespeare's demise as an actor with Prospero's breaking his staff and drowning his book and assert that Shakespeare is avowing his intent to leave the theatre omit two parts of the equation: the nature of the dukedom Shakespeare turns to after the resignation of his theatrical career, and its bearing on the interpretation of the play.

One of the most challenging critics, Anne Righter, accuses Shakespeare of "a perplexing habit of posing conundrums." She points to two numerical references that have no meaning for her and suggests that his "mathematical precision ... positively asks for speculation." She concludes that an answer cannot be supplied. "The dramatist knows, but is not telling."[30] This study proposes that, on the contrary, with a knowledge of the facts to which Shakespeare alludes, one does find answers and those answers make for a more comprehensive interpretation, a widened vision of the play. Discovery of a comprehensive plot and an episodic plot for *The Tempest*—a discovery that includes the spectacles, absorbs the themes, affirms the time, and accounts for the music and the characters of the cast—has helped in developing the vision offered in this book.

Shakespeare's drama is a function of many variables: exploratory, classical, political, scientific, and societal sources. Those variables—shards with their time inscriptions and settings—are exhumed and codified in Chapter I. In that chapter their contributions are weighed and their inadequacy as basic sources for *The Tempest* are cited. Chapter II examines English society in the sixteenth and seventeenth centuries, identifies Shakespeare's basic sources and discusses the literary characteristics of those sources. Chapter III dissects Shakespeare's introductory scene and cites the clues he gives to what follows. Chapter IV examines Shakespeare's mode of characterization. Chapter V presents a detailed comparison of *The Tempest* with its sources. Chapter VI defines some notes that are struck. Chapter VII describes Shakespeare's episodic plot. Chapter VIII examines the play's structure. Chapter IX considers the central themes of the play. Chapter X explicates Shakespeare's time references and identifies the isle's locale. Chapter XI analyzes the emotional turning points of the play and affirms the structure and the mystery. At appropriate junctures throughout the text the imagery is elucidated, themes are noted, and comparisons are made with studies of other critics.

Chapter I

Bardic Shards, Artifacts and Sources

Literary archaeologists searching for basic sources for *The Tempest* have spaded up the soil in many locales and have unearthed a variety of shards. Digging in travelogues written about places as distant from one another as "the Bermoothes," Sicily, and Patagonia, they have, to their delight, excavated names like those in *The Tempest*: Alonso, Sebastian, Anthonio, Ferdinand, Gonzalo, and Setebos.[1] One text was Richard Eden's *History of Travaille* (1577), a translation of M. Antonio Pigafetta's Italian work describing Ferdinand Magellan's voyages. Another account of Magellan's voyages by Pigafetta (in translation) yielded shards that suggested Caliban's dress and activity: men dressed in skins of animals who danced and sang and who when locked in irons called on "Setebos, their Great Spirit" to aid them.[2] Other researchers turned up accounts of Sir George Somers's fleet off the coast of the Bermudas: William Strachey's letter or manuscript *Sea Adventure*, "known as the *True Reportory of the Wrack*, dated 15 July 1610 but published for the first time in *Purchas His Pilgrimes* (1625)," Sylvester Jourdain's *Discovery of the Bermudas* (1610), and the Council of Virginia's apologetic *True Declaration of the Estate of the Colonie of Virginia*.[3] Unearthed along with those relics were the bits and pieces in John Florio's translation, published in 1603, of Montaigne's essay "Of the Canniballes." (Kermode notes that the British Museum holds a copy of this work containing "what may be a genuine signature of Shakespeare."[4]) Although they provide evidence that islands inhabited by creatures similar to Caliban really do exist, these travelogues are peripheral and contribute little to an understanding of the play.

At least one new historicist, Paul Brown, examined context to find what he interpreted as traces of colonialism in *The Tempest*.[5] The title of his essay reveals where he situates his representation of power: "'This thing of darkness I acknowledge mine': *The Tempest* and the Discourse of Colonialism."

However, a colonialist bias is dubious since none of those who arrived on the island did so of their own will. Prospero's and Miranda's arrival was occasioned by earthly treachery, happenstance, and Providence. Caliban's mother, pregnant with him, was brought there by the sailors. Through magic Prospero brought the "ship of souls" to the island where they underwent sea and mind changes. Ariel appears to have been the only one on the isle when Sycorax arrived. He was promptly imprisoned in a "cloven pine" (1.2.277) by the witch for refusing "to act her earthy and abhorr'd commands" (1.2.273).

Survival, duty, work, change, and renewal, not colonialization or power, are themes central to the play's meaning. As Peter Brook asserted, "*The Tempest* ... is not about power, but the 'human spirit' divined 'behind the words.'"[6] Moreover, Prospero's first act was the release of the original occupant of the isle, Ariel, from his imprisonment by Sycorax, whose demonic magic could be contrasted with Prospero's beneficent magic which brings "souls" to "clearer reason." In exchange for Ariel's release Prospero requires limited service, after which he grants absolute freedom. Prospero put not only Caliban to work, but also Ferdinand, a prince. Both carry logs — one as a slave, unwillingly out of fear, the other as a love-slave who finds his duties "light.../ Might I but through my prison once a day/ Behold this maid" (1.2.492–493). One might write a treatise on equality and the importance of reining in desire and instilling the work ethic in the young, regardless of race, social standing, or ideology. Is there a complementary history text for those concepts? As noted in Chapter I, Hunt found it ironic that *The Tempest* was "so focused on industry."[7] Caliban, as an immature person, has to learn the limits of ownership, which do not extend to possession of another person — Miranda, "thy crying self" (1.2.132), who, buffeted by fierce winds and sea, arrived without consent or intent upon a lone and hostile island. Caliban claims he has learned to curse because Prospero taught him language, but it was not Prospero who bought his allegiance with alcohol, as some colonists may have done in other circumstances, and viewed him as a trading-piece. Rather, Prospero "us'd" Caliban "with human care; and lodg'd" him in his "own cell, till thou [Caliban] didst seek to violate/ The honour of my [Prospero's] child" (1.2.347–350). Thus it appears that Brown's essay is not only limited but, in some respects, inaccurate. This study proposes with Thomas that "an important part of a project entitled a new historicism is to place under scrutiny what is accepted as proper historical analysis."[8]

Other researchers have focused on the politics of the sixteenth and seventeenth centuries. Halliwell-Phillipps unearthed William Thomas's *Historie of Italy* (Pamplona, 1609) and identified it as a possible source of the political intrigue found in *The Tempest*, providing what Nosworthy refers to as a "causal plot" for Shakespeare's play.[9] More recently, after examining the seventeenth century's political climate, Breight warned against too euphemistic an approach in interpreting *The Tempest*. He found treason characteristic of

Shakespeare's time and a vital element in the play: "If recontextualized within one aspect of English history, *The Tempest* ... is a politically radical intervention in a dominant contemporary discourse."[10] He identified the construction of the play "as a series of conspiracies, [which] can be inserted into a vast discourse of treason that became an increasingly central response to difficult social problems in late Elizabethan and early Jacobean London." He concluded, "To respond fully to *The Tempest*, we must learn to read it in non-euphemistic contexts."[11]

Although it was treason that set Prospero and Miranda afloat in a leaky craft, their arrival on the island was part of another, more comprehensive design, "Providence divine" (1.2.159). Furthermore, the treason and physical injury intended by some of the shipwrecked were averted by Prospero and his spirit, Ariel. A major theme of the play is change, which implies not the persistence of treason, but a remedy that will afford the "peace of the present" and good "cheer" (1.1.2, 3, 22) predicated in the opening scene of *The Tempest*, a remedy not dominantly political in nature. A number of suggestions of treason are present in *The Tempest*, but a framework or concept for the play cannot be built from them.

Breight identifies a problem, but he does not incorporate the changes in the "sea-swallow'd" (2.1.246), changes brought about by Prospero's persecutory magic, which brings new awareness to his enemies rather than the destruction that would have resulted from Prospero's wrath. Nor does Breight note Prospero's change from obedience to a vengeful law to the law of forgiveness. Breight does not fit into his framework the elements of change that represent Caliban's obeisance to one god after another, his return to Prospero as Master, and his purpose to "be wise hereafter,/ And seek for grace" (5.1.294–296). Other important changes, not cited by Breight, take place when Prospero abandons his magic, dons his hat and rapier, agrees to make "every third thought his grave," and promises to find relief in "prayer." Antonio and Sebastian appear to be the only ones whose change does not go far enough. Their change is from murderous intent to opportunistic trade of Caliban. However, their later purpose is also thwarted by Prospero's claim: "This thing of darkness I/ Acknowledge mine" (5.1.275–276).

Both Wagner and Still, digging for intent and meaning, turned up shards form the religion of the times. Wagner rejected some shards that Still incorporated, and built an incomplete artifact, partly glued together with scientific rationalism. Wagner argued in great detail that the play is dealing with the "uproar" in the church and suggested that Shakespeare was dealing with the paganism that had been absorbed by Christianity. She found *The Tempest* to be, "under the guise of allegory, a violent protest against the ignorance, superstitions and corruptions of the time — a scathing arraignment of the institutions, religious and secular, which fostered and perpetuated them."[12] For her *The Tempest* became a drama of Christianity concerned primarily with that intellectual, moral and religious movement which came as a protest against the perversion of the simple yet profound teaching of Jesus into the worse than meaningless forms, rituals and corruptions of ecclesiasticism — the movement which culminated in the sixteenth century in that cataclysm or storm of human thought known as the reformation.[13]

Since Shakespeare's vision is inclusive here as always, some of Wagner's shards (and many others) may be fitted into the play without diminishing the relevance of any, but Wagner's arrangement of those shards and the sense that evolves from her arrangement is another matter. Few critics would agree that the tone of the play is "scathing" or that Shakespeare's integration of the shards is achieved through scientific rationalism. The wonder and mystical sense of *The Tempest* surpass human reason.

The church was in a state of flux in the sixteenth and seventeenth centuries. There were factions and fractures. There were pagan elements in both the culture and religion. Shakespeare surely was cognizant of the elements of paganism and magic which existed in the Christianity of his day, the efforts to purge or Christianize the pagan, the diversity in Christian practice in the time of the Renaissance, and the attempt by state and religious leaders to assimilate or discourage different forms of faith and worship. In identifying pagan and magical elements of *The Tempest* it is important to discover how much weight Shakespeare attaches to them and how they are used — whether they are central to meaning, provide comparative parallels or reinforce meaning. Before the play ends, Prospero's magic, even though it is "white," is rejected.

Colin Still, too, focused on religion. He integrated elements that Wagner rejected. He found Shakespeare "took some pains to conceal [the play's] inner meaning"[14] and stated that his "real purpose" was to show the "close affinity between the pagan myths and ritual on the one hand, and the mysteries of the Christian religion on the other." To do so outwardly, said Still, "would be to 'use strange fire at the altar of the Lord.'"[15] He found *The Tempest* to be "a synthesis of the main features of all mythology and ritual, whether Christian or non–Christian," noting that "it tells the story of man's upward struggle partly in Biblical terms and partly in terms of pagan myth and ritual," that "it not only presupposes, but actually demonstrates, that there is one universal tradition underlying all religious and semi-religious concepts."[16] Thus Still fell into the same mode of interpretation of which Draper accused the Romanticists and Victorians:[17] gluing together disparate elements, not of Jamesian or Elizabethan England, but of his own era's theorizing, which for Still was comparative religion. Medieval religious thought and Renaissance literature worked toward the assimilation, adaptation, or rejection of diverse religious concepts and practices rather than comparison. Still's and Wagner's assembly of the shards they unearthed supply us with incomplete and very different artifacts.

Focusing on nomenclature, Stokes discovered a reference to a horse named Prospero, and although that piece hardly fits into the reconstruction of the Shakesperean character, it may have been responsible for the horsepond through which Caliban, Trinculo, and Stephano wade on an island where no horses appear to exist.[18] Stokes also turned up a character named Prospero (Wellbred) in Jonson's *Every Man in His Humor,* but that character has none of Prospero's supernatural qualities, nor does he appear in as many guises as Prospero.[19]

Gonzalo and his banter about Widow Dido have sent other nomenclature specialists scurrying to examine to the *Aeneid.* There they have found plot similarities in the shipwreck and in Aeneas's encounter with a caring woman, his mother, Venus. Nosworthy claimed that Shakespeare used this encounter— rather than Aeneas's with Dido—in Ferdinand's encounter with Miranda, a finding significant in this interpretation.[20] (The various relationships and figurings of Ferdinand and Miranda will be discussed in Chapter IV.) Digging deeper into Virgil's *Aeneid,* researchers have turned up a storm and Harpies which they compare with Shakespeare's tempest and the banquet that appears and vanishes with Ariel's help (3.3).[21] In Virgil's Fourth Eclogue, Hirst found suggestions of Gonzalo's "golden age."[22] Thus several bits and pieces of Virgil's works combine nicely to give a better start in reconstructing an earlier work that resembles *The Tempest,* but there is not enough material there to complete one.

Romantically minded researchers have looked for love stories with similar plots and found Jacob Ayrer's *Die Schoene Sidea* and Antonio de Eslava's *Noches de Invierno,* both of which include magic, a father, and a daughter, and sparingly follow the plot of *The Tempest.*[23] Another romanticist points to Diego Ortunez de Calahorra's *Espejo de Príncipes y Caballeros,* which had "a magic island, ruled by a vicious witch who had a son by the devil; a log-bearing prince; magic storms; magic books and invisible sages."[24] A later archeologist excavated and identified Longus's *Daphnis and Chloë* as a romantic piece in the plot.[25] Gesner named that work "as another important influence on the genesis of the play,"[26] stating that "the supernatural machinery point[s] directly to Longus rather than to an intermediary source, except that omission cannot be a conclusive argument, and supernatural direction abounds in classical literature."[27] She found "a general parallel in theme, setting, and structure" between the two works. She uncovered other similarities, such as taking of "a central topic the idea of celebrating the innocence of youth," "island stories," structural unity, focus of attention "on the central situation of the lovers," and specificity of time (not found in other Greek romances).[28] After considering both Day's and Amyot's translations of *Daphnis and Chloë,* Gesner stated that

> The conclusion that Longus is an ultimate influence on *The Tempest* is based on the presence of the elements of the stock pastoral plot, from which it devi-

ates in only one instance. The conclusion that Longus is a direct influence is not so surely established, but coincidences in the storms and in the chief characters, and the similarities of the wedding festivities suggest that Shakespeare was familiar with Longus.[29]

However, Gesner's qualifying admissions are significant, revealing that even in combining her discovery with the observations of others she still found it impossible to point to a "true" source. She concluded:

> It is naive ... to think of Longus as having contributed more than a web for the weaving of a tapestry as complexly beautiful as *The Tempest*. The pages of *Daphnis and Chloë* abound with appreciation of natural beauty and fertility in the land and in the lovers, but not with the air of transcendental supernaturalism and magic that invests Prospero's island.[30]

She also observed that as a most likely source for the romance, *Daphnis and Chloë* failed to contribute to the meaning of the play: "There is no hint in Longus of the arcane knowledge and philosophy of Prospero that tantalizes and raises in the thoughtful questions about the meanings of the play."[31]

Gesner's admission of the failure of the Longus romance to contribute to the play's meaning and her identification of *The Tempest* as a woven tapestry (with her implied acknowledgment that many threads are missing) left room for others to continue research.

Woodman used black and white color codes to categorize Sycorax's and Prospero's magic: "Although the events are not actually dramatized in *The Tempest*, Prospero's initial struggle with the witch Sycorax for control of the enchanted isle was just such a contest — with Prospero's white magic defeating the black magic of the witch."[32] Woodman described the white magician as one who "can receive and transmit the sources of divine power only through supreme dedication and study and by undertaking acts of self-purification that prepare him to be the suitable agent of God."[33]

Woodman examined Prospero and his art and declared that "a popular response to Prospero as a white magician was ... assured."[34] He and others are justified in classifying Prospero's magic as "white" since Prospero was "for the liberal Arts/ Without a parallel; those being all my study" (1.2.73–74); was "transported/ And rapt in secret studies" (1.2.76–77); and rejected his baser nature ("Yet with my nobler reason 'gainst my fury/ Do I take part: The rarer action is/ In virtue than in vengeance" [5.1.26–28]). Thus he could be seen in terms of Renaissance magic as an agent of God.

Kermode found correspondences between *The Tempest* and Golding's translation of Ovid's *Metamorphoses*, VII. He found that both works fused classical, Neo-Platonic, and native supernatural elements and made "a silent differentiation of the good magic of the better nature and the ill magic of the vile who are without virtue."[35]

Another archaeologist, searching extratextually, dug into Shakespeare's consciousness for interstitial shards. Finding the persistence of certain word and image associations, he concluded that "Shakespeare's genius was of an intuitional and associative rather than a ratiocinative type."[36] An example in *The Tempest* is the horse named Prospero and the horsepond cited above.

In 1948 Nosworthy attempted to fuse together some shards:

> I suggest ... that *The Tempest* is an amalgam of three narrative sources combined by Shakespeare with the utmost perfection of his art. He set out, in the first place, with an older play or romance covering the adventures on the island, and then elected to lend those adventures a heightened purpose by developing the theme of the earlier wrong done to Prospero. For this he found another source, which may, as we have seen, have been Thomas's *Historie*. Finally, he unified these two plots by adapting a familiar and favourite tale to serve as a link.... Montaigne, and the rest will account for this and for that, but they will not account for the two hours' traffic of dramatic concord that Shakespeare, after due consideration, entitled *The Tempest*.[37]

Although Nosworthy attested to the unity of the play, he did not discover a comprehensive source. What he proposed was an amalgam, not an artifact. Since none of the excavations performed thus far have furnished enough shards from which to reconstruct an artifact that resembles the play, no text thus far explored can be named Shakespeare's primary ground.

While most of the excavations throw light on societal and political matters in Shakespeare's time or reveal similar romantic tales, none are as broad in scope as *The Tempest*, nor do any focus on the meaning of the play. Like new historicist readings, they do not present an artifact comparable to the play. The problem with attempts to excavate in contemporary records of man's adventures, or identify with scientific reason, colonialism or tyranny, is to forget that all persons arrived on a strange isle without being willing to do so and that something more than Prospero's magic is operating upon them. The play may be grounded in earth, but it is ordained by "Providence Divine." It looks beyond earth and the problems of tyranny, usurpation, colonialism, and reason to the heavens, where Prospero notes "a most auspicious star" (1.2.182) and in the "corollary" vision presents Nature's goddesses, Juno, Ceres, and Iris, in an example of godlike providence. Therefore, one or more texts that encompass both heaven and earth are required as basic sources.

Bethell recognized and Sypher affirmed the multiconsciousness of the Renaissance mind,[38] a mind that could identify with a variety of elements in *The Tempest*. However, the bits and pieces of possible sources heretofore identified do not account for the poetic atmosphere or background of *The Tempest*. No matter how many possible sources have been unearthed, no one has been able to assemble them into a meaningful pattern that resembles the play. *The Tempest*, like Keats's Grecian urn, has a radiance and aura that do not evolve from any arrangement thus far attempted of the various shards. Exploration, political intrigue, romance, colonialism, nomen, scientific rationalism, and religious division and controversy have all turned up, but they cannot be arranged artistically to echo or fabricate Shakespeare's play and imbue it with a "transcendental supernaturalism." Not only do we find pieces missing, but the unity, beauty, wonder, harmony and mystery that Gesner and others find in the whole are also lacking.

Coleridge, Wilson, Knight, and Sypher are among those who identified some of the characteristics that an artifact must possess if it is to resemble the play. They emphasized the harmony, expansiveness, unity and visionary character of *The Tempest* and of other Shakespearean plays. Coleridge described the manner in which the characters were introduced in *The Tempest* as "wonderful," and he found each scene "still preparing, still inviting, and still gratifying, like a finished piece of music."[39] (Although Coleridge was enthralled by *The Tempest* and its characters, he did not unfold their sources of wonder for other readers.) Chapter IV of this book unravels the skeins in character portraits, revealing multiple identities of cast members.

Wilson found in *The Tempest* Shakespeare's mood "of one, who, contemplating all time and all existence, sees them as some sublime dramatic poem, moving inevitably and harmoniously towards 'a full and natural close, like music.' It is, in a word, the mood of Peace." Wilson asserted that the "impression of serenity and peace" with which the "concluding scene of the play leaves us" is "only paralleled by that conveyed in some of Beethoven's latest compositions."[40] Wilson caught the spirit and recognized the expansiveness of the drama, but he did not describe the closure of space and time which are intrinsically related to the source and plot and which precede the "close." He left that task to other critics. (Chapters VIII, IX, and X of this book describe time and space closures.)

Knight claimed that "a Shakespearean tragedy is set spatially as well as temporally in the mind." He went on to explain that "there are throughout the play a set of correspondences which relate to each other independently of the time-sequence which is the story." He cited "the intuition-intelligence opposition active within and across *Troilus and Cressida*, the Death-theme in *Hamlet*, [and] the nightmare Evil of *Macbeth*" as examples of what he called "the play's 'atmosphere'" and suggested that "atmosphere" relates to Aristotle's "unity of idea."[41] He found the route to unity is through "interpretation [which] is passive" and the way to interpretation through "a reconstruction of vision."[42] He distinguished between "criticism," which he called "a judgement of vision," and "interpretation," which he defined as "a reconstruction of vision."[43] Although a sense of the wholeness of *The Tempest* is gained through passivity, the mood in which this study began, a reconstruction of the whole vision involves diligent research. In fact it was well nigh impossible in light of the numerous concurrences that aroused and effected a response to remain passive. (Pictures of real persons upon whom Shakespeare draws to endow the play with meaning are drawn in Chapter IV of this book. The picture of Shakespeare's new cosmology is presented in Chapter VIII.

Frye wrote:

> Structure is the aura of what Eliot would call unified sensibility: it is the unity which balances a variety of moods, conflicting with and to some degree neutralizing one another. Any fragment of the structure may evoke, by a kind of conditioned reflex, a certain mood or association.[44]

The cosmological picture, the structure of *The Tempest*, described in Chapter VIII was drawn from various fragments, words and phrases that produced a conditioned reflex. The reflex evoked both a unified sensibility and the concept of a real space-time framework across which was stretched the fabric depicting the activities of multirepresentational characters.

Sypher wrote:

> One of the miracles of the last plays is the revision of the unendurable Lear environment and the creation of scenes in which man is redeemed ... all in a new context, in a psychography that magically brings remission of sin.... The farthest reach of pictorial imagination is the sea change in Prospero's kingdom.... It is a transfiguration that takes us back to the grove in Colonus, that precinct where the afflicted Oedipus also found that time is a version of mercy and that man is eligible for some mysterious levitation that seems almost sacrosanct.[45]

Since none of the elements from possible sources thus far discovered have produced, alone or together, an artifact imbued with wonder that encompasses mercy and incorporates miracle and transfiguration — characteristics noted by the foregoing critics — other possible sources need to be located.

The mystery persists. Where are the missing shards buried? Where is Prospero's wonder-working rod? Where is the restored tempest-tossed vessel? Where are the suggestions of mercy? Where are to be found "the single words" which Coleridge claims "instill" the energy, "the power of poetry," "into the mind," the single words that "live" in Miranda's and the seventeenth century audiences' minds, words with which Shakespeare wishes to evoke "of any thing the image" (1.2.43, 42)? In which texts do cacophony and music pursue their parallel and "conflicting" courses? What kinds of structures and texts could Shakespeare find elsewhere which "unify" and cover Wilson's "all time and all existence" and, as Frye suggested, "balance a variety of moods, conflicting with and to some degree neutralizing one another"?[46]

According to T. S. Eliot, "Our first duty as either critics or 'interpreters,' surely, must be to try to grasp the whole design, and read *character* and *plot* in the understanding of this subterrene or submarine music," which he refers to earlier as the "richer design" woven "*organically*" in the "genuine poetic drama."[47] This study identifies the scriptural tradition, the Bible and its derivatives, as the source of the "subterrene music" heard in the play and of its design which unites character and plot, providing the warp and woof, the fabric of Shakespeare's vision. The scriptural tradition invests the play with "the air of transcendental supernaturalism."

Of all Shakespeare's plays, *The Tempest* sets forth most fully and delightfully the biblical story of humankind: the tempestuous nature and thorny way of fallen man, the good news of the law of forgiveness as a means of reconciliation, proper order and right relationship which involves equality, "the peace of the present" (1.1.22) and the "cheer" which is to be "Good" (1.1.2–3). To quote the Bible exactly would be too overt for a seventeenth century audience. In the early seventeenth century, a king's translation of the Bible was being made; already there existed the Great Bible, the Geneva Bible, the Bishop's Bible and the Coverdale and Tyndall Bibles. Shakespere's society was pervaded by biblically based epigrams and emblems and religious art, and religious festivals were celebrated with masques and drama. Thus allusions to and inversions of scriptural passages would be easily recognizable to Shakespere's audience. Single words could "bring to remembrance" stories of characters with similar traits living under similar circumstances.

The varied sounds heard in *The Tempest*— sweet airs, solemn music and even cacophony — are also found in religious drama, a fact that provides good reason to examine religious plays as possible sources. A careful study of the Mystery cycles makes clear that *The Tempest* owes much more to the Mystery Plays than has been heretofore acknowledged and has more in common with them than with the sources cited earlier. Some of the characters, action and themes of *The Tempest* are derived directly or indirectly from the Bible. Allusions to stories chosen from the Old Testament for inclusion in the Corpus Christi play are hidden in *The Tempest;* imagery from the Corpus Christi play is woven into its fabric. Those images provide a sense of wonder not available in nonbiblical texts that have been excavated. The Mystery Plays are a gold mine for retrieval of word senses and imagery lost to modern audiences but used by Shakespeare.

Although elements and the continuities of the metaphor contribute to an understanding of the play and its artistry, tracings of them are not as central to its meaning as the characters and imagery found in the Mystery Plays. What provides meaning in *The Tempest* is the way Shakespeare hones in on the essentials; the provision for harmony amidst the complexities of political, ecclesiastical, and personal disturbances; and his ordering of authority, time, masters, and values. Shakespeare's mode of integration is comparable to, though not identical with, that of Spenser in his *Epithalamium*, where Spenser calls in the pagan gods to celebrate Christian marriage. The spirit of *The Tempest* is not so much a celebration of Christianity as an abstraction of its essence from its trappings. In a stance far more evident in the sixteenth century than today, two witnesses to truth were given man: nature (including human nature) and the sacred scriptures. While the Renaissance embraced two modes of ascent, today we have all but lost both through biblical illiteracy, adaptation of the culturally cold Copernican system and rationalism, and our drowning out of nature with our overwhelming earth lights and industrial smog. Spenser's integration came before Shakespeare's; Milton's came after, for the latter wrote:

> Well hast thou taught the way that might direct
> Our knowledge, and the scale of Nature set
> From centre to circumference, whereon
> In contemplation of created things
> By steps we may ascend to God. [*Paradise Lost*, V.508–512].

The passage speaks of the part nature plays in man's ascent to God. Colin Still traces the ascent of specific men in *The Tempest* through experiencing the elements of nature. However, neither the above passage nor Still speaks of the "descent" of God to man. (Milton, of course, includes the descent of God to man elsewhere in *Paradise Lost* and *Paradise Regained.*) In order to determine whether *The Tempest*'s "secret subject" was comparative religion and its denouement mortal, or whether *The Tempest*'s dénouement is immortal and the play specifically Christian, it is necessary to search for specific textual references that affirm the descent of God to man in the play. With Prospero's dismissal of the creatures of nature, "elves," "printless" footed ones, "demi-puppets," and the "midnight mushrumps" makers, he lacks the "weak masters" upon whom he has depended for his "rough magic" (5.1.33–50). He is left without fantastic helpers to assist him. Does that mean the loss of supernatural aid?

Colin Still brought together diverse elements in the play which had appeared extraneous and disconnected, but it would appear that Shakespeare's appeal to the audience in the Epilogue is not, as Still infers, to recognize Shakespeare's comparative religion design, but to acknowledge the place of normalized man in the world as both supplicant and servant. In the many references he cited, Still provided undeniable evidence of Shakespeare's recognition of pagan rites throughout the play. At times throughout his book he related biblical and pagan rites, pointing to their similarities and differences, but he did not formally document *The Tempest* as a Christian play in the way he documented it for pagan rites. Although the title of his book, *Shakespeare's Mystery Play: A Study of "The Tempest,"* suggested a likely source, he made little effort to prove that *The Tempest* was a mystery play, inconvertibly and profoundly, a biblical play. He stopped short of identifying numerous Christian elements which, though similar to, common with, or contrasting with pagan rites, give the play a distinctly Christian tone. His assignation of "mystery play" was appropriate, but he failed to carry through with a proof.

The Tempest is indeed a mystery play. It is a greatly condensed version of the Corpus Christi play.[48] Although some nonbiblical material is included in both the Corpus Christi play and *The Tempest*, they both are essentially Bible plays.

The Tempest works toward synthesis and unity, achieved through sublimation, subordination, transposition and providential ordering, which supersedes the equivalence of Still's approach. A comparison of a mystery play and *The Tempest* is made in Chapter V. The following pages will examine the fabric of Shakespeare's vision following the threads of which it is woven; attune to its harmony by recognizing the resonances of lost notes; and plumb the depths to discover the submerged portion of the iceberg, for *The Tempest* goes further into time "than did ever plummet sound" (5.1.56).

Chapter II

The English Cultural Climate and Mystery Play Scholarship

Before focusing on the specifics of *The Tempest*, this study will consider the English cultural climate at the time of the play's production and the contributions made by recent scholarship to our understanding of the literary characteristics of the Mystery Plays.

In the Renaissance the plight of man was affected by the struggle for power; by the introduction into society of natural or barbaric man through exploration; and by a new emphasis on materialism occasioned by new trade routes and the introduction of Arabic numbers. Added to these earthly concerns were challenges to belief systems by diverse religious factions and by scientific discovery. Many English religious reformers, eager to do away with medieval ecclesiastical practices, felt that changes in the newly established English church did not go far enough. Recusants wanted conformity with the Roman Catholic church. Belief systems were also being challenged by the new scientific concepts of the heavens, which catapulted people out of their position at the center of the universe and sent them spinning in an unprotected orbit. The fracture of the space-time cultural system, the cosmological order, by the invention of the telescope and the culturally cold Copernican system eventually led to the separation of science and imagination and to rationalistic modes of thought.

When *The Tempest* was first played, however, reason had not yet replaced belief in the fantastic natural and the supernatural, nor had knowledge been compartmentalized as in later societies. Many different forms of the supernatural were available to the Renaissance mind. Belief in both white and black magic still existed and fascinated some in spite of King James's *Daemonologie*, written in the form of a dialogue of inquiry with one of his stated purposes to show "what exact trial and seuere punishment they merite."[1] In fact, the King's detailed descriptions of the wonders accomplished by magicians and witches suggest that, he, too, was fascinated by their magical works.

English elves and fairies, the little folk, were part of May Day and Midsummer Night celebrations. Medieval society had allowed the incorporation of pagan rites and festivals into Christian practices. Pagan modes of initiation, with their emphasis on earth, water, air, and fire or light, which led to self-knowledge, were absorbed into Christian experiences of baptism and illumination. A society accommodating so many types of supernatural agencies in its celebrations would have as little trouble accepting Shakespeare's use of parallelism in the portrayal of providence in the Judeo-Christian figures (which will be cited in this book) and the pagan gods and goddesses of the vision provided Ferdinand and Miranda — unlike later societies whose knowledge would be compartmentalized and where reason would, if not replace, at least obscure the suprarational.

Many in Renaissance society, fearful of being displaced from the center of the universe, still clung to the revised Ptolemaic cosmology whose Greek and Roman gods and goddesses had been replaced by the medieval church with a hierarchy of angels. The average citizen, forced by law to attend the English church services or pay a penalty, would have been more familiar with the biblical tradition and the hierarchies of angels than with Greek and Roman gods and goddesses. However, some vestiges of the gods remained even in biblical writ. When a lame man was healed under Paul's ministry, the amazed crowd called Barnabas "Jupiter" and Paul "Mercurius" (Acts 14:9–10, 12).

While new historicists and cultural materialists in practice appear to be more concerned with politically marginalized, resistive, and secular forces and hegemonic, feminist, and colonialist readings, their emphasis on historical contexts validates an examination of the religious practices and belief systems pervading the culture in the Renaissance. Critiques that claim the early seventeenth century was free of the orthodoxies of the Middle Ages have not accounted for the religious symbolism and language found in Shakespearean dramas, particularly his later works. Historians designate periods of time as Middle Ages, Renaissance, and Modern, basing their designations on revolutionary changes effected by exploration, scientific discovery, and the resurrection of classical texts; yet from age to age there were continuities, particularly in belief systems. Some of those continuities may have been marginalized, but they did exist. The many new historicist readings of a Shakespearean play attest to Shakespeare's ability to integrate many cultural phenomena. These phenomena should include the intent and direction of popular drama written in the fourteenth and fifteenth centuries and played well into the sixteenth century. If the early seventeenth century was free of the orthodoxies of the Middle Ages as at least one new historicist has claimed,[2] why have critics found Shakespeare's later dramas fraught with religious symbolism, religious language, and biblical quotations, and why are there so many records of persons having been tortured for persisting in the practice of their beliefs?

It is possible to trace continuity in belief even with change in institutional authority. Middle Ages orthodoxies derived from the biblical text, and although there were new translations and new interpretations, the Bible still provided the basis for belief. Religious dimensions of Renaissance culture and their representations in literature are particularly important in situating texts, for religious issues were at stake with dominant and resistant strains clearly at work. The rise of Protestantism and the transfer of church authority to the crown consolidated power but did not silence the voices of Puritans and recusants. Moreover, in England medieval belief systems persisted in the form of popular drama well into the Renaissance. The Bible was the basis of the religious English tradition. It was mouthed, heard, and enacted in the Mystery Plays in the streets of towns and cities in England as late as 1569 in York, 1575 in Chester (Whitsun), and 1579 in Coventry.[3] Some members of a 1611 audience certainly would have seen one or more performances of the Corpus Christi play, and it is likely that some members of Shakespeare's audience would have participated in one of the plays, for "there is the likelihood that two hundred and forty-three different actors would have been required to fill all the roles" in the forty-eight plays of the York cycle.[4] The last performances of the Mystery Plays took place in Shakespeare's lifetime; therefore it is possible that he saw one or more performances. It is also possible that he had access to one or more of the extant manuscripts of the four cycles: York, Chester (Whitsun), Wakefield (Towneley), and *Ludus Coventriae* (N-Town).[5] There are five manuscripts of the Chester cycle that are of the late sixteenth and early seventeenth centuries.[6] That Shakespeare had the Mystery Plays in mind at the time he was writing his final plays is confirmed by Perdita's observation in *The Winter's Tale*, "Methinks I play as I have seen them do/ In Whitsun pastorals" (4.3.133–134). The question is, who was thinking of the Whitsun pastorals? Was it Perdita, Shakespeare, or his audience? At a performance of the play, it would be all three.

The later date of the last performance of the Coventry cycle, the fact that it "had gained a national reputation and had succeeded in attracting royalty on several occasions," suggests it as a most likely source for *The Tempest*.[7] However, Shakespeare's use of "Whitsun pastorals" suggests the cycle which was moved from Corpus Christi day to Whitsuntide either to reduce competition for merchants and playgoers or for Protestant reasons.[8] Changes in the procession involved "a procession not from one church to another but through the principal streets of the city with stops at Northgate and the Castle prisons for the distribution of alms to the prisoners. The two stops are significant because they acknowledge symbolically the two major legal jurisdictions, the city's and the earl's."[9] According to this study Shakespeare's play is concerned with more than one type of authority. As will be shown later, in the chapter on time, a passage taken from the Wakefield play, which has no counterpart in the other three cycles, corresponds to Prospero's dissolution speech.

Shakespeare's depiction of Ferdinand as a grown man suggests a possible debt to the York cycle. Shakespeare's reference to the Whitsun play and the particular correspondences with other plays suggest he had access to more than one cycle manuscript.

Since the performances of the Mystery Plays took place out of doors, whole communities experienced them. In their production and enactment the material world and a formerly marginalized group of people were linked with a belief system, for it was the artisans and tradesmen of the bourgeois who constructed the platforms, arranged the scenery, and spoke the parts of biblical characters.

To relate properly the many factual references which Shakespeare makes in his plays it is necessary to appreciate the tremendous impact that the English church and its liturgy, seasons, sacraments, festivals, and its biblical derivative (*The Book of Common Prayer*, 1559) had on him, his audience, the court, and the society in the period in which he wrote. It is also necessary to acknowledge his apparent intimacy with the Mystery Plays. In Shakespeare's England the Act of Supremacy had made Elizabeth the supreme head of the church, and adults were legally required to attend church and to receive communion. Frye pointed out that the law required "that lists be kept of the names of those who did not attend the Church of England, and there is no evidence, either in London or in Stratford, that Shakespeare absented himself from the services, sermons, and sacraments of the established Church."[10] For many who attended the theater in Shakespeare's day, even the time which governed their day rang out from the cathedral's belfry, since watches and domestic clocks were owned chiefly by royalty and wealthy citizens.

The early church's worship was organized around events in the life of Christ. As the cyclical church year developed, it came to have seven seasons or tides. (The number had varied in earlier times.) Those seasons and the festivals associated with them were rooted in Jewish customs and rearranged with the adoption of the Roman calendar. The festivals were infiltrated by and absorbed pagan practices. Throughout the centuries after Constantine, changes were made in the church year. Saints' days began to be celebrated and a calendar developed for a year of celebration of saints. The seven seasons in the year became known as Advent, Christmas, Epiphany, Septuagesima, Lent, Easter, and Pentecost.[11]

During the Reformation sweeping changes were made and in the Anglican Church a limited number of saints' days continued to be celebrated. Later the calendar year came to be divided into two parts, those celebrating events in the life of Christ and those celebrating the church. Allhallowtide became a collect for the celebration of many of the saints formerly assigned specific days. It extended until Adventide, which included the four Sundays before Christmas and was a period of expectancy. Christmastide encompassed the twelve days of Christmas, which ended in Epiphany (January 6), the day commemorating the coming of the wise men to the Christ child. For four or five Sundays after January 6, lessons regarding that day were taught. Shrovetide occupied the days, usually three, before Ash Wednesday and was a time for confession preparatory to Lent. Lententide followed. Later it absorbed Shrovetide. Eastertide encompassed the period from Easter to Ascension Day (40 days), Whitsunday (50 days), or Trinity Sunday (57 days). Ascensiontide covered the period from Ascension Day to the Day of Pentecost, the beginning of Whitsuntide, which commemorated the descent of the Holy Spirit on the day of Pentecost. Trinitide, with its focus upon the Three Persons of the Trinity and its emphasis upon the fruits of the Christian faith, was an alternate name for Whitsuntide. Adventide through Ascensiontide made up the first half of the church year, and Whitsuntide (which began with Pentecost) and Allhallowtide made up the second half.

Changes were made from time to time, and the *Book of Common Prayer* referred to "Terms" rather than Seasons or Tides. Nevertheless, the names of church seasons and the festivities associated with them were familiar to Shakespeare's audiences, and Adventide, Christmastide, and Eastertide are terms commonly used today in many churches.

In addition to the seven tides of the church year, there were seven sacraments and rites. They were baptism, confirmation, communion, penance, marriage, orders (in priesthood), and extreme unction.[12] *The Tempest* provides correspondences with all of these, as Shakespeare dramatizes the church's sacraments, makes reference to its seasons, and depicts the order and essence of its service. Recognizing that exemplars of rites and rituals may be either comical or serious makes identification easier. In *The Tempest* as in the Corpus Christi play, burlesque parodies of sacred events were played. Drunk Caliban's High-day mocks a Christian ritual. All of the occupants of the "ship of souls" are immersed (baptized). A banquet, symbolizing communion, appears, but is not available to "the three men of sin." A wedding is performed. Caliban is taught a supreme lesson in mastership and becomes a candidate for "grace"—confirmation. A "holy" man and the king enter the magic circle to receive orders of a kind. (In Shakespeare's day both clergy and kings were set apart for a specific and holy function in society, the latter under the divine right of kings.) Alonso undergoes a sea-change, a spiritual form of extreme unction. As penance, Caliban, Trinculo, and Stephano trim Prospero's cell "handsomely."

Shakespeare's multiplicity of concerns is matched by his range of moods and exemplar. Although Wilson, Coleridge, and others focus on the wonder of it, the play is not acted continuously in the realm of the sublime. It is at times very earthy, at times uproariously funny, and at times mystical. Nor does it end with a mere "show of benevolence" as Bright intimates. Some very real changes are effected in the minds and behaviors of some of those in the isle.

However, no priest, parson, friar, novice, nun, bishop or cardinal plays an impressive role in Shakespearean drama unless it is the duke in disguise in *Measure for Measure*. Even in that play, however, the church fares poorly as an institution, for its representation is carried on outside its doors in a government hall, in a garden, and within prison walls, chiefly by individuals rather than in a Mass. Although they are not introduced as churchmen, certain characters in *The Tempest* figure heavily as biblical personages or saints and Shakespeare associates them in a unique way with the English church. Other ways in which Shakespeare drew upon the English church, its sacraments and seasons, and the scriptural lessons in its *Book of Common Prayer* will be discussed in later chapters.

The English church was associated with dramatic presentations. Masques and plays were written for and enacted at the religious festivals that occurred during the church year. In a significant work Hassel correlated the themes, narratives, and images of Renaissance masques and plays performed on festival days with those of festival liturgy. Hassel claimed that "starting around 1605 court masques begin to be commissioned for annual performance on Epiphany and Shrovetide" and that "these masques with their pronounced thematic and allegorical bias and their genesis within the festival context might be expected to grace their holy days with particular if subtle aptness."[13] Hassel found that "the details of this whole tradition of festival masques and plays would seem to deserve more attention, for their implications could establish a new and major context for the understanding of Renaissance drama."[14] He added: "Since many in the Renaissance audience still understand that joy and value in basically Christian terms, it would hardly be surprising if their masques should sometimes parallel the liturgical celebrations they are designed to grace."[15] Since Hassel's correlations cover a large number of Renaissance dramas (including 13 of Jonson's masques) and the various festivals, his treatment of *The Tempest* is limited. Hassel focused on *The Tempest*'s correspondence with the "Hallowmas liturgical festival."

Although *The Tempest* is a play, it contains a masque and in some ways the whole play resembles a masque. The times of its playing — Hallowmas, November 1, 1611, and the "winter of 1612–13, as part of the festivities at court to celebrate the marriage of the Princess Elizabeth to the Elector Palatine"[16] — suggest a close association with seasons of the English church year. However, *The Tempest* deserves closer scrutiny for festival relevance, for it is more closely related to the Christmastide festivals than *Twelfth Night*, whose title begs comparison.

Moreover, a custom practiced at the time of the first performance of *The Tempest* has correspondences in the play. In the Middle Ages on November 1 a Lord of Misrule was lodged in one of the great houses in England. A similar mock ruler in Scotland was called the Abbot of Unreason: "In every case these mimic dignitaries represented the highest authority in the Church. They masqueraded in the vestments of the clergy, and exercised for the time being some of the functions of the higher clergy."[17] The Lord of Misrule began his rule on All-hallow Eve, Hallowmas, or the day after. In England he presided over the Yuletide revels. On the day marking the end of Christmastide, Epiphany, the true lord of the great house was reinstated.

The custom can be applied to the play on several levels. *The Tempest* opens with an anti-lord, Antonio, ruling in a great house in Milan. On the literal level Antonio is one of the Lords of Misrule. Shakespeare combines both the English and the Scottish aspects of the mock ruler, for Antonio is Lord of Misrule in his usurpation of the dukedom of Milan and the Abbot of Unreason in the defuming which brings him to "clearer reason," if not to repentance. As in festival practice, the true lord of the greathouse, Prospero, is acknowledged as the rightful Duke of Milan by Alonso before the play ends. In the location assigned the isle in Chapter VII of this book, Caliban's claim that he was king of the isle before the arrival of Prospero makes him a Lord of Misrule. Prospero, as magician, is a Lord of Misrule, if one considers King James's ruling against magic. Before the play ends, Prospero turns over his authority and submits to the Rightful Lord (Christ). That replacement is associated with one of Prospero's identities (discussed in Chapter IV). The time of Prospero's reclamation of the dukedom and hence of the deposition of the Lords of Misrule in the play corresponds in the church year to the time of the manifestation of Christ to the Gentiles, divine revelation, and Epiphany.

Other associations can be established with the festivals and church rituals associated with the second performance of *The Tempest* in the winter of 1612–1613. The celebrations and events of the twelve days of the festival of Christmastide which ended with Epiphany have many correspondences in the play.

In order to identify specific references and allusions, it is necessary to understand not only the divisions of the English church year, but the nature of the celebrations and sacraments associated with those divisions. Epiphany was a favorite day for baptism for Gnostics before Catholics began to regard it as an appropriate day for that rite.[18] In the Middle Ages it was the time for the announcement of the date of Easter, was associated with dramatic representations of the Magi, and was linked not only with the rite of Baptism, but also with the stilling of the tempest, the miracle at the wedding in Cana, and the resuscitation of Lazarus. In *The Tempest* Shakespeare includes a "resurrection" of a son, presumed dead, "buried i' the ooze"; a "negative" dramatic presentation of the Magi in "the three men of sin"; an involuntary immersion (baptism) of all members of the ship of souls, excepting Ferdinand, who dove into the waters; a wedding; and the stilling of the tempest in the minds of wayward men. Kolve noted that one of the reasons all of the cycles "play the Flood" is its "major figural importance" which "derives from I Peter 3:20–21, in which Noah's ark, which brought some few souls to safety through the water, is compared to the waters of baptism, by which many are saved."[19] The ship's master, the crew and the boatswain, who appear on deck wet, may be assumed to have received the rite while performing their duties.

There was, in fact, a "tendency to regard it [Epiphany] as a celebration of all manifestations of the Divine nature of Christ."[20] Thus Epiphany came to include a celebration of the entire church year with its tides. Chapters IV and V will show how Shakespeare references and exemplifies the celebrations. Nevertheless, although Epiphany had a tendency to unite all the celebrations of the church year, it was associated, in particular, with a time of celebration for the manifestation of Christ to the Gentiles. There appears to be a link between the "three wise men" and "three men of sin," to be sure an opposite rather than an apposite link. Both groups of three do have in common the fact that they are Gentiles. In Ariel's appearance to the "three men of sin" as a "minister of Fate" the three are associated with Greek (Gentile) rather than Hebraic belief. Lessons with appropriate biblical readings regarding the effect of the manifestation to the Gentiles are drawn out in the 1959 *Book of Common Prayer* for the Sundays after Epiphany.

Not all of the festivities of the twelve days of Christmastide were solemn, nor were they fully Christian. The Feast of Fools began on Innocent's Day, December 28, and lasted until January 1, the day of the Feast of Asses. Innocents' Day, December 28, was a commemoration of the slaying of the innocent children by King Herod. "The Feast of Asses was a combined celebration of the flight into Egypt, Baalim's ass, and Jesus' entry into Jerusalem."[21] The incorporation of three widely scattered biblical events into one feast illustrates the integrated nature of religious observances in Shakespeare's time. It compares with the density of biblical allusion in *The Tempest* and the interconnections observed by recent critics in the Mystery Plays. The Feast of Fools and the Feast of Asses, as well as Saint John's Day and Epiphany, were mixed heavily with Roman midwinter festival activities. A similar mix with the Christian elements of *The Tempest* occurs with the appearance of Roman gods in the vision and the references made to the widow Dido and to Carthage, which was destroyed by the Romans in 146 B.C.

The English church accepted the Feast of Fools as an opportunity to parade the follies of men which needed to be purged through religious ritual. The feasts were supposed to mark man's folly, imperfection, and worldliness and to celebrate God's forgiveness through the humility of Christ. They were intended to encourage mortification, but they often became riotous. "The Liberty of December extended to New Year and Epiphany, covering the whole of the Christmas festival. The 'Misrule' called forth constant protests. In England the excesses of the Feast of Fools were abolished by proclamation of Henry VIII, July 22, 1542, though restored by Mary in 1554."[22]

In *The Tempest* Shakespeare parades some of the follies of men before his audience in the "troops" which Ariel "dispers'd ... 'bout the isle." The antics of the various faulted characters correspond to those occupying certain festival days during Christmastide. Antonio and members of his troop exemplify some of the follies of men; Stephano, Trinculo, and Caliban exemplify others. Whatever their assumed authority, it is subordinated to another's before the play ends. In fact, at all levels of island society presumption of authority has been attempted. Antonio usurped Prospero's dukedom. Caliban attempts to assume conjugal rights in his predacious pursuit of Miranda. Even Ferdinand, who for Wagner is an ideal, in an action corresponding to that of the disciple Peter's reaction in Gethsemane, exhibits folly in attempting to take Prospero's kingdom with a sword. While the king and Gonzalo sleep, Antonio tempts Sebastian to murder to gain authority. Prospero assumed magical authority with his books and staff. Stephano and Trinculo are prepared to follow Caliban to overthrow Prospero. Before the play ends earthly authority is restored rightly and the subjection of all to appropriate heavenly authority is delineated. Some are placed under the law, line and level; some receive the grace of forgiveness; and Prospero, bereft of his magic book and staff, finds his strength will come through prayer.

Reconsiderations of the cycles by twentieth century critics of the unity, content, purpose, meaning, and structure of the Mystery Plays and recent interest in their imagery, symbolism, and representational modes also have highlighted what was familiar to sixteenth and seventeenth century audiences and the frame of mind the audience brought to the theater, Bethell's "multi-consciousness." The detailed examination of the literary characteristics of the Mystery Plays has helped to disclose the literary usages which *The Tempest* has in common with them and has provided a basis for an analysis of *The Tempest* as a mystery play.

A considerable amount of recent scholarship has been devoted to studying the Mystery Plays. In fact, there has been such a proliferation of studies of medieval drama that a comprehensive account of it would not serve the purpose of this book. Some scholarship has been devoted to uncovering the literary qualities of the plays, some to comparison of extant manuscripts, some to an exhaustive examination of individual plays or a single cycle. All have been concerned with their unifying qualities and hence have contributed to an understanding of their meaning. The studies provide insights into cultural consciousness that made possible a more comprehensive view of *The Tempest*. They have not as yet been explored for their relevance to an interpretation of *The Tempest*. Greenblatt's identification of "a 'whole reading'" as a "satisfying illusion"[23] is real. However, his claim that time places limits on the construction of "a unified interpretative vision"[24] should not negate the search for one in light of the recent insights deriving from unification studies of the Mystery Plays. Moreover directors, while delivering the "whole" play, must decide how to present it. Peter Brook discovered "through a growing awareness that the overall unifying image was much less than the play itself"[25] and recognized that "a whole area of living experience that seems close to one's own concerns is also close to the concerns of the people in the world around one."[26] Brook also asserted, "Shakespeare forged a style in advance of any style anywhere, before or *since*, that enabled him, in a very compact space of time, by a superb and conscious use of varied means, to create a realistic image of life."[27] The compactness of Shakespeare's vision depends in part on the awareness of beliefs about time, human nature, and character which were available to persons living in the sixteenth and seventeenth centuries. The Mystery Plays, and the twentieth century discourses on their sources of unity, characterization, time frames, imagery, and purpose, afford abundant sources for comparable studies of Shakespeare's play. The brevity and complexity which underlie *The Tempest*, in spite of its airiness, are in part possible because Shakespeare used time concepts and modes of character representations and drew upon imagery and language with which his audiences were familiar, much of which had filtered down through years of Mystery Play enactment.[28] Studies dealing with the mode of character representation used, selection of biblical story, and time concepts are fundamental in establishing *The Tempest* as a mystery play. The recently edited texts of the Mystery Plays have also provided glosses to a vocabulary unfamiliar to today's readers. All these basics, woven into the fabric which is *The Tempest*, will be treated in depth in separate chapters.

Two early twentieth century works exemplifying different kinds of studies are E. K. Chambers's *Medieval Stage* (1903), a comprehensive discussion of custom as well as drama, and Marie Lyle's *The Original Identity of the York and Towneley Cycles: Studies in Language and Literature* (1919), showing the relationship between the York and Towneley plays.[29] In 1957 Purvis translated a version of the York cycle into its nearest equivalent in modern English and contracted it into a form "which might be acted in something under three hours."[30] With his contraction, Purvis showed that the themes and purpose of the whole cycle can be conveyed in the same length of time taken for the playing of *The Tempest*. Purvis found in the Mystery Plays "a noble simplicity and a direct and powerful handling which belong only to great art" and "a sincerity, a natural aptness of expression, a grandeur and unity of theme, a sweeping movement, and a nobility, which are never found together, and seldom even separately, except in great art."[31] The qualities he describes are characteristic of *The Tempest*. Behind the apparent simplicity lies a profound and unified complexity.

Recent discourses on the Mystery Plays have revealed patterns of thinking about time and biblical characters which made possible Shakespeare's compact vision in *The Tempest*, a vision that has more meaning than is readily available to today's audiences. A close analysis of the characteristics of the Mystery Plays and a comparison with Shakespeare's use of similar features in *The Tempest* bear heavily on the sense of the play. Focusing on the literary characteristics of the Mystery Plays, the twentieth century's scholarship uncovered their sources of unity, their time frames, and their purpose.

Kolve was one critic whose findings have provided insight into the basics of the Mystery Plays. He focused "on the Corpus Christi *kind*, on the elements essential to the tradition," identifying and exploring major themes and strategies.[32] His emphasis on "*kind*"[33] is à propos to this interpretation and its attempt, not to identify a particular cycle as source, but to show what *The Tempest* shares with the Mystery Plays and the Bible and to isolate the elements they contribute to Shakespeare's play.

Kolve disagreed with A. C. Cawley's conclusion that the Corpus Christi play "took the form of an elaborate dramatic presentation of 'every phase of the Christian story as a commentary on the daily ritual of the Mass.'"[34] He found a similar error in Hardin Craig's statement that "'the Corpus Christi play tells this story in its completest possible form.'"[35] Rather, Kolve found the cycle to be "highly selective" and that "it is selective in formally coherent ways."[36] He identified and commented on two principles of selection:

> the doctrine of figures, and the idea of the world having seven ages, can together do much to explain the hierarchic importance in the Middle Ages of these specific Old Testament stories. But the correspondence is so exact that something like intention seems implied. Somehow these cycles took form; somehow they took substantially the same form; and the form can best be explained and described in terms of these two organizing ideas.[37]

Thus Kolve accounts "for the obligatory presence of certain Old Testament plays, for their formal meaning and their hierarchic importance prior to the local dramatic meanings developed *within* the plays themselves."[38] Shakespeare's references to corresponding Old Testament plays and his portrayal of one character who appears in all of the cycles point to the Mystery Plays as a basic source and to Shakespeare's intent to present the same Mystery.

Davies, along with Kolve, found "two principles of selection and organization can be observed in the extant Corpus Christi plays."[39] He found those principles to be "that the arrangement is predominantly chronological ... [and] that the material is relatively comprehensive,"[40] not all-inclusive, "but that the story of man's destiny begins at the beginning and goes on to the end."[41] He cited the need for other principles of selection, acknowledged several that have been proposed, and pointed to their usefulness and inadequacies. He noted that "one of the latest [theories] is that a cycle can be conceived of as 'one vast sermon on repentance.'"[42] Happé concurred with that theory of purpose, averring that the Mystery Plays' intention was not literary, but "a religious and didactic one," celebrating "the Christian story from Creation to Doomsday with two central peaks in the Nativity and Passion of Christ." However, he compared the cycles' literary characteristics. He found that the "Towneley plays are much more complex than those of York" and that the Wakefield Master "exhibits a fine sense of dramatic effect, especially of comedy."[43] Shakespeare's dramatic effects and comical portrayal of Caliban, Stephano, and Trinculo share those characteristics, although they surpass anything done by the Wakefield Master.

In 1975 Meyers focused on the interrelationships of the plays within a cycle and identified and described a second typology within them: the diabolical, with key figures Lucifer, Pharaoh, Caesar, Herod, and Pilate, whom he identifies as negative antitypes of Christ.[44] The form of representation adapted from the Bible for use in the Mystery Plays is referred to as typology or figuration. Both type and antitype are used to describe one who prefigures Christ. Antitype is also used to describe characterizations that contribute to what Meyers calls diabolical typology. Shakespeare's use of types and antitypes (in both senses of the word — like and unlike) extends to his use of plays within plays in some of his dramas. The corollary in *The Tempest*, the vision of provision with Roman gods and goddesses as actors, can be taken as a typical vision or antitype of the Judeo-Christian providential design of the whole play. Many of the characteristics described by Mystery Plays critics compare with those of *The Tempest*.

Meyers concurred with Kolve's two organizing principles:

> the individual types actually used in the cycle dramas did not produce the theory of unified time found there: rather, all of typology, the work of St. Augustine, St. Irenaeus, St. Justin Martyr, etc., produced both the theory of time found in the plays and the elements of typology in the plays.... The unification of the plays is achieved through what may be called a typological outlook, rather than through the rigid application of the particular types. Types indeed have a major part in tying the plays together, but they extend primarily to the sacred material found there. The typological outlook, seeing history as the repetition of patterns, brings together the secular material and unites it with the sacred.[45]

Meyers identified typology as a key to the cycle plays, connecting the patriarchs of Israel in their foreshadowing of Christ.[46] Kolve's "doctrine of figures" and Meyers's typology describe the same usage. It should not be surprising to find Shakespeare's adaption of this common usage in *The Tempest*.

Rose noted, "The frequency of the journey motif is characteristic of drama in the round, and the Wakefield Plays and the *Ludus Coventriae* share this characteristic to a high degree."[47] It is a round — the circle scribed by Prospero — to which *The Tempest*'s shipwrecked souls journey. Within Prospero's circle members of the court party experience a renewing of their minds and Prospero rejects vengeance, accepting the law of forgiveness, Christ's law, celebrated in the Corpus Christi play.

Rose also distinguished the kinds of music accompanying various scenes. He noted, "In the *Ludus Coventriae Massacre of the Innocents*, ... even the entry of a banquet dish is the occasion for a fanfare," and that "fanfare sounds his [Herod's] last farewell.... On the other hand, it is the ringing of bells that attend the Nativity and the resurrection."[48] Thus he distinguished the kind of music used in association with good and evil characters and events. A similar distinction in sounds can be heard in *The Tempest*. There are so many sounds in *The Tempest* that a detailed examination of them and a comparison with those in the Mystery Plays with the help of the findings of the foregoing critics will be made in Chapter VIII.

Scholarship continued to flourish, with some critics comparing cycles while others focused attention on a single cycle. Woolf made a detailed literary and historical analysis of all four cycles, noting their interdependence and their differences.[49] Her findings did not negate the possibility that Shakespeare may have had access to the four cycles in one way or another.

Happé noted "a remarkable consistency in the four cycles and in the Beverley list. They are

> The Fall of Lucifer
> The Creation and Fall of Man
> Cain and Abel
> Noah and the Flood
> Abraham and Isaac
> Moses (not Beverley)
> The Prophets (not Beverley; Balaam at Chester)
> The Nativity — Annunciation, Suspicion of Joseph, Shepherds, Purification, Magi, Flight into Egypt
> Massacre of the Innocents
> The Baptism (not Chester)
> The Temptation (not Towneley)
> Lazarus
> The Passion — Conspiracy, Judas, Last Supper, Caiaphas, Condemnation, Crucifixion, Lament of Mary, Death
> The Resurrection and Ascension
> The Assumption and Coronation of the Virgin (not Towneley)
> — Doomsday."[50]

Elements from these plays which can be found in *The Tempest* will be cited in Chapter V where a comparison of *The Tempest* with *Ludus Coventriae* is made.

Pointing to differences in choice in the French *Mystères* which include the Old Testament characters Joseph and Job, Happé stated, "The English selection is determined by the intention to represent the important episodes of scriptural history which prefigure the life of Christ."[51] Thus Happé pointed to typology as a determinant in selection. All of these studies have provided a basis for comparison with *The Tempest*.

Claiming that *The Tempest* is a mystery play implies more than Northrop Frye's statement that it "would have a general Christian shape."[52] In his examination of the York, Wakefield, Chester, and N-Town cycles Stevens uncovered more than their "general Christian shape." He provided insight into their distinctive features, including their structures and their particularized interpretation of salvation history.[53] *The Tempest*, if a mystery play, would be Shakespeare's own interpretation of that history.

Of particular importance in a search for a basic source for *The Tempest* is Stevens's assertion "that the Corpus Christi play was the root of the native dramatic tradition," that it was "primarily from the religious theater of the Middle Ages that the later English stage, especially that of the High Renaissance, gained its sense of time and space and, therefore, its dramatic form — one that is, in many respects, the antithesis of the classical drama."[54] He wrote, "I perceive that this debt was the product of a world view more than a direct influence. Shakespeare, as is widely speculated, may have seen the Coventry plays. But what he knew about the *theatrum mundi* of the Middle Ages probably comes less from being a spectator than it did from *the absorption of the environment in which the drama was bred*"[55] (emphasis added). "Shakespeare and other playwrights inherited a stage that accommodated all the varieties of medieval drama, and they lived in a world that was influenced by a uniform salvation history, based on the Bible and its multiple interpreters and reflected in the liturgy, the art, and the social context of the late Middle Ages."[56] Stevens's assertions validate the appropriateness of a comparison between *The Tempest* and the Mystery Plays. The discovery of many similarities between *The Tempest* and the Mystery Plays led to the claim in this book that Shakespeare condensed the Corpus Christi play, giving his audiences a play which encompasses all human time and "o'ertops" treason when a "schoolmaster" (1.2.172), submitting to "a most auspicious star" (1.2.182), uses, then abandons, white magic, and imbues *The Tempest* with "transcendental supernaturalism," wonder, and beauty, and a sense of peace.

In the Bible, Old Testament characters pointed to Christ. Stevens wrote, "The Corpus Christi play ... is by definition concerned with the ubiquitous presence of the body of Christ in all of his shapes. It is this many-faceted Christ who is indeed the protagonist and the focus of the play."[57] Stevens, like Meyers, recognized a diabolical impersonation of God which he called "*simia Christi*, a figure that we recognize as a deliberate parodic impersonation. The playwright thus makes the very nature of impersonation, whether true or false, the pivotal aesthetic and moral concern of his play. His question, simply put, is, What is the proper form of *imitatio Dei*?"[58] There are parodic impersonations in *The Tempest*: Setebos, Sycorax's god (though only referenced), and Stephano, whom Caliban makes a god.

Similarities in selection of story, characterization, vocabulary, imagery, and duration in *The Tempest* and the Mystery Plays may become a means of determining how much Shakespeare relied on the Mystery Plays. Chapter IV uncovers Shakespeare's use of typology in *The Tempest*. Chapter V compares the biblical stories selected for use in one Mystery Play cycle with references to those stories in *The Tempest*. Chapter VI compares a common vocabulary and shows how glosses of obsolete words in Mystery Plays contribute to the meaning of *The Tempest*. Chapter VIII explores distinguishing sounds in both dramas and changes in masters and men. The time frames of the cycle plays and *The Tempest* are examined in Chapter X.

Throughout, the intermingling of the comic with the serious and the sublime will be noted, as well as themes and images. The correspondences cannot be fully explored in one chapter; therefore Shakespeare's mode of character portrayal will be compared first with that used in the Mystery Plays after a brief look at Shakespeare's own introduction.

Chapter III

Shakespeare's Turbulent Overture

In the preceding chapters the inclusiveness of Shakespeare's vision was affirmed by the enumeration of the many shards which have been unearthed by critics and by the identification of the Bible and its derivatives, the Mystery Plays and *the Book of Common Prayer* (1559), as basic sources for *The Tempest*.

The varied insights and interpretations of critics are illuminating, but no introduction can compete nor is as replete as the one Shakespeare provides in the first scene. Perhaps no opening scene of a Shakespearean play has been so lightly treated by the critics as that of *The Tempest*. It is difficult to assess why critics have not alluded to the several biblical tempests upon which Shakespeare draws. More understandable, perhaps, is the critics' diminution of the storm in their eagerness to escape the noise and explore the magic of the "yellow sands" and the wonders of the enchanted isle. In *The Meaning of "The Tempest"* Wilson confessed that Shakespeare's "opening scenes generally give us in broad and simple statement the main theme of the drama that follows," but he claimed that in *The Tempest*,

> the first scene serves as contrast, not as an initiation…. So overwhelming is the realism and so convincing, that the dramatist has us completely at his mercy for the wonders he means later to put upon us…. It serves as a kind of back-cloth to the Enchanted Island…. It is as if Shakespeare had packed his whole tragic vision of life into one brief scene before bestowing his new vision upon us.[1]

Wilson ignored the details of the first scene to the extent that he claimed falsely that the "king [was] lurking unseen in his cabin,"[2] whereas the king actually is the third person to speak on stage and when he does, he asks a question which involves a major theme of the play. It is ironic in a work titled *The*

41

Meaning of "The Tempest" that the point of the king's question, "Where's the Master?" is lost, for there is a search in the first scene for an authority effective in the storm. Not only can the king's question be taken to apply specifically, but in light of the universality of Shakespeare's dramas, it can be understood to imply the king's lack of control in this situation — the lack of control of the highest earthly authority. A king, too, needs a master with more control than he possesses, for as is revealed in Scene 2, the ship is laden with "souls."

Wilson was not alone in devaluing the first scene. Coleridge claimed, "The first scene was meant as a lively commencement of the story."[3] In "The Mirror of Analogy" Brower suggested that the first scene is significant for its *noise* which is juxtaposed against the serenity of the island, and passing over it he found that "all of these continuities" — which he has named previously as "strange-wondrous," "sleep-and-dream," "sea-tempest," "music-and-noise," "earth-air," "slavery-freedom," and "sovereignty-conspiracy" — "appear during the second scene of Act I, which is an exposition of Shakespeare's metaphorical and dramatic designs for the entire play."[4] However, unless we measure noise merely in decibels of sound and not in the amount of cacophony and confusion, we find considerable noise in many of the ensuing scenes. The tempestuous sounds of nature in the first scene are symbolic of the human disturbances, particularly of the disturbances in men's minds. The first scene is important for what it reveals about the characters of the ship's passengers as Tillyard[5] suggests, but its relevance is far greater than that.

The first scene is potent. A careful examination of it reveals that Shakespeare has not broken the pattern of disclosure found in the first scene of other plays and that he reveals the climate, themes, and thrust of the whole play at its onset. The words and questions in Shakespeare's introductory scene provide evidence of its sources, describe the human predicament, and predicate the means to a resolution. The first scene raises the question of control and mastery and the effectiveness of work, name, and advice in the face of disaster. It calls attention to men in a tempest, which for all we know upon a first reading or observing is a very real tempest of the elements, not a tempest induced by a man's (Prospero's) design.

Before we get to Master Prospero, we meet the ship's master. He is the first on stage and the first to speak. He it is who sets the tone for the play with his answer to the question, "What cheer?" which tells us it is to be "Good" (2, 3). The ship's master, not the king, is the authority in the craft that carries "souls."

The questions asked in the first scene are significant, not only in regards to the storm and the play, but to its meaning. The master is being sought and there is a question of his being heard. "Where's the Master?" "Where is the master, boatswain?" and "Do you not hear him?" (9, 12, 13) emphasize the themes of master and hearing and, together with "What cares these roarers for the name of king?" (16–17), raise the question of authority and where it is to be centered in the drama. Indeed, the controlling forces named in the scene are significant. They reveal who each character thinks is in charge. They are as diverse as the "sea," the "roarers," the work of the mariners and the boatswain, "good Fate," "destiny," the "name of King," "prayer," and "the wills above"–almost every kind of authority sought or feared by men in distress. The thrust of the whole scene is to question who is in charge and to whom each character ascribes authority. And if, as proposed in this vision, the play is talking about something greater than the enchanted isle and the storm, the answer to "Where's the Master?" will be someone other than Prospero even after his discourse in the second scene.

The mariners have a unique function in the play. They work to save those on board. They endeavor to bring them safely to the isle. They are not out of place in the play as the usurping duke is, and they do not get out of place on the ship as the king and company do. Their only words uttered, when they appear on stage, "wet," state the condition of those on board, "All lost!" and direct the men to a viable solution to their problems: "To prayers, to prayers!" (51). Having performed their mission, they enjoy "sore labor's bath" and arise refreshed at the end of the play to convey the company home to their rightful places in society. The importance of the prayers called for by the mariners is reflected in the Epilogue, when the restored duke of Milan confirms his need to pray, "Now I want/ Spirits to enforce, Art to enchant;/ And my ending is despair,/ Unless I be reliev'd by prayer" (Epi. 13–16). Neither identification of persons as "souls" nor a beginning and ending in prayer suggests merely an earthly dilemma or solution to humankind's predicament.

The boatswain had ordered the men to keep below. That is where they belong, not only on the ship during a storm, but in the hierarchical order of beings. Their despicable behavior places them *below* other men. Not only is the usurping duke out of place by being on deck, but he is out of place as duke in the proper order of rule and authority. For medieval and Renaissance man, place was important in the scheme of things. According to Gregory the Great, Noah's Ark "had three levels arranged in the shape of a pyramid, with reptiles and beasts below and birds and man above." He likened the ark to "the Church, which contains a greater number of carnal men, along with a smaller number of spiritual men and with one man, Christ, who is without sin, at the highest level."[6] The audience would probably catch the significance of the boatswain's order to keep "below."

Shakespeare's craft, unlike Noah's, is broken. It bears its cargo of "souls" close enough to the isle, so that with some effort on their part, they can reach it. In a length of time appropriate for the image Shakespeare conveys, it is fully restored.

Later in the first scene, when the usurping duke appears on deck with his brother and the honest old councillor, the boatswain asks other questions: "Yet again?" "What do you here?" "Shall we give o'er and drown?" and "Have you a mind to sink?" (38, 39). "Yet again?" suggests repeat offenders. The question is prophetic of the intended, though thwarted, behavior of these men in the play. "What do you here?" addresses both the reason for the three men's being on deck and the further question of what they are doing on the "ship of souls." Likewise, "Shall we give o'er and drown?" takes on a wider meaning when the company is identified as a "ship of souls." It inquires of the men whether they wish to be left to their own fate or submit to the continued efforts on the part of the mariners to save them. "Have you a mind to sink?" plays on the double meaning of *mind*. It questions the offenders' determination to be lost souls in spite of all efforts to save them, and asks whether they are aware of their own circumstances. It also questions the proper functioning of their minds. The reference to *mind* is significant on another level as we see later in the play when Prospero endeavors to bring some of the occupants to "clearer reason" (5.1.68). Used in connection with "to sink," it suggests the base mind that is in them may be destroyed, allowing the knowledge of good to take possession of their minds. These later questions deal with the human condition and choice.

After the mariners state the condition of the souls on board, Gonzalo, the councillor, introduces Shakespeare's theme of equality: "The King and Prince at prayers, let's assist them/ For our case is as theirs." The usurper is not shown praying, but cursing his fellowmen and choosing to "sink wi' th' King," with whom he has made a pact to usurp earthly authority. His evaluation of the situation is not reliable: "We are merely cheated of our lives by drunkards." He blames others for his plight. Gonzalo, however, true to character, calls for "mercy," submits to the "wills above," and correctly describes the immediate situation as well as political, religious, and social conditions which threaten the human family and a particular family (the ruling family of Milan), the Christian world and the church in Shakespeare's day: "We split, we split!" It may be assumed that if the initial condition (splitting) and the end (good cheer and "the peace of the present" [22]) are to be compatible, some kind of union and unity will be achieved and a master of the storm will be found before the play comes to a close. In the beginning of the scene, at his only appearance, the boat's master specifies who is responsible: "we run ourselves aground" (4). The passengers' contribution to the present disturbance is further called to our attention with the boatswain's "You mar our labor," "you do assist the storm," and "they are louder than the weather" (more noisy and tempestuous) (13, 14, 36–37). These statements point to the fact that the noise is not just elemental and that it is likely to persist wherever these persons are found. In the Mystery Plays noise and cacophony were associated with the rabble and silence and prayer with the master, Christ.

In the first scene Shakespeare also designates the time of the play and the condition existing at that time, "mischance of the hour" (25–26). It is important to recognize the time limit placed upon the storm. The storm is not an eternal mischance, and we may expect that the ensuing unpleasantries of the play will not be enduring. We can expect rescue and salvage of the *souls* who are aboard the ship. Shakespeare states the dual purpose of the play: "command these elements to silence, and work the peace of the presence"[present?] (21, 22). Although in the midst of the storm, the silencing of the elements carries specific meaning, as the play develops the meaning behind that phrase is amplified when Prospero bids farewell in the "ye elves" speech to the "weak masters" "by whose aid" he "bedimmed/ The noontide sun, called forth the mutinous winds,/ And 'twixt the green sea and the azur'd vault/ Set roaring war" (5.1.40–44). The "peace of the present" also emphasizes the time of the play — the present, which is echoed throughout the play in the abundant "now."

Shakespeare designates the types of people we may expect to meet in the play. They are master, boatswain, mariners, king, councillor, "uncharitable dog," "insolent noisemaker," "wench" (Sycorax), prince, drunkards, "widechopp'd rascal," wife, children, brother. The appellations in the mouths of the cast are not necessarily properly applied and in the perverse characters tend to be self-reflective.

Almost every word of the first scene is freighted with meaning and usually with layers of meaning. Moreover, the tempest is a biblically composite tempest. Key words and phrases taken from the biblical text of tempest scenes in Jonah, Matthew, Mark, Luke, and John evoke memories of those scenes, suggesting a biblical base and the cosmic emphasis of the drama. In the Hebrew Scriptures tempests were a means of breaking a man's will, as in the story of Job (Job 9:17); changing his course, as in the story of Jonah; or punishing an entire people for their sin, as in the story of the flood. There is great similarity between the first scene of *The Tempest* and Jonah's account of a storm, for in that account "the mariners were afraid, and cried every man unto his god" (Jonah 1:5). In the play, as we have already pointed out, all kinds of gods or authorities are invoked as possible sources of relief. In the Jonah story the cessation of the tempest was not achieved through the seafarers' prayers, but upon the disembarkation of the disobedient. Further, it was within the *circle* of the whale's belly, a place of isolation and disenchantment with his own wishes, that Jonah made his peace with the wills above. Although the first scene does not present the circle of the island or the circle drawn by Prospero where minds are defumed, those in Shakespeare's audience who recognized the similarities with the Jonah story could anticipate some kind of enclosure where a change would occur in the minds of those who "are louder than the storm."

In the New Testament tempests were evidences of the miraculous, such as the Pauline tempest (Acts 28:34) referenced in the second scene of the play: "Not a hair perish'd" (1.2.217). In the Gospels they were affirmations of the power of The Master to control the elements of nature. Indeed, the Gospel records of tempests are always associated with The Master "that even the wind and the sea obey" (Matthew 8:27). He it is who calms the storm and, when seen "walking on the sea," calmed men's fears with the words "good cheer" (Matthew 14:27).

Although the master of the New Testament commands, "Peace, be still" (Mark 4:39), the councillor cannot "command these elements to silence," nor can he "work the peace of the present" as instructed by the boatswain. The councillor can not use his "authority" to stop the storm, but the New Testament master did still the storm and "taught ... as one having authority" (Matthew 7:29).

The Psalmist declares, "Upon the wicked he shall rain snares, fire, and brimstone, and an horrible tempest" (11:6), words which correspond quite closely to Ariel's description of his own performance: "flam'd amazement," "burn[ed] in many [a] place," "lightnings," "dreadful thunder-claps," "the fire and cracks/ Of sulfurous roaring the most mighty Neptune/ Seem to besiege, and make his bold waves tremble,/ Yea, his dread trident shake" (1.2.198–206).

Similar associations of tempests with God's judgments were held in the Middle Ages. Tillyard noted that the medieval concept that fortune and nature were the "tool[s] of God and the educator of man" continued to be held in Renaissance thought and that "for the Elizabethans the moving forces of history were Providence, fortune, and human character."[7]

Still further clues to the nature of the play are given in the first scene, and a society that had seen Miracle and Mystery plays, been exposed to biblical art and narrative, and participated in the rituals and festivals of the English church year would recognize these clues. Gonzalo's remarks about the boatswain, taken out of context, are reminders of Judas Iscariot, who was "born to be hanged" (32–33) and of whom it could be said, "the rope of his destiny [is] our cable" (31). If the story to which Gonzalo's remarks call attention is not so, then "our case is miserable" (33). Lifted completely out of context, "If he be not born to be hang'd, our case is miserable" can also have reference to the crucifixion of Christ. It is just such phrases that would induce resonances in the minds of a seventeenth century audience, especially in connection with the rescuing of a ship of "souls."

One more allusion in the first scene, properly understood, illuminates further the inclusiveness of Shakespeare's presentation. The curse that Antonio inflicts upon the boatswain — "would thou mightst lie drowning,/ The washing of ten tides"— has not been explained in full. A note in the Arden Shakespeare calls this curse "an exaggerated form of the sentence passed upon pirates by the English court of Admiralty, which was that they should be hanged on the shore at low water mark and remain there until three tides had flowed and ebbed."[8] The editor fails to consider that the other seven tides can be accounted for by the seven tides of the church year, of which Shakespeare's original audiences would have been very aware, since church attendance was required and absence punished. One might also take into account that the tides celebrated by the medieval church numbered eleven at one time and changes made to reduce that number may have been gradual. Furthermore, sacraments were associated with tides. Rust lists ten items under Ritual: litany, suffrages, baptism, confirmation, matrimony, visitation of the sick, extreme unction, burial, purification, and Ash Wednesday.[9] It appears that Shakespeare forecasts his intention to include either the washings of nature, the tides of the church, or both in the play.

In just sixty-eight short lines, Shakespeare presents the themes of hearing, master-authority, equality, tempest (internal and external); designates the time (now); describes the human predicament; acknowledges the seasons or rituals of the church year; and paraphrases a part of the Lord's Prayer: "The wills above be done!" In these brief lines Shakespeare gives a comprehensive introduction both to his drama and to the plight of humankind, contemporary and universal, and alludes to a means of resolution of the human problem. Scene One is a remarkable proem to *The Tempest*.

Chapter IV

Shakespearean Typology: The Several Identities of Characters in *The Tempest*

"Who's there ?" "Are you a man?" Macbeth *2.3.8, 3.4.57*

Bethell averred, "More has been written about character than about any other theme in Shakespearean criticism.... [B]ut there is still some haziness about the principles governing Shakespeare's presentation of character."[1] Brook noted that "Shakespeare's verse gives density to the portrait."[2] The density may be explained in part by what Bethell described as "The mixed mode of character presentation favored by Shakespeare and the popular dramatic tradition [which] depends for its validity upon the principle of multiconsciousness."[3]

Shakespeare's use of the multiconsciousness mode of representation has led to a wide variety of identifications for Prospero. Almost two hundred years after the First Folio appeared with *The Tempest* as the lead play, Clark asked, "Who is Prospero?" and pointed out that his question "has agitated the minds of countless thousands who have been charmed by *The Tempest*. Some have wondered whether he is intended to be the personification of Destiny. Others have conjectured that he is Shakespeare himself."[4]

Being somewhat confused by Prospero's many traits, James found Prospero is "Jupiter ... of *Cymbeline* ... in a heavy disguise of mortality. Here is no crude descent of a god. God Prospero may be; but he is also a very human, impatient old gentleman. His humanity is as perfectly set out as his divinity.... But [Shakespeare made] ... an all too human character of his divinity in *The Tempest*."[5]

Prospero has been described by Tillyard as a ruler who has made a tragic

49

mistake and then repented of it, and interpreted as a "Superman" by Knight, "an harmonious and fully developed *will*" by Dowden, "an artist of a kind" by Zimbardo, as "the representative of Art" by Kermode, as "the instrument of judgement" by Traversi, as "a philosopher" by Clark, as "the prototypical Supreme Being, whom indeed the pagan hierophant was deemed to represent" by Still, and as the symbol of "reason" or the "thinking, understanding mind with its crowning faculty, reason" by Wagner.[6] Although it may appear as Traversi suggests that Prospero is judging, his role is not as judge, but as "schoolmaster," who brings awareness of the law to the untaught and the recalcitrant.

Wagner's identification of Prospero with reason not only reduces him from man to symbol, but divests the play of its divinity in exalting man's reason. Wagner does extend her description of Prospero—"He is reasoning mind plus knowledge"—but she sees Prospero's books as "a symbol of scientific knowledge" rather than books of magic. This interpretation is not compatible with either Prospero's drowning of his book (5.1.57) or Shakespeare's comments about the separation of the branches of knowledge and Leontes's rationalism gone irrational in *The Winter's Tale*.

Wagner emphasizes reason in her thesis that Shakespeare is concerned in *The Tempest* with the expulsion of pagan ideas that have crept into Christianity. Reason and the new scientific thinking appear to her to be the method by which Shakespeare expunges error and spurious ideas from Christianity.[7] She fails to recognize that it was science in the first place that provided a false framework on which both Paganism and the church could build their cosmologies. Copernicus did not create an entirely new pattern for the heavens. Much earlier Heraclides of Pontus (born c. 400–380 B.C.) assumed "that only the interior planets, Mercury and Venus revolved around the sun, while the sun and the other planets revolved around the earth." Aristarchus (c. 217–c. 145 B.C.) "placed the sun in the center of the planets."[8] For centuries mainline scientists rejected the possibility of a heliocentric model and subscribed to the erroneous Ptolemaic model of the heavens. Shakespeare, unlike Wagner, subordinates the new science, magic, and reason to human need and plays the music of the spheres in a different key with new authority figures. Those figures — masters, not gods — will be described in this chapter; their spheres of influence, in Chapter VIII.

Prospero does not figure primarily or fit solely into any of the aforementioned designations. They err who make Prospero only a symbol or equate him with divinity. In *The Tempest* as in some of Shakespeare's other plays, characters exhibit aspects both of divinity and humanity, yet they should not be seen as gods.

Hassel's view of Prospero as a man is broader than that of Wagner or James: "He has tasted his finitude and his infinitude to the lees, and he has learned that he must be something of both to be a man." Hassel points to the revels passage and the Epilogue as evidence of both Prospero's awareness of his mortality and his "human weakness with the paradoxical blessings of humility and forgiveness." Hassel sees the last plays as a "return to the comic–Christian sense of human life as an insubstantial pageant with a benevolent, forgiving auditor," urging "upon their Renaissance audience a comforting old response to the new scientific rationalism that may be threatening their composure."[9] Hassel's view of the last plays thus concords with this study in rejecting Wagner's rationalism and scientific purgation and in ascribing to the Christian sense of human life in *The Tempest*. (Chapter VIII describes the specific nature of that comfort.)

Bethell, too, finds Shakespeare inclusive in his outlook. He compares Shakespeare's mode of character presentation with a more limited mode:

> The change from conventionalism to naturalism, from multiconsciousness to what we might call theatrical monism, reflects not only a change in technical resources but also a profound change in metaphysical outlook. Theatrical naturalism ... is a product of philosophical materialism, which monistically denies reality to the supernatural. Scientific interest in individual case history, as displayed by Ibsen and the naturalists, is the only sort of interest in humanity possible when humanity has been ousted from its central position in the universe. But the Shakespearean presentation of character depends on a multiconsciousness related to that balance of opposites which constitutes the universe of Christianity: God and man; spirit and matter; time and eternity.[10]

Although Bethell, Hassel, Still, and Wagner acknowledge that the play is concerned with Christianity, Wagner's and Still's ideas of Shakespeare's purpose differ markedly from Bethell's and Hassel's. Neither Bethell nor Wagner nor Hassel associated the play with the Mystery Plays. Although in the title of his book *Shakespeare's Mystery Play: A Study of "The Tempest"* Still identified it correctly, he did not make a comparison of the play with one or more of the Mystery Plays; rather, he compared it with pagan rites of passage. If *The Tempest* is a Christian play, however, then Prospero, the principal character, must be associated in some way with Christianity.

Presenting Christianity posed a problem since Shakespeare could not use freely the name of God or of Christ in the theater.[11] If the name of the deity could not be mentioned, how could Shakespeare bring the idea of divinity into the play? In the Mystery Plays, as was pointed out earlier, Old Testament characters typified some aspect of Christ. The plays also used Christ's name anachronistically in the Old Testament. If Shakespeare's characters, in what has been identified herein as his Mystery Play, are intended to typify some aspect of divinity, they would have had to have traits and functions similar to scriptural characters since Shakespeare did not use biblical names. Similar behavioral characteristics, along with imagery and a vocabulary familiar to the audience, would convey the sense he intended. For an audience whose members were required to attend church and listen to homilies and to the reading of most of the Bible every year, and where, all about them they saw biblical scenes engraved in masonry, carved in wood, painted in frescoes and arranged in collages of stained glass, a word or phrase could bring to remembrance many biblical stories, interlocking themes and character figurings. Part of the compactness and inclusiveness of the vision that is *The Tempest* can be attributed to Shakespeare's use of words, which not only had dual or triple senses but also brought to mind particular dramas, art, or texts with which audiences were familiar.

Prospero is severally associated and should be severally identified. He functions in the play as a magician, and describes himself as the deposed duke of Milan, Miranda's father, and her "schoolmaster" (1.2.172). He confesses both his neglect of duty as duke and "being transported/ And rapt in secret studies" (1.2.76–77). Awareness of the multiconsciousness operative in *The Tempest* should enable us to recognize Prospero's several identities and shuttle from one of his personalities to another. Shakespeare assists us by using changes of apparel for Prospero. (The dual or multiple identities of other characters must be comprehended without that kind of help.) Prospero alternately wears a mantle called a "magic garment" (1.2.23) or a "robe" (1.2.169), wears his magic robes (5.1, beginning of scene), carries a staff and a book (5.1.54, 57), wears a hat and carries a rapier (5.1.84), or appears disrobed as Miranda's father before he puts on his schoolmaster's robe.

After the "ship of souls" is "dash'd all to pieces" (1.2.8), Prospero assures Miranda

> No harm:
> I have done nothing, but in care of thee,
> Of thee, my dear one; thee, my daughter, who
> Art ignorant of what thou art, nought knowing
> Of whence I am, nor that I am more better
> Than Prospero, master of a full poor cell,
> And thy no greater father [1.2.15–21].

Prospero's "what thou art," "of whence I am," and "more better than" forecast there will be a revelation of his and Miranda's identity. It will go beyond Milan. Prospero asks Miranda to help him remove his magician's attire: "Lend thy hand,/ And pluck my magic garment from me. So./[*Lays down his mantle.*]/ Lie there my Art" (1.2.23–25). Disrobed, as her father, he relates his experiences as "once" duke of Milan and his care of Miranda under the adverse circumstances occasioned by his "neglect of duty" and his brother's treachery. Disrobed, he is simply — or not so simply, if we consider one of Miranda's identities — her father, once duke of Milan. After giving her a Milan family history lesson, he changes his attire: "[*Puts on his robe*]"[12] (1.2.169), which may differ from the mantle he laid aside earlier or be the same garment serving differently. Robed, he rises and announces another identity, that of "school-master"(1.2.172). In that capacity he apprises Miranda that his "prescience" (1.2.180) is more far-reaching than Milan, for he is aware of "a most auspicious star" in his "zenith" (1.2.182, 181). In his heaven-oriented role, he is Miranda's "careful" tutor (1.2.173) as well as that of others in the play.

As a schoolmaster Prospero has a wide range of protégés. After Miranda falls asleep, he continues in the role of schoolmaster, checking on Ariel's performance, repeating his monthly lessons, and rebuking him for forgetting: "Hast thou, spirit,/ Perform'd to point *The Tempest* that I bade thee?" (1.2.194) and "I must/ Once in a month recount what thou hast been,/ Which thou forget'st" (1.2.261–263). He teaches Caliban to distinguish the lesser and bigger lights by naming. He teaches Stephano, Trinculo, and Caliban the consequences of foolish and gluttonous behavior by leading them through a bog. He teaches Ferdinand restraint, communal responsibility, and respect. With thunderous sounds and a banquet he teaches Sebastian and Antonio that everything they plan and see is not within their grasp. His prime pupil, whom he takes great care to instruct, is Miranda. Under his tutelage she has become a sensitive and caring person, who pleads with her father to show mercy on the "fraughting souls." Not least among those instructed by Prospero are members of the audience, who along with Miranda are encouraged to remember what "lives in" their minds from the "dark backward and abysm of time" (1.2.49–50) and who are reminded throughout his lengthy recounting to "heed," "hear," and "listen." Prospero's constant reminders to Miranda to pay attention and his suggestions that she is not listening are also directed at the audience. Schucking stated that Prospero "unintentionally appears in the light of a schoolmaster," but at considerable length he gives examples of Prospero's pedagogy.[13] The evidence he offers abrogates his claim that Shakespeare's portrayal was unintentional.

If Prospero's appearance as magician, dressed in a mantle and equipped with a staff, did not arouse suspicions, his designation as "schoolmaster" should have for a biblically literate society, as well as for those familiar with the Mystery Plays; for Prospero has still another identity, that of an historical character, which is subtly presented by Shakespeare. Recognition of that identity is important to a fuller understanding and appreciation of the play. That unnamed identity establishes *The Tempest* as a mystery play. It has escaped the attention of critics but may well have been obvious to seventeenth century audiences. The "haziness" Bethell found in Shakespeare's presentation of character is dissolved and the divine attributes critics have ascribed to Prospero are properly assigned when the mode Shakespeare uses for representation of historical characters is identified as figuration or typology. Throughout *The Tempest*, Shakespeare uses that biblical mode of representation, referred to earlier as a unifying factor in the Mystery Plays. With it he provides correspondences between his characters and historical personages without loss of contemporaneous individuality. In the Old Testament many characters figure some aspect of divinity, foreshadowing Christ. No doubt it is Shakespeare's use of this mode of representation that is partially responsible for critics' sense of the divine in Prospero, who is, in fact, in all of his representations a man.

In the use of figuration, correspondences and differences exist between characters, and although the person figures another, he is a person in his own right in an historical or dramatic context. Figuration is a far more distinctive and sophisticated approach than abstracting the quality of a person as in *Everyman* or attempting to impersonate another. Moreover, its use adds dimensions to the play, since it brings awareness of two or more personalities even though they are not visible on stage as separate actors. Along with the use of dual, triple, and obsolete word meanings, figuration provided a way for Shakespeare to tap into what lived in the minds of his audience, and it accounts for part of his success in conveying a great variety of ideas in a relatively brief script. It also imparts meaning. The compactness and inclusiveness of the vision that is *The Tempest* can in part be attributed to Shakespeare's ability to draw on the audience's familiarity with the modes of character representation used in the Mystery Plays and on the cultural concepts of time.

Shakespeare's mystery play covers the same human time period as the medieval plays. However, his typology differs from that of the medieval plays in that his cast of characters do not have biblical names or belong to biblical times. Some of them figure biblical persons who in turn are types or antitypes of Christ. Shakespeare's failure to use biblical names for his characters does not make them nontypical. In the Mystery Plays, contemporary characters portrayed biblical characters, who figured as types or antitypes of Christ. Ira Clark noted that some sixteenth and seventeenth poets, e.g. Donne, Herbert, and Vaughan, were using what he called "neotypology," "devout personal lyrics based in types" which amounted to the insertion of personal experience into biblical settings.[14] Clark pointed out that one of the ways allegory differs from typology is that in typology "both type and antitype have independent historical existence."[15] Shakespeare also used contemporized typological events in relating beliefs established by the church and promulgated in the medieval plays.

Shakespeare's use of nonbiblical names did not imply loss of the sacred meaning of the play. The comic aspects of both the Corpus Christi play and Shakespeare's play served a dual purpose. Kolve wrote, "The Corpus Christi drama is an institution of central importance to the English Middle Ages precisely because it triumphantly united man's need for festival and mirth with instruction in the story that most seriously concerned his immortal soul."[16] Miranda and Prospero identify those brought to the isle by Prospero as "poor souls" (1.2.9) and "fraughting souls" (1.2.13), not as men or fools as in Brant's *Ship of Fools*.

Shakespeare did not depend only upon costume and function for clues to Prospero's historical identity. He provided a nominal and a numerical clue. Biblical names were indicative of character or associated with events and their place in history. Name changes were indicative of changes in persons' lives, e.g. Abram and Sarai became Abraham and Sarah and Saul of Tarsus became Paul. Methuselah, who was the oldest man to have lived, died in the year of the flood. His long life suggests the mercy of God in delaying the destruction of humankind.

The name Prospero is suggestive. Prosper is a word associated in Scripture with one of the major themes of the play, that of hearing. Prospero's name and his emphasis on hearing and heeding can be associated with a biblical character. His name is as significant as Angelo in *Measure for Measure*. Angelo is not an angel unless he is a fallen one, and certainly in terms of banishment Prospero is not very prosperous. However, Prospero's words, like those of God's law, do not return void, but they "prosper in the thing whereto ... [they were] sent" (Isaiah 55:11). Before Moses took leave of the Israelites and after he had repeated the Ten Commandments, he said, "Hear therefore, O Israel, and observe to do it; that it may be well with thee, and that ye may increase mightily" (Deut. 6:3). King David of Israel instructed his son, Solomon, "Then shalt thou prosper, if thou takest heed to fulfill the statutes and judgments, which the Lord charged Moses with concerning Israel" (I Chron. 22:13). The Psalmist associated God's law and prosperity: "his delight is in the law of the Lord; ... and whatsoever he doeth shall prosper" (1:2, 3). Job's struggle with his losses was in part due to the concept promulgated in the Old Testament that the righteous would prosper. Hence, "Prospero" suggests an Old Testament rather than a New Testament character. If *The Tempest*, like the Mystery Plays, is a Bible play, then in the expanded plot of *The Tempest* the most appropriate figuring for Prospero, who stands for the law in Milan and identifies himself as "schoolmaster," would be Moses, who in biblical writ and the Mystery Plays was both lawgiver and teacher. In Chapter V of this study the comparison of Shakespeare's selectivity of biblical reference with specific plays in the *Ludus Coventriae* cycle helps to establish the correspondence between Prospero and Moses as lawgivers and teachers.

Moses is called a "figure" in the Bible: "Nevertheless death reigned from Adam to Moses, even over them that had not sinned after the similitude of Adam's transgression, who is the figure of him that was to come" (Romans 5:14). Although this passage may present an ambiguity and raise the question of who is the figure of whom, both Adam and Moses figured, in one respect, the One who was to come. The antitype could be positive or negative; that is, the antitype of the failed son of God, Adam, could be the unfailing Son of God, Christ. But Adam's repentance made him a lately obedient son and he would then be a positive antitype, the first created human son of God. Moses, the lawgiver, was a teacher and a type of Christ, who taught his disciples a new law, the law of forgiveness — even of enemies. Therefore, when Clark wrote of Prospero, "In this spirit realm Prospero's word is law," he came close to suggesting Prospero's historical identity.[17] In pictorial and dramatic representations Moses carried a staff and book, the book of the law and a shepherd's staff that was used magically before Pharaoh and his court magicians.

One of the finer details of similarity involving numbers, which a seventeenth century audience might be more aware of than a twentieth century audience and which called forth "speculation" for Anne Barton Righter, intimates Shakespeare's figuring of Prospero as Moses. Righter claimed, "Within the play itself, [Shakespeare] has a perplexing habit of posing conundrums: 'I/ Have given you here a third of mine own life' (4.1.2–3), or the declaration that once returned to Milan 'Every third thought shall be my grave' (5.1.311). Mathematical precision of this kind positively asks for speculation as to the nature of the other two-thirds. In neither case can an answer be supplied. The dramatist knows, but is not telling."[18] Righter's claim provides a challenge. This study proposes that with a knowledge of the facts to which Shakespeare alludes, one does find answers, and those answers make for a more nearly complete interpretation of the play and a widened vision of it. If the exact numerical proportion, "third," does have significance, Shakespeare's use of it here may have been to identify with the number of years assigned to the divisions of years in Moses' life and to the proportion of his life devoted to the leadership of the children of Israel. The several corresponding biblical facts are recorded in Acts and Deuteronomy: "And when he was full forty years old, it came into his heart to visit his brethren the children of Israel.... Then fled Moses at this saying, and was a stranger in the land of Madian, where he begat two sons. And when forty years were expired, there appeared to him in the wilderness of mount Sina an angel of the Lord in a flame of fire in a bush" (Acts 7:23, 29–30). "And Moses was an hundred and twenty years old when he died: his eye was not dim, nor his natural force abated" (Deut. 34:7). Moses visited the children of Israel at age forty. Subsequently, he killed an Egyptian and fled to the wilderness where he remained for the next forty years. Taken together the two forty-year periods make up two-thirds of his life. He devoted the rest — one hundred and twenty minus eighty, i.e., one-third of his life (the proportion mentioned by Prospero) — to the deliverance and teaching of Israel.[19]

Although at first we may not relate Prospero's magic to the Bible, we may with a closer reading and biblical knowledge become aware of other similarities between Moses and Prospero. Prospero, who at times wears a magician's mantle and carries a staff, performs a function similar to that performed by Moses. Although we still have available to us the Book of the Law of Moses, we do not have his wonder-working rod, so we tend to forget that aspect of Moses' authority. In the miracle of the burning bush, recorded in Exodus 3 and 4, when Moses casts his shepherd's rod on the ground at divine command, it becomes a serpent, frightening Moses. When Moses picks the serpent up by the tail, again at divine command, it becomes a rod once more (Exodus 4:2–4). In Pharaoh's court with his rod Moses proved himself a greater magician than Egypt's magicians, and later with his staff he visited ten plagues upon the Egyptians. Prospero simulates Moses in using a magician's staff that controls factors in nature. Caliban acknowledges that Prospero's power is superior to that of Sycorax's god, Setebos: "His Art is of such pow'r/ It would control my dam's god, Setebos,/ And make a vassal of him" (1.2.374–376). Miranda refers to Caliban's "vile race" that "had that in't which good natures/Could not abide to be with" (1.2.360–362). These remarks may have been meant to help promote the association of Prospero with Moses and distinguish between the Egyptians, represented by Sycorax and Caliban, and the Israelites. In *The Tempest* Caliban recounts the plagues Prospero visits on him:

> his spirits hear me,
> And yet I needs must curse. But they'll nor pinch,
> Fright me with urchin-shows, pitch me i' th' mire,
> Nor lead me, like a firebrand, in the dark
> Out of my way, unless he bid 'em: but
> For every trifle are they set upon me,
> Sometime like apes, that mow and chatter at me,
> And after bite me; then like hedgehogs, which
> Lie tumbling in my barefoot way, and mount
> Their pricks at my footfall; sometime am I
> All wound with adders, who with cloven tongues
> Do hiss me into madness [2.2.3–14].

Although Frye glosses Caliban's curse, "The red plague rid you" (1.2.366), as the bubonic plague,[20] the red plague may well be a reference meant to remind Shakespeare's audience of the last plague inflicted by Moses, the death of the Egyptian firstborn and the attempt by Pharaoh to drive the Israelites into the Red Sea. The bubonic plague is usually referred to as the black plague. Prospero also plagues some of the recalcitrant in *The Tempest* by having Ariel lead them through a bog, *their* wilderness wandering. The humor and ridiculous behavior that occur when Stephano and Trinculo discover Caliban parallels scenes in the Mystery Plays where the follies of human nature are paraded. One example is found in the Noe play where Noah's wife rebels against going into the ark and sits among "gossips" who discuss the foolishness of Noah's endeavors, a scene which has no counterpart in the Bible.

The seventeenth century was exposed to and maintained an ambivalent attitude to white magic, and dramatists used it in various ways to impress their audiences. Woodman noted "the almost simultaneous appearance of *The Alchemist* and *The Tempest*. In one, the white magician, as charlatan, was used as an admirable tool for social satire; in the other, he was made genuine, and seen as a symbolic, mythic figure."[21]

Woodman suggested that because the English body politic was vulnerable, the possibilities of achieving order through the aids of white magic were strongly appealing to audiences. Just as healing through white magic was shown to bring health to the diseased individual, so it might also promote order in the diseased body politic. The traditional white magician might conduct his benevolent works ... to reconcile rebels or usurpers and thus bring order to a foundering state.... Prospero's power over his spirit Ariel enables him to accomplish a series of triumphant maneuvers that culminate in a harmonious reunion as well as in his restoration to a usurped throne. Not only does he cure some of the diseased minds of the rebels but he also cures the diseased body politic of his kingdom.[22]

In *The Tempest* both the body politic and the minds of men are diseased. Prospero uses his white magic to cure both.

Citing Moses as a prototype of the white magician, Woodman wrote, "Moses ... demonstrated his skills to prove that the all-powerful God was on his side, and also to destroy the enemies of the Israelites. By miraculously producing water and food in the desert, he also revealed himself as the tribal medicine man."[23]

Prospero, a mythic figure, uses his magic as Moses did to achieve a release from bondage. In the play that release is from the bondage of the characters' hearts and minds, which are held captive to murderous intents or foolish, self-aggrandizing thoughts. Prospero not only prevents the evil forces from taking over the isle, but he prepares a banquet. Thus Woodman places Prospero in the same tradition as Moses, although he does not suggest that the former figures the latter.

Both Moses and Prospero could be described as "neglecting worldly ends" (1.2.89). Under somewhat different circumstances than Prospero, Moses turned from the responsibilities of Egyptian rule — which would have been his, since he was brought up in Pharaoh's house — to the shepherding of Jethro's sheep. Prospero, neglecting earthly governance, was "transported/ And rapt in secret studies" (1.2.76–77). There appear to be more correspondences between Moses and Prospero than between any other Old Testament character and Christ in the Mystery Plays. Perhaps the number of correspondences was necessary to establish the relationship in the minds of the audience.

The association of Moses and Prospero does not curtail the uniqueness or humanity of either character, and Shakespeare makes this clear in *The Tempest* by having Prospero change garments each time he assumes a different role in the play. Thus Shakespeare uses the biblical mode of representation available to him, in which a human being can be both a figure of another and a living person in his own right. Shakespeare juggled human characteristics so that no one can be identified exactly with another person. Differences between Prospero and Moses allow the audience to perceive both characters at the same time, and to perceive meaning that is only available through typology.

Typology is suggestive, but there is never a one-to-one comparison between the figure and the one figured, type and antitype. In Prospero's reason for using magic and his reason for losing his rulership, Shakespeare used figuring as a means of representation rather than substitution. Moses used magic to persuade a king to release a people from physical bondage that denied them time for worship. Prospero used magic to bring the release of individuals from the perversion of their own wills and minds. Moses abandoned his opportunity as Pharaoh's adopted son to be ruler of Egypt, choosing instead to identify with his blood brothers; Prospero was banished from his dukedom by his brother after his absorption with art and books caused him to neglect his duty. As duke of Milan, Prospero was too careless about his duty and put too much trust in his brother, thereby putting temptation in his brother's way. Not so Moses, who chose "rather to suffer affliction with the people of God, than to enjoy the pleasures of sin for a season" (Hebrews 11:25). However, the similarities between Moses and Prospero are striking and much greater than the differences. Prospero brings each man, not just to enchantment, but to knowledge of the truth about the human condition and human relationships. With his magical staff, his book, his own knowledge and his airy servant he accomplishes this task with means similar to those of Moses, who used his rod to change natural phenomena and taught God's laws to the Israelites.

The figuring of Prospero as Moses allows us to evaluate him less harshly than did Wilson, who found him to be "a terrible old man, almost as tyrannical and irascible as Lear at the opening of the play."[24] Prospero is dealing with would-be repeat murderers, not only with a would-be murderer of himself and his infant daughter, and with natural man, uninhibited by law, who would violate his daughter. His "neglect of duty," which afforded his brother the occasion for evil, is hardly so serious a crime as willful plotting of murder or rape. The equality of retribution of the law expressed in "an eye for an eye and a tooth for a tooth" would not allow for the equating of neglect with murder. Even Tillyard's amelioration of Wilson's description, which limits the evaluation to "Prospero as he once was, not the character who meets us in the play, in whom these traits are mere survivals," does not seem to be an appropriate evaluation of one who preferred art and magic to governance.[25] They better apply to Moses, who killed an Egyptian before fleeing to the desert. Only the figuring of one as the other allows us to infer a murderous intent in Prospero—unless, of course, we accept anger or "vexation" as equivalent to the deed, a New Testament concept. However, Moses' reluctance to deal with Pharaoh and lead Israel out of bondage might be compared to Prospero's distaste for governing. As Prospero had Ariel, Moses had a mouthpiece: Aaron, his brother, who unlike Prospero's brother did not usurp authority.

Prospero, as Lord of Misrule in the biblical tradition, masquerades as one of the highest authorities in the Judeo-Christian religion. He puts on vestments to represent Moses and carries a book and a staff as Moses did, so that in appearance he can been seen as a magician or as a leader and teacher of Israel. A distinction is necessary between the representations of a magic book and the book of the law when Prospero dismisses the elements of nature, breaks his staff and drowns his book. Prospero appears in the former performance to be acting as a magician only. The book of the law is not dispensed with, for it appears in another guise as Prospero heads back to Milan. On the typological level, as the figure of Moses, Prospero turns over his rule to another before the play ends. His abandonment of magic is recorded and his recognition of the true lord is implied in the "ye elves" speech in his reference to the "printless" characters.

The sixty scenes carved on the spandrels in the chapter house of Salisbury Cathedral end with five depicting Moses: Moses on Sinai, the miracle of the Red Sea, the destruction of the Egyptians, Moses striking the rock, and the law declared.[26] The emphasis on Moses as a figure in the Mystery Plays, the New Testament and the *Book of Common Prayer* (1559), and in medieval art account for Shakespeare's figuring of Prospero. The two episodes staged in the Mystery Plays — the exodus from Egypt and the giving of the laws — have associations in *The Tempest*. Vestiges of Egypt's bondage remain in Shakespeare's portrayal of Caliban and the mention of Sycorax. In accordance with scripture: "All in Moses were baptized, in the cloud, and in the sea" (I Cor. 10:2). The service for baptism in the *Book of Common Prayer* also refers to the Red Sea.[27] "The Red Sea becomes a figure for the waters of baptism, and Christ the leader of the new Exodus which frees men from the bondage of the devil."[28] Prospero, like Moses, initiates the "ship of souls" in a comparable rite of baptism and proclaims the law through his spirit, Ariel. Thus Shakespeare's choice of Prospero as the principal character in his Mystery Play is appropriate. The identification made by comparing Moses and Prospero will be further substantiated in the following chapter where comparisons are made between the *Ludus Coventriae* cycle and *The Tempest*.

Gonzalo, who is called councillor and is a visionary as well as the instrument of Providence for the preservation of Prospero, his books, and Miranda, figures a prophet. Gonzalo confirms his penchant for prophesy in the play with "I prophesied,.../ This fellow could not drown" (5.1.217–218) when Ariel returns with the boat's master and the boatswain. As a prophet Gonzalo is not always accurate about history, as when, equating Tunis and Carthage, he is ridiculed by Antonio and Sebastian. Rather than recounting past happenings, a prophet looks at the present, interpreting current happenings, and to the future, foretelling coming events. In the latter respects Gonzalo functions well. His outlook for the future is good, for he is a prophet of good news. He describes the condition of man on the isle where he would have his "commonwealth" as free from human control and human bondage.

Shakespeare probably expected his audience to recognize a specific Old Testament prophet, Isaiah, for Isaiah does not come into *The Tempest* by slight inference only. Isaiah could be called the prophet of the isles, for he addresses and references them often: "Listen, O isles, unto me" (49:1). "Keep silence before me, O islands" (41:1). "I will send those that escape of them ... to the isles afar off ... and they shall declare my glory among the Gentiles" (66:19). "The isles shall wait for his law" (42:4). It appears from the outcome of *The Tempest* that the new law of forgiveness does come to the isle, for Prospero forgives his enemies and asks forgiveness. Isaiah also writes of a tempest, and in his tempest there is "great noise" and "the flame of devouring fire" (29:6). In the same chapter, Isaiah also writes of "a dream of a night vision," "a book that is sealed," "the spirit of deep sleep," being "brought down," "speech ... low out of the dust, and a voice ... as of one that hath a familiar spirit, out of the ground," "an hungry man" dreaming of eating and awaking, "and his soul is empty," "a marvellous work among this people" and "their works are in the dark, and they say, Who seeth us?" all of which have correspondences in the play. The concluding verse of the twenty-ninth chapter of Isaiah describes the outcome of the play: "They also that erred in spirit shall come to understanding" (Alonso, Sebastian, and Antonio), "and they that murmured shall learn doctrine" (Caliban, Stephano, and Trinculo). At the end of the play Alonso understands enough of what has happened to say, "Thy Dukedom I resign, and do entreat/ Thou [Prospero] pardon me my wrongs" (5.1.118–119). These words beg to be put into the mouth of Antonio rather than Alonso, since he has held Prospero's office of duke. However, if it is Alonso who speaks, Antonio and Sebastian nevertheless hear the truth, and although their conversion is not complete (being only a transition from murderous thoughts to those of profit-making), they are subject to a changed King Alonso, who will have control of dukedoms. Caliban remains under Prospero's tutelage and Stephano and Trinculo are also put under the law, "line and level."

One of Isaiah's prophecies of the coming of Christ uses the phrase "dyed garments" (Isaiah 63:1), and Gonzalo calls attention to the freshness of the clothes of those who have been immersed in the sea with "our garments, ... being rather new dyed" (2.1.59, 61). He encourages Sebastian and Antonio to "weigh/ Our sorrow with our comfort" (2.1.8–9) as the prophet Isaiah promulgates comfort to the people of Israel and declares the end of warfare (Isaiah 40:1, 2). The latter decree is in agreement with Shakespeare's "the means to peace." Many passages in Isaiah describe the coming of a more benign society which compares in essence with Gonzalo's "commonwealth."[29] "Aliens from the commonwealth of Israel" have "no hope" (Ephesians 2:12). Antonio and Sebastian, who ridicule Gonzalo for trying to persuade them "the King his son's alive," have "no hope" (2.1.231, 233, 234). Through their evil intent and unbelief they alienate themselves from Gonzalo's prophesied commonwealth. As Gonzalo stands with the others within the magic circle which Prospero has drawn, Prospero calls him "holy" and his "true preserver, and a loyal sir/ To him thou follow'st" (5.1.62, 69–70), which refers in the immediate situation to whoever may be the duke of Milan, but also may imply "the wills above" (1.1.66). Gonzalo as a councillor cannot use his kind of authority to control the storm, but as a prophet, he can foresee the means to peace, one of which is "the washing of ten tides" (1.1.57). Each being has its proper sphere of activity or influence.

The number of descriptions in Isaiah that are compatible with the behavior and experiences of the characters in *The Tempest* are indeed numerous, and Gonzalo is the one who sees what is happening in the present and foresees what is possible. Figuring Gonzalo as Isaiah enhances his image, whereas Wagner's symbolism, which makes him "a symbol of conscience," is reductive of both his manhood and his vision.[30]

Through his schooling Prospero has brought Miranda out of "her bondage to the elements of the world," which Shakespeare uses in the sense of elements of nature, of human nature, and of earthly sovereignty or authority. Among those would be the elements of paganism that had crept into Christianity (a parallel with the deliverance of Israel from Egyptian sovereignty). Miranda's "schoolmaster made [her] more profit,/ Than other princess' can, that have more time/ For vainer hours, and tutors not so careful" (1.2.172–174). It may be noted here that Moses' nurse and "careful" tutor was his own mother, even though his adoptive parent was Pharaoh's daughter, a member of a pagan culture. When Miranda first appears, she is free to recognize the worth of and to love all humankind. Later hers is the universal acceptance of "Oh brave new world,/ That has such people in't!" (5.1.183–184). This sounds naive, but invokes a possibility if not a probability. Her remark is consistent with Isaiah's prophesies that the Lord "will do a new thing" and "Behold, the former things are come to pass, and new things do I declare" (43:19; 42:9). She is characterized as a virgin, and a lady with "piteous heart," who "suffered/ With those that I saw suffer" (1.2.5–6). Such phrases, her innocence, and her pleas for mercy for the shipwrecked, along with Prospero's continued concern for her virginity, suggest the Virgin Mary. As a descendant of one who figures highly in Israel, she further qualifies to figure as Mary, although Mary's lineage is traced through the kings of Israel rather than through Moses in both the Bible and the Corpus Christi play. However, in the stained glass of the Fairford Church Mary is associated with Moses.[31]

Ferdinand's appraisal of Miranda as "admir'd, … so perfect and so peerless" and his request for her name "chiefly that I might set it in my prayers" (3.1.38, 47, 35) provide more associations with Mary. Medieval Christians and recusants prayed to the Virgin Mary. The word "screen," which Prospero uses in describing his brother's playing the part of duke probably would have made his audience think of the Virgin Mary, for the screens that separated the statues of Mary from view had been removed and much discussion had centered about their use and removal.

The intricacy of Shakespeare's art and his use of it to bring awareness perhaps is nowhere more subtle than in the delicate scene where Ferdinand asks Miranda why she weeps. She answers:

> At mine unworthiness, that dare not offer
> What I desire to give; and much less take
> What I shall die to want. But this is trifling;
> And all the more it seeks to hide itself,
> The bigger bulk it shows. Hence, bashful cunning!
> And prompt me plain and holy innocence!
> I am your wife, if you will marry me;
> If not, I'll die your maid: To be your fellow
> You may deny me; but I'll be your servant,
> Whether you will or no [3.1.77–86].

The language Miranda uses to express her desire to marry Ferdinand — "bigger bulk it shows" and "holy innocence"— are reminders of the Virgin Mary's "being great with child" and yet being a virgin. Although we have every reason to believe Miranda is not with child, Mary was. Only Shakespeare could incorporate so much suggestive imagery in what might otherwise merely be an expression of love between two characters in a play.

Ferdinand, who thinks his father, King Alonso, drowned in the storm, says to Miranda, "O, if a virgin,/ And your affection not gone forth, I'll make you/ The Queen of Naples" (1.2.450–451). The condition that Miranda be a virgin and the fact that in Renaissance times the Star of Naples was the Star of Bethlehem[32] provide other links between Miranda and Mary. When Prospero tells Alonso, who believes his son is dead, that he lost a daughter in the last tempest, Alonso responds, "O heavens, that they were living both in Naples,/ The King and Queen there!" (5.1.149–150). However, Miranda cannot be equated directly with Mary. In the figurative sense of the play, Miranda typifies Mary and Ferdinand shadows Christ. The relationship between the two in the figurative sense compares with the parallels Nosworthy drew between *The Tempest* and the *Aeneid*.[33] In the vision of provision which Prospero provides for Ferdinand and Miranda, Ceres requests, "Tell me, heavenly bow,/ If Venus or her son, as thou dost know,/ Do now attend the queen?" (4.1.87–89). Although in the description of the son and in the setting of Roman goddesses, one would infer Cupid, in the context of the play Shakespeare may have been thinking of the *Aeneid* as well. Although in the play Ferdinand and Miranda wed, typologically they figure mother and son, Ferdinand as a type of Christ and Miranda, Mary, Queen of Naples and star in the Bethlehem scene. The density of the play is enormous.

On the literal level in the Milan-Isle-Naples milieu Miranda and Ferdinand are human lovers. In any case Miranda should not be taken as Wagner suggested "as the symbol of the Christian ideal" and "as an ideal rather than a woman."[34] As symbols Shakespeare's players would lose all the warm humanity with which he richly endows them and which endear them to his audiences.

Shakespeare's treatment of Ferdinand is also superb. Francisco's report that "he trod the water" (2.1.111) brings up the imagery of Christ walking on water (John 6:19). Alonso's anguish, which causes him to cry out, "O thou mine heir,/…what strange fish/ Hath made his meal on thee?" (2.1.107–109), instills a vision of Jonah's engorgement by the whale, which in turn, for a biblically aware audience, could be a reminder of Matthew 12:39–40, where Jonah's experience is designated as a type of Christ's entombment in the earth. The question also calls attention to the symbol used by early Christians, the fish.

In his capacity as a wood-carrying and willing servant Ferdinand further figures Christ, who was willing to become a servant "that he might present it [the church] to himself a glorious church, not having spot, or wrinkle" (Ephesians 5:27). Prospero's demands upon Ferdinand and his concern for the preservation of Miranda's virginity are consistent with such an interpretation, as well as with the importance given in Scripture and the Mystery Plays to the virginity of Mary, Mother of Jesus, as confirmation of Christ's divinity. Ferdinand also figures as the New Testament husband, who is the "saviour" of the body, and is thus a figure of Christ. Although work, represented in *The Tempest* by wood carrying, was part of the curse, it was also a means to life. Ferdinand must carry wood for Miranda. Both Ferdinand's wood carrying and his being "stain'd/ With grief" (1.2.417–418) suggest Christ, who carried a wooden cross and was "a man of sorrows, and acquainted with grief" (Isaiah 53:3) in order to bring new life to humankind. In the Mystery Plays Christ's carrying a wooden cross was prefigured by the story of Isaac carrying the wood to the mount where Abraham was prepared to sacrifice his son. No doubt at least some in a seventeenth century audience would make a triple link: Isaac to Christ and Ferdinand to Isaac to Christ.

Wagner's thesis that Ferdinand, who was the first to leave the ship of souls in *The Tempest*, was in the forefront of the movement of the Reformation should be given credence insofar as that movement represented a return to the simplicity of the early Christian believers.[35] Ariel's description of Ferdinand as "the first man that leapt; [and] cried, "Hell is empty,/ And all the devils are here'" (1.2.213–214) exemplifies both the extremes and concerns of some Puritans in Shakespeare's England. As a Puritan, Ferdinand's concerns appear more weighty than those of Malvolio, whose attention is focused on apparel and "cakes and ale." Whereas Malvolio is the subject of ridicule, Ferdinand is comforted and reassured. Wagner's description of Ferdinand is limited by the singularity of her thesis. Therefore, it precludes the several tones and overtones evoking the more important figurings of Ferdinand. Traversi saw in Miranda's "is't a spirit?" and "a thing divine" (1.2.412, 421) recognition of Ferdinand "as something supernatural, the representative of a humanity exalted above the normal condition of man."[36] It is in the context of Miranda's remarks that Prospero uses a phrase associated with Christ's suffering, "stained/ With grief" and that his "soul" (1.2.415–416, 423) is prompting the turn of events which will culminate in Ariel's freedom "Within two days" (1.2.424). Although as the son of a king, a prince, and a wood-carrying servant Ferdinand is a type of Christ, he is not the only representation of Christ in the play. Shakespeare depicts the Redeemer using imagery drawn from the Mystery Plays. That imagery will be discussed in the next chapter.

A minimal number of passages in *The Tempest* have been cited for their biblical counterparts. Throughout the play, however, key words and biblical typology or figuration allow us to see the shadow or outline of one person in another. There are similarities in the shadows cast because, while each is known in the flesh as a distinctive person, the real persons are illuminated by the same light. In biblical figuration different characters foreshadow Christ; no one is a full representation, but each shadows in some way the promised one who was described as light (John 1:7–8), the full figure or revelation. The Mystery Plays and *The Tempest* move through typology from shadow to reality. In Prospero as lawgiver and teacher, in Gonzalo as counselor and prophet, and in Ferdinand as burden-bearer and prince, then, it is possible to identify characteristics of the unnamed master of the play, which no one of these characters fully portrays, for no mere man could. Shakespeare varies the use of figuration somewhat, letting persons from Milan figure biblical characters, who in turn figure the master.

The use of typology permits multifiguring; therefore Ferdinand and Miranda figure Mary and Christ, Mary and Joseph, and Christ and the church as they do in the Mystery Plays. Joseph's obedience to the heavenly vision makes him a type. Together, in their innocence, Ferdinand and Miranda in their obedience to and reverence for their earthly fathers remind us of Joseph and Mary. Ferdinand claims that "by immortal Providence" Miranda is his (5.1.189), which implies a broader meaning than the immediate betrothal of the two in question. The plan for their lives exceeds mortal planning. Bethell's concept of Shakespeare's multiconsciousness is illustrated in these multifigurings.

Ariel has been variously identified as "a symbol of the imagination," "the spirit of the sensible soul, ... attribute of Prospero," as Shakespeare's "art," Prospero's "poetry in action," as "one of those elves or spirits," "the swiftness of thought personified," "the agent and minister of an inscrutable Providence, [who] becomes ... a symbol of the spirit of poetry found pegged in the cloven pine of the pre–Shakespearean drama, brought into the service of the creative imagination, and employed for his term in the fashioning of illusions to delight the eyes and move the hearts of men," and "one who acts as the messenger for Prospero." Ariel must be reconsidered, for he has more than one aspect.[37] He qualifies as a spirit since he flies from place to place in the play, is at times invisible, and has a name that suggests he is airborne. The description of Ariel's history as given in the play does seem, at first glance, to suggest a nonbiblical figure. Yet his name is found in Isaiah and described in that book as "the city where David dwelt" (29:1). The latter definition invokes another overtone, for Christ was born in Bethlehem, "the city of David" (Luke 2:4).

Ariel has been defined as meaning the "altar hearth."[38] The latter definition, his chirping, and his darting from one place to another suggest a cricket, an association which would satisfy the imagination of an audience that was prepared to hear Prospero's "ye elves" speech (5.1.33–57). He can be taken, too, for the messenger of God, for his description is compatible with that of Psalm 104:4, which is quoted in Hebrews 1:7: "Who maketh his angels spirits, and his ministers a flame of fire." His representation both as a "flaming one" and as a singer fit angelic descriptions. Indeed, his first song, like the song of the angels in Bethlehem, is a song of invitation.

If Prospero figures Moses, who in turn represents the law, then Ariel, as Prospero's messenger, figures the spirit of the law. Now "by the law is the knowledge of sin" (Romans 3:20). The law reveals truth and brings conviction to the sinner. Ariel serves Prospero in this capacity, for after he has caused the banquet which appeared before Alonso, Antonio, and Sebastian to disappear, he identifies them as "three men of sin" (3.3.53). Alonso, who is of the "lower world" whose "instrument" is "destiny" (3.3.53–54) and hence of the elements, hears the winds singing and "that deep and dreadful organ-pipe," of "thunder" "bass" his "trespass" (3.3.97–99) But the law is also the messenger of hope to the obedient son, Ferdinand.

Jan Kott comes close to defining the dual nature of the law as exhibited in Ariel's behavior when he says, "Ariel is [the island's] angel and its executioner."[39] However, although Ariel identifies sin, alarms, raises a tempest, and leads through a fen, he doesn't execute anyone, for we are told "not so much perdition as an hair/ Betid to any creature in the vessel" (1.2.30–31) and again, lest we missed the first reference, "Not a hair perish'd" (1.2.217). He is, in fact, a "minister," who although he says "of Fate" and appears as a harpy, is a minister of Prospero and the messenger of the law. The law served two purposes, direction and prevention, and provided for blessing and curse. In discovering the minds of the "three men of sin," Ariel exemplifies the Word which reveals the "thoughts and intents of the heart" (Hebrews 4:12).

Missing Shakespeare's many biblical references and his typology, Curry dismissed Christian myth in *The Tempest*, making Ariel nothing more than a "minister of Fate," a Neo-Platonic spirit. Curry's interpretation of the play is limited by his failure to recognize its biblical elements:

> in *The Tempest*, with its Neo-Platonic concepts serving as artistic pattern and with its unities of time and place, the artist is revealed as having passed definitely under the influence of Renaissance thought. He no longer employs Christian myth as the integrating principle of tragedy; here he creates an altogether different world, which is dominated by a purely pagan philosophy.[40]

Kermode found Ariel had

> the qualities allowed to Intelligences in medieval theology, which include simultaneous knowledge of all that happens; understanding of the cause of things; the power to alter his position in space in no time, and to manipulate the operations of nature, so as, for example, to create tempests; the power to work upon a human being's will and imagination for good or evil ends; and total invulnerability to assault by material instruments.[41]

Davidson cited Chambers' speaking of Ariel "as from one point of view, 'the agent and minister of an inscrutable Providence' ... which providence operates to maintain order and justice in the world."[42] In his description of Ariel, Davidson thus affirms indirectly, but certainly, this author's assertion of both law and Providence in *The Tempest*. The law is providential since it distinguishes that which is beneficial from that which is harmful to the individual as well as to the whole human family. Coleridge wrote, "a state of bondage is almost unnatural to him [Ariel] yet we see that it is delightful for him to be so employed.... In air he lives, from air he derives his being, in air he acts; and all his colours and properties seem to have been obtained from the rainbow and the skies.... Hence all that belongs to Ariel belongs to the delight the mind is capable of receiving from the most lovely external appearances."[43] There are several references in the Bible to "delight" in the law, (e.g. Psalms 1:2 and 119:77, 174; Jeremiah 6:10; Romans 7:22). Ariel's wish to be free from the duties required of him by the master of the law does not change the fact that he represents the spirit of the law, for the *spirit* of the law was emphasized by the new master who represented freedom from bondage. It is freedom from bondage to the Old Testament law-giver, the Prospero-Moses figure, that Ariel craves. When Prospero releases him, he chooses to live under a new master (who is described in the next chapter).

Caliban is variously described in *The Tempest*. Prospero calls him "thou earth," "tortoise," "poisonous slave," "hag-seed," "born devil," and "a thing of darkness." To Miranda he is an "abhorred slave." Trinculo calls him "a most ridiculous monster" and a "deboshed fish." Tillyard, stating that Caliban "in the end shows himself incapable of the human power of education," found that Prospero's claim to him represents the bestial in man.[44]

Chambers rejected the idea of Caliban's signifying "the spirit of prose" in contrast to his acceptance of Ariel's symbolizing "the spirit of poetry." He found Shakespeare "adumbrat[ing] in Caliban such a general conception of primitive humanity as the expanding knowledge of his day had opened out to him. Caliban is an earthy creature. He has the maliciousness of a troglodyte, and must be taught the first elements of human knowledge ... and even the first principles of articulate speech."[45] But as Hirst points out "the situation is not so simple. Caliban stands firmly at the center of the play, the pointer to the different criteria of two worlds. He represents

... the noble savage as well as the brute; and it is his unspoilt nature which throws into relief the viciousness of the civilization which both trains the political unscrupulousness of Antonio and corrupts the morals of Trinculo and Stephano."[46] Shakespeare may have had in mind John 3:31: "he that is of the earth is earthly and speaketh of the earth" when he referred to Caliban as "earth," when he describes the places on the isle where Caliban finds his food. Caliban, like "the first man, Adam," of the first age of man, "is of the earth, earthy" (I Cor. 15:45, 47). But he can hear the music of the spheres, for "the heavens declare the glory of God; ...Day unto day uttereth speech.... There is no speech nor language where their voice is not heard" (Psalms 19:1–3).

Chambers identified Sycorax, Caliban's dam, as "controversial theology."[47] Sycorax hardly seems to represent theology, but probably, as suggested in the discussion of the Prospero-Moses connection, she represents Egypt's black magic, and Egypt, the oppressor of the Israelites.

Traversi wrote, "The 'state of nature' is less an idyllic simplicity, of the kind already evoked by Gonzalo, than a void waiting to be filled in accordance with a purpose stronger, more potent for either good or evil, than itself. The rule of Prospero is an alternative, not to natural spontaneity, but to the power of Sycorax."[48] Caliban's descriptions of nature come closer to "idyllic simplicity" than Gonzalo's commonwealth where people live together in peace as equals. Prospero's rule differs from Sycorax's in its submission to a heavenly authority. Sycorax-Egypt enslaves, Prospero-Moses frees from bondage both the spirit of the law (Ariel) and the minds of wayward men.

As in the Mystery Plays and the Bible, characters with both holy and diabolical intent can be found in *The Tempest*. Traversi identifies Antonio and Sebastian as "courtly cynics" whose "intelligence [is] applied exclusively to purposes of destruction," and as "the natural successors to Iago."[49] The means of grace are available to the pair in the prophet's description of a more desirable, if unattainable, visionary commonwealth, in the saints' (Adrian's and Francisco's) benign sense of the isle, in Prospero's forgiveness and in the resurrection of Ferdinand, recognized by Sebastian as "a most high miracle!" (5.1.178).

Throughout, however, Sebastian is inclined to the physical aspects of life. When the banquet appears, both Antonio and Sebastian, being exposed to the unusual phenomenon, express belief: "Now I will believe/ That there are unicorns; that in Arabia/ There is one tree, the phoenix' throne; one phoenix/ At this hour reigning there." Antonio adds, "I'll believe both" (3.3.21–24). Alonso receives a message from their "excellent dumb discourse" which expresses "sound." However, whereas Francisco notes that the providers of the banquet "vanish'd strangely," Sebastian's basic interest is "They have left their viands behind; for we have stomachs" (3.3.37–39, 41).

The murderous activities of the apparently unrepentant Antonio will be curtailed under the jurisdiction of the confessed, defumed Alonso. Resigned by Alonso as usurping duke, his interests, along with Sebastian's, when Caliban appears, are now those of merchant, trading in men:

> SEBASTIAN: Ha, ha!
> What things are these, my Lord Antonio?
> Will money buy 'em?
> ANTONIO: Very like; one of them
> Is a plain fish, and, no doubt, marketable [5.1.263–266].

The pair's designs on Caliban in their new occupation are frustrated by Prospero, who claims, "This thing of darkness I/ Acknowledge mine" (5.1.275–276).

In the end Caliban owns the Prospero-Moses figure as his rightful master, showing he has learned something about masters. Under the schoolmaster, he will learn to distinguish right from wrong and thus be made ready for the "grace" which he promises to seek, for "the law was our schoolmaster to bring us unto Christ" (Galatians 3:24). As a newly apt pupil, Caliban represents the three ages of man: natural man, man under the law (where he now belongs), and man in the age of grace, where he should seek to be.

Adrian and Francisco are not bent upon "usurpation" of power. They both have hope of the good. Adrian knows that appearances can be deceiving, and his senses are attuned to delicacy, tenderness and the temperate (the mean rather than the extreme). He has a knowledge of historical facts and appreciates perfection. Adrian recognizes that the island is not a place to be lived in: It is "unhabitable" (2.1.38). Men experience truth on the enchanted isle, but they must go back, as they do in the end, to take their place in a world of responsibility. Adrian recognizes that it only seems to be a desert, for nothing is absolutely impossible for him. He senses the meaning. He does not depend upon one sense alone. Although it looks like a desert, he *feels* the air breathing sweetly. He leaves open the possibility that one may have a false impression, and he is open to truth. Moreover, for him, the wonders that the isle "fortends" are "almost inaccessible" (2.1.38). It has taken more than the plans of men, "immortal Providence," to make the isle available.

Schucking, who claimed "we can take interpretations in which the action of *The Tempest* is explained as a symbol of the moral order of the world in the Christian sense" "still less seriously," thinks Adrian and Franciso "speak only just enough to prevent a clever expositor from supposing that they have lost their speech in consequence of the excitements of the shipwreck; for the rest, they are nothing more than 'supers.'"[50] Yet they do represent a distinction in attitude and present another response to the isle. It is never safe to assume anything in Shakespeare is superfluous. That is especially true in this very compact, complex play.

History records three popes named Adrian (I, IV, and VI). Adrian I supported Empress Irene in her struggle against iconoclasm and sent legates to the Second Council of Nicaea. The association of Adrian I with the Adrian of the play would give credence, but not centrality, to Wagner's thesis. Adrian IV was an Englishman named Breakspear. Adrian VI was an ascetic and pious man who tried to curb the abuses he found. Shakespeare and some in his audiences may have been aware of some of the foregoing facts. Certainly Adrian shows his awareness of history in the dialogue.

Francisco does "not doubt" that the King son is alive (2.1.117–118). Francisco is a man of faith. His one speech might be taken as a statement of belief. It may have been that Shakespeare expected his audience to associate him with Saint Francis of Assisi. Francisco's single speech could be taken as a mini-sermon.

Shakespeare's inclusion of two historical types in a biblical setting is consistent with the neotypology practiced by some of his contemporaries.[51] Failure to recognize Shakespeare's use of typology detracts from the complexity and meaning of the play and has led to mortal conclusions about the denouement. Responding to the resonances enhances appreciation of Shakespeare's artistry and the play's sense and its immortal as well as its mortal emphases.

In his "ye elves" speech Prospero dismisses all forms of the creaturely supernatural and dispenses forever with his magic paraphernalia. By inference at this juncture and later with his reference to prayer in the Epilogue, he does acknowledge divinity, the only form of the supernatural that is left.

The shadowing and multi-character representation ascribed to here is compatible with some of Bethell's findings in *King Lear*. Bethell quotes two passages from that play:

> …Thou hast one daughter
> Who redeems Nature from the general curse [4.6.201–202]

and

> Fairest Cordelia, that are most loved despised,
> Most choice forsaken, and most loved despised [1.1.250–251]

"where … Cordelia seems to be compared with Our Lord" and another "which directly echoes a saying of Our Lord from St. Luke's Gospel" (Luke 2:49):

> …O dear father,
> It is thy business that I go about [4.4.23–24].

Bethell finds a similar shadowing that does not involve a biblical character. He writes, "it seems more than likely that, in this constant association of Cordelia with Christian doctrine, Shakespeare wished to suggest the foreshadowing of Christ in pure natures before His coming; as medieval thought looked back to Virgil, and as the Church has always regarded Moses and the prophets."[52] He averred, "Characters may also be symbolic of some aspects of Deity." However, he found "only two examples of this" in Shakespeare: the duke in *Measure for Measure*, and Prospero. He found both represented "divine providence." He did not recognize the shadowing of other biblical characters in *The Tempest* cited in this interpretation. Although he did not recognize the four specific identities here assigned to Prospero, he did see the necessity for more than one apprehension of a character: "The audience needs to attend simultaneously to two diverse aspects of the same character: the representational and the symbolic." He acknowledges that "the Duke in *Measure for Measure*, and Prospero, are endowed with characteristics which make it impossible for us to regard them as direct representations of the Deity, such as we find in the Miracle Plays. They are human beings, however they may signify the Divine; and Prospero, at least, has human imperfections."[53]

Biblical Fabrics: *Ludus Coventriae* and Descriptive Portraits in *The Book of Common Prayer* and the Bible

Since the Mystery Plays were of necessity selective, it is easier to trace the elements *The Tempest* holds in common with them than to delineate its biblical sources, although this interpretation has proceeded in the opposite manner, identifying biblical textual elements in *The Tempest* and discovering later its debt to the medieval plays. A close examination of the Mystery Plays has afforded a confirmation of Shakespeare's use of biblical concepts and modes of representation found in the Mystery Plays and pointed to the likelihood that they, along with the Bible and *The Book of Common Prayer*, were Shakespeare's immediate sources. This chapter emphasizes correspondences in selectivity of story and scene and in character likenesses in the Mystery Plays and *The Tempest*. It also compares biblical texts and those of the 1959 *Book of Common Prayer* with *The Tempest*. Later chapters deal in greater detail with themes, imagery, time and word usage common to Shakespeare's play and the Mystery Plays.

Although various elements in *The Tempest* appear to reference different Mystery Play cycles and some elements appear more closely related to the biblical text, in a short study it is easier to follow one cycle and note the contributions of other cycles at various junctures. The text chosen for comparison is that printed in R. T. Davies's *The Corpus Christi Play of the English Middle Ages*.[1] Although scholarship has agreed that the Ludus play was erroneously associated with Coventry and has assigned to it the name N-Town, and although even the later supposition that it was played in Lincoln has come into question, its locale is not the prime concern of this study. Neither questions about its staging nor Potter's assertion that it is not a "pure" Corpus Christi play need be addressed in this study whose prime concern is the comparison of its elements with elements in *The Tempest*.[2] The following pages show that Shakespeare makes reference to many of the biblical stories used in the text of *Ludus Coventriae*. He also portrays characters in *The Tempest* whose actions and traits simulate those of characters in the cycle, forming a typological link with them.

Both *Ludus Coventriae* and *The Tempest* cover all human time. Human time in the *Ludus* play begins with "Creation and Fall," which includes the creation and the fall of Lucifer, Adam and Eve (73–86).[3] The other extreme of human time is portrayed in *Ludus* as Doomsday (368–373), when the obedient and disobedient are respectively rewarded and punished. Shakespeare describes the end of human time in Prospero's dissolution speech in 4.1.146–158. It will be discussed in the chapter on time. Some descriptive terms used to distinguish types of characters from others in the Mystery Plays, such as obedient and disobedient, are not used as such by Shakespeare, but the distinction is clearly made in Shakespeare's depiction of the attitudes and behaviors of *The Tempest*'s cast.

Shakespeare registers the fall of humankind with "sweat" (2.1.156), awakening what lives in the audience's mind, the story of Adam and Eve's disobedience in eating of the tree of the knowledge of good and evil with its consequences. The Bible account reads: "In the sweat of thy face shalt thou eat bread, till thou return to the ground" (Genesis 3:5). The *Ludus* play reads, "Go! till thy meat with swink and sweat,/ Unto thy lifes end" (83).

The Eden temptation was "ye shall be as gods" (Genesis 3:4), an appeal to pride (Lucifer's downfall) to assume authority and power rightly belonging to God. *The Tempest* begins after Antonio assumes authority which belongs to Prospero. Caliban rejects an appropriate master, Prospero, but later returns to Prospero, acknowledging his own foolishness. Adam and Eve, too, are repentant after the Fall. Adam says "My weeping shall be long fresh," and Eve expresses regret: "Alas! that ever we wrought this sin" (85, 86). Both Caliban and Adam look forward to "grace." Caliban declares "I'll be wise hereafter,/ And seek for grace" (5.1.294–295). Adam says, "Let us walk forth into the land,... Till some comfort of Godes sand [sending]/ With grace relieve our careful mind" (85). Both Adam and Caliban belong to the first age of man, that of natural man.

The word sweat is repeated in the *Ludus* play "Cain and Abel." Unlike the biblical Cain, the *Ludus* Cain complains about giving his best sheaf to God, who "does neither sweat nor swink" (89). "Cain and Abel" is a story of brotherly treachery. In Antonio's usurpation of Prospero's dukedom Shakespeare typifies the *Ludus* characters. However, Shakespeare's story ends differently, since it takes place in the third age of man, the age of God's grace, which followed the second age of man, the age of the law.

The next *Ludus* play, "Noah," describes a terrible storm and the survival of "eight soules" (95). The souls in Shakespeare's ship, like those in Noah's ark, reach land safely, although their vessel, unlike Noah's, is wrecked. In "Noah" God's punishment of Cain and of those who hurt Cain is told in a story of Lamech, Noah's father, who accidentally shoots Cain. Prospero, unlike Lamech, does not kill his enemies and thus is spared the curse pronounced on those who hurt such as Cain. (As early as the second human generation warning was given against man's taking revenge on a transgressor.) Noah explains that the "floodes" are sent "for sin of mannes wild mood [heart, disposition]" (98). Prospero's tempest is directed toward the evil dispositions of some of those aboard the ship.

The *Ludus* "Abraham and Isaac" play follows "Noah." In it Abraham's willingness to sacrifice his son, and Isaac's submission to God's will and to his father and his bearing the "fagot" and "fire" for his own sacrifice, look forward to Christ's carrying a wooden cross and sacrificing his life to redeem humankind. Isaac is referred to as a "buxom [obedient]" (104) child. Abraham says to Isaac, "I pray to God send thee good mind." As in *The Tempest* the condition of the man's mind is of prime importance. Apparently both the Mystery Play writers and Shakespeare understood that the Edenic tree was not an apple tree, but one which would pervert or contaminate the mind. The Bible describes it as the "tree of the knowledge of good and evil" (Genesis 2:17). The assumption is that before partaking of the tree, Adam and Eve had knowledge of good only.

The evil in the play is in the minds of men. Antonio, Sebastian, Caliban, Stephano, and Trinculo are all intent on murder. Antonio not only sets his brother and niece adrift in a leaky craft, but he entices Sebastian to murder good Gonzalo and the king when he says to Sebastian, "My strong imagination sees a crown/ Dropping upon thy head" (2.1.203–204). Caliban tells Stephano and Trinculo that Prospero takes an afternoon nap and explains that "there thou mayst brain him" (3.2.86). Prospero has a different interest in man's brain. He draws a magic circle, which the court party enters; he requires "a solemn air" and bids "the ignorant fumes that mantle/ Their [the court party's] clearer reason" depart (5.1.58–68).

In the *Ludus* and two of the other cycles Isaac appears as a child. In the comparable York play Isaac is 30 years old, the age at which Christ began his ministry. The York play suggests an age closer to that of Ferdinand, who in his wood-carrying is typologically related to both Isaac, who carried wood for his own sacrifice, and to Christ, who carried a wooden cross.

"Moses" is the next *Ludus* play. Both Abraham and Moses acknowledge God's creation of the sun and moon, the former in "Abraham and Isaac" (101–108) and the latter in "Moses" (109–115):

> Most mighty maker of sun and of moon,
> King of kinges and Lord over all,
> Almighty God in heaven throne ["Abraham & Isaac" 101]

> He that made all thing of nought,
> Heaven and earth, both sun and moon,
> Save all that his hand has wrought,
> Almighty God in heaven throne! ["Moses," 109].

In *The Tempest* Caliban acknowledges that Prospero attempted to teach him and refers to the sun and moon as part of his instruction: "When thou cam'st first,/ Thou ... wouldst ... teach me how/ To name the bigger light, and how the less,/ That burn by day and night" (1.2.334–338).

The *Ludus* "Moses" proceeds with an account of God calling to Moses from a burning bush. When Moses encountered the burning bush he was tending the flock of his father-in-law, Jethro. It is likely, then, that this mystery play would have presented Moses in a robe and carrying a shepherd's staff. Shakespeare uses "staff" and "stick," not wand, to describe what Prospero carries: "For I can here disarm thee with this stick" (1.2.474) and "I'll break my staff" (5.1.54). The Bible account uses "rod." The biblical story goes on to evince the magical or miraculous at the burning bush with Moses' use of the "rod." The *Ludus* "Moses" does not include the rod-serpent episode. In it the biblical account of God's dealings with Moses is greatly foreshortened and the giving of the commandments introduced, erroneously, in the burning bush scene. The emphasis in *Ludus* is on the laws of God and Moses' function as teacher or "schoolmaster" (1.2.172).

The play's constant reference to Moses as teacher of God's law is significant when comparing Prospero and Moses. The lengthy instructional passage compares with Prospero's long speech in the second scene of *The Tempest*. After Moses' reception of the tables of the law, he says,

> Every man, take good *heed*,
> And to my *teaching* take good intent,
> For God has sent me now in deed
> You for to *inform* his *commandment*.
> You to *teach* God has me sent
> His *lawes* of life that are full wise.
>
> . . . .
>
> And *print* theses *lawes* well in thy *mind* [110–111, emphasis added].

The play closes after Moses has taught the ten commandments with

> Friendes! these are the *lawes* that you must keep.
> Therefore every man set well in *mind*,
> Whether that thou do *wake* or *sleep*,
> These *lawes* to learn thou *hark* full hend [readily],
> And Godes grace shall be thy friend,

He succour and save you in wealth from woe!
Farewell, good friendes, for hence will I wend:
My tale I have *taught* you, my way now I go [115, emphasis added].

The emphases throughout the previous quotes from "Moses" highlight matters which are similarly associated in *The Tempest*. Both Moses and Prospero put great emphasis on heeding or listening (second scene of *The Tempest*) and teaching, Moses in repeated reference to it in the *Ludus* play and Prospero in deed and word in *The Tempest*. As *The Tempest* proceeds the audience is made aware of what is in the minds of the various characters that Prospero and Ariel operate on, and it is the "minds" that are cleared of "ignorant fumes" (5.1.67) and brought to "clearer reason."

The Moses play from York portrays the burning bush, the ten plagues, and the crossing of the Red Sea. Unlike Wakefield, Chester, and *Ludus Coventriae*, it does not include the giving of the law. The Ten Commandments are recited in *Christ with the Doctors* in the York play. Moses recites some or all of the commandments in Ludus, Wakefield, and Chester, and the exodus is played in York and Wakefield.

The recital of Moses law in the York New Testament play brings the Old Testament law and the New Testament lawgiver together. In *Ludus* "Moses" the link is made simply by Moses' use of "figure":

A green bush as fire does flame,
And keepeth his colour fir and bright,
Fresh and green withouten blame.
It figureth [is a figure for something] of right great fame
    [traditionally, the Incarnation] —
I cannot seyn what it may be [109].

The Old Testament characters have only the figure or shadow of who is to come, so Moses cannot say (explain) its meaning. He only knows it is important, "of right great fame."

Augustine's seven ages of man provided the act divisions of John Bale's *Tragedy or Interlude manyfesting the chief promises of God unto man by all ages in the old law, from the fall of Adam to the incarnation of the Lord Jesus Christ,* written in 1538. The first six acts of this play portray the promises made by God to Adam, Noah, Abraham, Moses, David, and Isaiah; the final act mentions some of the minor prophets, John the Baptist and Christ's sacrifice.[4] Bale's most famous play, *King John*, shows the transition from the medieval morality play to Renaissance historical drama, allegorically describing the fate of England rather than the fate of man's soul.

A similar association of these persons could be seen in a fifteenth century transept window in Great Malvern Priory Church. In Hamand's illustration of the window, Adam, David, and Noah appear on the left of the coronation of Mary and Moses, an unknown and Abraham on the right. Curiously, the coronation is not centered, which makes the arrangement more noticeable.[5] There are links in *The Tempest* with all of these characters, and Moses and Isaiah are represented typologically as explained in Chapter IV. Prospero, the central Old Testament figure in *The Tempest*, accompanies and oversees Miranda, who figures Mary.

Although some theologians group Moses with the prophets, he is distinguished from them in *Ludus Coventriae*. In that cycle "Moses" is followed by "Jesse," in which the prophets are grouped with the kings of Israel. In *The Tempest* the prophet Gonzalo travels with King Alonso.

The Jesse play of *Ludus Coventriae* begins with the prophecy of Isaias: "That a clean maid, through meek obedience,/ Shall bear a child" (115). The next speaker in "Jesse" is the primary source or root of the clean maid, "Radix Jesse." He proclaims,

> A blessed branch shall spring of me,
> That shall be sweeter than balmes breath.
> Out of that branch in Nazareth
> A flower shall bloom of me, Jesse root,
> The which by grace shall destroy death,
> And bring mankind to bliss most sweet [116].

In the remainder of the play speeches by prophets alternate with the speeches by the lineal kings. Unlike "Jesse" Shakespeare has only one prophet, Gonzalo, whose "commonwealth" corresponds with aspects of the kingdom proclaimed by the biblical Isaiah.

Salamon Rex's speech is particularly significant:

> I am Solomon, the second king,
> And that worthy Temple forsooth made I,
> Which that is figure of that maid young
> That shall be mother of great Messy [116].

Davies glosses "Messy" as "Messiah." Although the Jesse play refers to the "mother of great Messy" as "that worthy Temple," the New Testament presents Christ as the new temple and associates his death and resurrection with the destruction of the temple: "in this place is one greater than the temple" (Matthew 12:6) and "Destroy this temple, and in three days I will raise it up. Then said the Jews, Forty and six years was this temple in building, and wilt thou rear it up in three days? But he spake of the temple of his body" (John 2:19–21). In *The Tempest*, following more closely the biblical text, Miranda describes Ferdinand as "a temple": "There's nothing ill can dwell in such a temple" (1.2.460). However, the figuring in the *Ludus* play is appropriate, since Mary carries the Christ child and Solomon's temple was the dwelling place of God in Israel.

The use of "figure" continues as Daniel and Jonas predict scenes from the life of Christ:

> DANIEL PROPHETA: I, Prophet Daniel, am well apayed [pleased]
> In figure of this I saw a tree —
> All the fiendes of hell shall be afraid
> When maidenes fruit thereon they see [117].

❖

> JONAS PROPHETA: I, Jonah, say that on the third morn
> From death he shall rise — this is a true tale —
> Figured in me the which long beforn
> Lay three days buried within the whale [117].

In "Jonas" a numerical typological link is made between Jonah's entombment in the whale and Christ's death and resurrection. It follows the biblical comparisons made in Matthew 12:39 and Luke 11:29. The former reads, "As Jonas was three nights in the whale's belly; so shall the Son of man be three days and three nights in the heart of the earth." The latter identifies Jonah as a "sign." Shakespeare uses grieving Alonso's question, "What great fish has made his meal on thee?" to suggest the same meaning to his audience.

After the gathering in and near Prospero's circle, as Gonzalo ends his prayer with "amen!" Ariel appears with the master and the boatswain. Gonzalo reminds the audience of his prophecy in the first scene that "this fellow could not drown" and continues, "Now blasphemy,/ That swear'st grace o'erboard, not an oath on shore? ...What is the news?"(5.1.217–220).

The boatswain responds with, "The best news":

> our ship —
> Which, but three glasses since, we gave out split —
> Is tight and yare, and bravely rigg'd, as when
> We first put out to sea [5.1.221–225].

Alonso acknowledges that something supernatural has taken place: "These are not natural events; they strengthen/ From strange to stranger" (5.1.227–228).

The boatswain describes the strange happenings:

> We were dead of sleep,
> And — how we know not — all clapp'd under hatches;
> Where, but even now, with strange and several noises
>
> . . . .
> And moe diversity of sounds,...
> We were awak'd; straightway, at liberty;
> Where we, in all our trim, freshly beheld
> Our royal, good, and gallant ship; our master
> Cap'ring to eye her: — on a trice, so please you,

Even in a dream, were we divided from them,
And were brought moping hither [5.1.230–240].

The "dead of sleep," "awaked," "royal, good, and gallant ship," and the uses of "trice," which indicates an instantaneous event, and "three glasses," which measure time, are significant in a typological setting. *The Tempest* craft carries the "fraughting souls" to the isle, where they are made aware of the possibility of forgiveness and of grace and where the craft, being broken and miraculously restored to wholeness, serves as a symbol. As Noah's ark was a symbol of salvation, so Shakespeare's craft, symbolic of the broken and resurrected body of Christ, is a figure of redemption.

Throughout "Jesse" emphasis is placed on the virginity of Messy's mother with the use of "clean maid Mother," "clean maid," "quod virgo concipiet," "maid young," and "of maiden be born" "maidenes fruit" and "maidenes child" (115–119). Shakespeare's and Prospero's emphasis on Miranda's virginity corresponds with the many references and attempts at proof of Mary's virginity in the Mystery Plays. Shakespeare uses "virgin" twice ("O, if a Virgin/ And your affection not gone forth, I'll make you/The Queen of Naples" [1.2.450–451] and "The white cold virgin snow upon my heart" [4.1.55]). Moreover, Prospero's prime concern is that Miranda's virtue not be violated either by Caliban or Ferdinand.

Both Manasses Rex and Baruch Propheta refer to the "maidenes child" as the "Prince of Peace" (119). Ferdinand is a son and prince and the purpose of *The Tempest* is to "work the peace of the present" (1.1.22).

In the churches of the twelfth and thirteenth centuries there were windows with "gorgeous Jesse-trees, in stately rows of prophets and kings."[6] Thus, reminders of what had been heard on the streets of England in Mystery Play presentations could be seen in church windows.

In the play following "Jesse," "Mother of Mercy" *"Mary is shown in the Temple, presented at three years old to God"* (121). This corresponds to Miranda's age when she arrived at the aisle. *"Mary is then shown at fully fourteen, again in the Temple, unwilling, because of her dedication, to marry, though the law requires it. An angel bids all the kinsmen of David to bring white rods, and Mary to marry the man whose rod blossoms"* (121). It is Joseph who holds the blossoming rod.

There is a time gap between the two scenes. A similar gap involving comparable ages occurs in the presentation of Miranda. When *The Tempest* opens twelve years have elapsed since Miranda arrived on the isle at age three. Since in the *Ludus* play, Mary was "fully fourteen" and the annunciation had not yet taken place, it may be assumed that in the Middle Ages it was believed that Mary was fifteen years old when Christ was born. Mary is to be attended by three women, Susana, Rebecca and Sephor, at age fourteen (120–122), rather than at age three when Miranda remembers, "Had I not Four or five women once that tended me?" (1.2.46–47).

The "Parliament of Heaven and Annunciation" play (123–134) begins with

> Four thousand, six hundred, four year I tell,
> Man for his offence and foul folly
> Has lain yeares in the paines of hell [123]

and declares that "Time is come of reconciliation" (124). Some degree of reconciliation occurs in *The Tempest* when Prospero forgives Antonio. Full reconciliation of humans with God did not take place with the coming, the revelation, of Christ. In the play as in life, some characters fail to respond favorably.

In the "Trial of Joseph and Mary" (147–160), Joseph is tried and Maid Mary's virginity is questioned. A test is performed and both are exonerated and Mary is called "Blessed Virgin." Prospero's trial and constant surveillance of Ferdinand is comparable to the severity displayed in that *Ludus* play. In "Birth of the Son" (160–170) Mary's virginity is proven by the midwives who arrive after the child is born. Since, according to this study, Miranda figures Mary, Prospero's insistence on Miranda's virginity is significant.

The same symbolism for Christ as that used in the "Jesse" play, "flower" and "maidenes fruit," appears in "The Shepherds" (170–175), where Christ is referred to as "flower of friendship," "fair fresh flower," "flower fair and free," "flower of flowers," "bloom on bed," "Light from Trinity," "Prince of Paradise," "flower over flowers founden in frith [superior to flowers in the meadows]" and "flower of all." Both the "blossom" (flower) and a "Prince of Paradise" appear in *The Tempest*, one in Ariel's choice to *"live now/ Under the blossom that hangs on the bough"* (5.1.93–94) when he is set free by Prospero, and the other when Ferdinand, who is a prince, claims, "So rare a wonder'd father and a wise/ Makes this place Paradise" (4.1.123–124). *Primus pastor* says, "I saw a great light with sheen shine,/ Yet saw I never so selcouth [wonderful] sign" (171). Prospero notes the importance of "a most auspicious star" in his "zenith" (1.2.182, 181). In "Herod and the Three Kings" (176–186) the star is mentioned many times. *Primus rex* speaks of "Godes fruit free" (180), thus linking freedom and fruit as Ariel links blossom and freedom in *The Tempest*. Secundus rex, Melchizar, says, "In hot love my heart is hid,/ To the blossom upon his bed,/ Born by beastes bin" (177). He associates the bloom, star and maid when he says,

> The child is born and lies here by,
> Bloomed [flowered] in a maidenes body.
> A star has streaken upon the sky,
> And led us fair by fen [181].

The repeated use of blossom and flower suggests that imagery would be so familiar in the sixteenth century that Shakespeare's audience would instantly recognize the meaning of his "blossom that hangs on the bough," a meaning lost in recent centuries.

The use of "fen" in the above quotation is interesting since it occurs twice in *The Tempest* in the singular and once in the plural. Davies associates it with "difficult country" (gloss, 181). Caliban, Stephano, and Trinculo come through a fen before being sent to Prospero's cell to decorate it.

The "Raising of Lazarus" immediately precedes "Passion I" and leads into it. It ends:

> JESUS: Now I have showed in open sight
> Of my Godhead the great glory,
> Toward my passion I will me dight [dispose]
> The time is near that I must die.
> For all mankind his soul to buy,
> A crown of thorn shall piercen my brain,
> And on the Mount of Calvary
> Upon a cross I shall be slain [234–235].

In his speech about "weak masters" Prospero claims, "graves at my command/ Have wak'd their sleepers, op'd, and let 'em forth/ By my so potent Art" (5.1.48–50). Ferdinand, who Alonso believes "i'th' ooze is bedded" (3.3.100) for Alonso's "trespass," is, in a sense, resurrected in keeping with his typological identity.

The plots against Prospero by Caliban, "demi-devil" (5.1.272), and against the lives of Alonso and Gonzalo by Antonio and Sebastian are related typologically to the plots in *Ludus* "Passion I: Prologues" (235–240) and "Passion I: Council of Jews I" (241–247) against Jesus by demons and by those in power who feel threatened by Christ's following and his miracles.

In "Passion I: Betrayal" (261–264) Judas plans to sell his master:

> JUDAS: Now counterfeited [contrived] I have a privy treason,
> My masteres power for to fell.
> I, Judas, shall assay by some encheson [excuse]
> Unto the Jewes him for to sell.

In *The Tempest* Caliban, who has been Prospero's understudy, intends to turn Prospero over to his new master, Stephano.

In Passion I: Maundy III (264–271), Jesu speaks of the "old law," not in its replacement, but of its spirit:

> In the same form as the old law does specify,
> As I show by ghostly interpretation [giving it a spiritual
>   interpretation: I Cor. 5:7–8],
> Therefore, to that I shall say, your willes look you reply [265].

The law is not replaced in *The Tempest*, but the spirit of the law, Ariel, is set free and joyfully takes his place under the master of the new law.

The emphasis in Passion II: Crucifixion (306–315) is on forgiveness of enemies:

> JESUS: Oh! Father almighty, maker of man,
> Forgive these Jewes that do me woe,
> Forgive them, Father, forgive them then,
> For they wit not what they do [308].

Prospero, too, in keeping with the spirit of the law must forgive his enemies.

> Though with their high wrongs I am struck to th' quick
> Yet with my nobler reason 'gainst my fury
> Do I take part: the rarer action is
> In virtue than in vengeance: they being penitent,
> The sole drift of my purpose doth extend
> Not a frown further. Go release them, Ariel [5.1.25–30].

In *Ludus* several plays describe Christ's appearance after the resurrection to those who had been close to him. Although Prospero typifies Christ only in that he typifies Moses who typified Christ, his unexpected appearance to the court party is a typical event. More directly, Prospero's discovery of Ferdinand and Miranda playing chess (5.1) typifies an appearance of Christ. Alonso fears it is "a vision of the island" of "one dear son" (5.1.176) and Sebastian can only exclaim, "A most high miracle!" In the last scene of *The Tempest*, as described earlier, the boatswain's description of the "gallant" ship that had been broken also typifies the broken body and the resurrection of Christ.

Shakespeare's world's end is less personal and less traumatic than that of the *Ludus* "Doomsday." Although that play has been associated with II Peter 3:10–12 and could be associated with Isaiah 51:6, its immediate source may have been "Noe" in Wakefield Cycle. (Those passages and the *Tempest* passage are compared in Chapter X, which deals with time.)

Blossom, virginity, "bough" (branch) and the Christ child were also linked in church drama.

> Prospero acknowledges a star in his zenith:
> and by my prescience
> I find my zenith doth depend upon
> A most auspicious star, whose influence
> If now I court not, but omit, my fortunes
> Will ever after droop [1.2.180–184].

The star mentioned here obviously differs from the one which led the three Kings "fair by fen" (181).

In the Mystery Plays Old Testament events were typologically directed toward the Christ and salvation history. Similarly in *The Tempest* Prospero's recollection of past events serves as a backdrop for the restoration of proper relationships through forgiveness and clearer reason in the isle. Forgiveness was the law of the Christ in the Mystery Plays: In "Passion I: Council of the Jews I" (241–247) Moses' law is referenced many times, and Christ is accused of breaking that law by forgiving sin. The gloss on "old" law reads, "i.e. Jewish, Mosaic law (as contrasted new law of Christ)" (241). In the earlier play, "Woman taken in Adultery" (211–220), Mulier, the woman who was taken in adultery, appeals to the "high grace" of Christ and asks for "mercy" (219).

Although *The Tempest* is biblically based, like Corpus Christi, it is not a liturgical play. *The Tempest* is a popular play in which Shakespeare juxtaposes, as Corpus Christi does, the sublime and the ridiculous and, like the latter, in one of its plots, disregards the unity of place, or rather plays out human history in one place, the isle, rather than on the streets of England. (Actually Shakespeare uses the isle to represent more than one locale, as will be described in Chapter VII.) In one sense both the Mystery Plays and *The Tempest* unify time. As in the Mystery Plays, contemporary persons and biblical characters with similar attitudes or mindsets combine to represent ever-changing, ever-like humankind. Episodes or subplots in *The Tempest*, with change of scene and action, suggest past and future but take place in present time.

While *The Tempest* follows the selectivity of the Mystery Plays, it also reflects the teachings and the cyclical emphasis of the English church. Descriptions of characters and incidents in certain readings from the 1559 *Book of Common Prayer* have correspondences in Shakespeare's text.

The 1559 *Book of Common Prayer*

> came into being in the sixteenth century as a result of the demands of reformers, such as Archbishop Thomas Cranmer, for a simplified, more Biblical, and more "modern" order of worship. *The Elizabethan Prayer Book ...* was the third and most endurable of the earliest editions and provided the context in which Elizabethans, from Queen Elizabeth and William Shakespeare to the village housewife and yeoman farmer, lived and died.[7]

The Prayer Book or *Book of Common Prayer* assigned "Proper lessons" from the Bible to be read on specific dates during the church year at both matin and evensong, so that "all the whole Bible, or the greatest part thereof, should be read over once in the year" (14). It also provided for the order of service and the administration of sacraments, rites, and ceremonies.

In the Prayer Book under "Of Ceremonies, Why Some Be Abolished and Some Retained," one reason given for "the abolishment of certain ceremonies" that had been at the base of many of the religious controversies of the fifteenth and sixteenth centuries was their abuse, "partly by the superstitious blindness of the rude and unlearned and partly by the insatiable avarice of such as sought more their own lucre than the glory of God" (20). Whether he did so consciously or unconsciously, Shakespeare offered images of these types of persons in *The Tempest*, the former as Caliban, Stephano, and Trinculo and the latter as Antonio and Sebastian. Stephano and Trinculo are linked with Caliban in the play, for they, like him, are still without law and grace.

"Of Ceremonies" also speaks to persons who might be offended by the retention of some ceremonies and recommends that such persons "declare themselves to be more studious of unity and concord than of innovations and new fangleness" (20). "Of Ceremonies," like Shakespeare, focuses on the essentials or basics of Christianity. The article asserts the need to retain discipline and order, but affirms that they "are not to be esteemed equal with God's law." The emphasis is not on church order, but on God's law. It dispenses with "dark and dumb ceremonies" (20). While "unity and concord" (20), the projected ends for the "spelling" in *The Tempest*, are in conformity with the above passage, the dumb discourse, which Alonso finds "such sound expressing — /Although they want the use of tongue" (3.3.37–38), is not. The latter words might be a hidden cue to recusants for whom tropes were very meaningful. However, the trope cannot be used to prove Shakespeare was of Roman Catholic persuasion anymore than a Puritan (if he attended the theatre) could claim that Shakespeare favored Puritanism just because Prince Ferdinand spoke, acted, and sounded like one when he jumped overboard, crying, "'Hell is empty,/ And all the devils are here!'" (1.2.214–215). However, *The Tempest* is basically a drama and is suggestive, and, as will be shown later, the banquet has Christian significance.

Collects and Scriptures[8] assigned to be prayed and read during the Epiphany season have as many manifestations in Shakespeare's play as the rites and sacraments celebrated during that period. It is particularly significant, in light of Gonzalo's figuring in this interpretation, that *all* of the "Proper Lessons to Be Read for the First Lessons Both at Morning Prayer and Evening Prayer on the Sundays,"[9] beginning with Advent and running through Christmastide and the Sundays designated as Sundays after Epiphany, are taken from Isaiah (27). Several texts from Isaiah whose themes, phrases, and characterizations have correspondences in the play have been cited in previous chapters and others will be referenced later because of their bearing on *The Tempest*.

The times of the first two records of performance of *The Tempest*— November 1, 1611, in Whitehall, the day of ascendancy for the Lord of Misrule and the beginning of the Feast of Fools, and the winter of 1612-13,[10] which includes the twelve days of Christmastide — invite comparisons of the play with activities of both seasons. Shakespeare uses the specific number twelve, even though with more than one possible inference. A comparison of the play and the Scripture lessons and the collects assigned in *The Book of Common Prayer* for Advent and the twelve days of Christmastide and the celebrations observed during those times reveal many correlations between them and the play.

The Epistle lesson for the first Sunday in Advent, taken from Romans 13, includes "It is time we should now awake out of sleep" (77), and the collect for the second Sunday in Advent referring to the Holy Scriptures advises "Read, mark, learn and inwardly digest them" (79). The Epistle lesson, Romans 15, for the second Sunday includes "Isaiah saith, There shall be a root of Jesse" (79–80), and the Gospel lesson, Luke 21, reads, "There shall be signs in the sun and in the moon, and in the stars, and in the earth the people shall be at their wits' end, through despair. The sea and the water shall roar, and men's hearts shall fail them for fear" (80). The relationship of Jesse to the imagery of the play has already been discussed in the comparison with the *Ludus* play. The importance of staying alert, not sleeping, and of learning are stressed by Prospero in the second scene of *The Tempest*. The storm and men's fears in the first scene compare with the Luke reading. Prospero's advice to heed, listen, and mark compare with the collect.

One Scripture for the third Sunday in Advent, I Corinthians 4, includes, "Let a man on this wise esteem us, even as the ministers of Christ, and stewards of the secrets of God. For herewith it is required of stewards that a man be found faithful" (80). The relevance of this passage to *The Tempest* will be discussed in the next chapter in a discussion of an obsolete meaning of "grave."

The collect for Christmas Day acknowledges the virgin birth and that "we" are made God's "children by adoption and grace" (83). Prospero's claim that Caliban is his could be taken to mean he has adopted Caliban: Caliban, who served as a wood-carrying slave and whom Prospero attempted to teach as he would a child, and who was expelled from Prospero's cell for attempting to violate Miranda, is later owned by Prospero. Having received Prospero's pardon, Caliban will become a candidate for grace. The first Scripture reading for the day, Hebrews 1, recalls how in "times past" God spoke through the prophets and affirms that He now speaks through "His own Son." It acknowledges that ... the Lord "laid the foundation of the earth and the heavens are the work of [His] hands" (83), that He is everlasting and that the earth and heavens will "wax old as doth a garment" and "they shall be changed" (84). This passage, read yearly, harmonizes both with the biblical passage in the Peter Epistle, often cited in connection with the revels speech, and with a Mystery Play passage. According to this interpretation Gonzalo figures a prophet from "times past." The second Scripture reading for the day, taken from John 1, identifies Christ both as the "true light" and "the Word" (84). In this play there is a light above Prospero to which he submits.

When Prospero returns to Milan, he no longer carries a magic stick, but is equipped with a rapier, a two-edged sword. Hebrews 4:12 describes the "word of God" as:

> quick, and powerful, and sharper than any two-edged sword, piercing even to the dividing asunder of soul and spirit, and of the joints and marrow, and ... a discerner of the thoughts and intents of the heart.

Shakespeare may have meant the rapier to be symbolic of the word of God, including the law of Moses, which through Prospero and Ariel has been operating upon the minds of the recalcitrant, discerning the thoughts and intents of their hearts. The lessons to be read at matin and evensong (29) include "Behold a virgin shall conceive, and bear a son, and shall call his name Immanuel" (Isaiah 7:14) and "For unto us a child is born, unto us a son is given: and the government shall be upon his shoulder ... The Prince of Peace" (Isaiah 9:6). Ferdinand is a prince and Miranda a virgin and the purpose is to "work the Peace of the present." Also included were the "good tidings" passage from Luke 2 and a passage from Titus 3:4–5 (29): "after that the kindness and love of God our Saviour toward man appeared,/ Not by works of righteousness which we have done, but according to his mercy he saved us, by the washing of regeneration, and renewing of the Holy Ghost." "Mercy" and celebration, rather than "good works," are stressed in the resolution of the play.

Christmas was followed by St. Stephen's Day, December 26. The collect for that day began "Grant us, O Lord, to learn to love our enemies by the example of thy martyr St. Stephen, who prayed for his persecutors" (84). Its exemplar in *The Tempest* is Prospero, who, according to the "figuring" in this book, represents the Old Testament law which allowed "an eye for an eye, and a tooth for a tooth" (Matthew 5:38), but who accepts the new master's law of forgiveness of enemies and thus submits to the demands of Christ. St. Stephen prayed for his enemy, Saul of Tarsus, who not only persecuted him but "consented to his death." Saul's conversion followed. He became Paul. Prospero exemplifies — although he is at times vexed — both mercy and humility, one in his conduct toward his enemies and the other in accepting the responsibilities of his stewardship as duke of Milan, rather than continuing the pursuit of his private studies. There are two sides, of course, to this commitment and at this point in the dénouement Prospero is acting not as the Moses figure, but as the rightful duke. Like Stephen his submission to the light above helps to effect a change in some of his enemies.

The first Scripture for St. Stephen's Day, from Acts 7, describes the vision of Stephen in which he saw the "heavens open, and the Son of man standing on the right hand of God" (85). In his dreams Caliban thought "The clouds ... would open" (3.2.139). Although his vision is not of the Son of God, it is an opposite link to the Scripture. The second Scripture is taken from Matthew 23 and deals with the persecution of the prophets, wise men, and scribes, whom God sent (85). Typifying Moses, who inscribed the law, and Isaiah, who prophesied, Prospero and Gonzalo can be identified with this passage. In the play Prospero has suffered at the hands of his enemies and Gonzalo is ridiculed by the unbelievers, Sebastian and Antonio. Both men are persecuted and perform a spiritual duty: Gonzalo in adumbrating and effecting design and Prospero in arresting men in their waywardness with truth. The New

Testament lesson, Acts 7, listed for Evensong for St. Stephen's Day (30) is peculiarly relevant to this interpretation of *The Tempest*. It has already been cited in Chapter IV as supplying facts which resolve numerical references Shakespeare makes. It recounts the bondage of Jacob's family in Egypt, and the signs and wonders Moses showed. It mentions the molten "calf," which was compared with Caliban, "moon-calf" in Chapter IV. It even mentions "the star of your god Remphan" (43). Remphan was the Egyptian name for Saturn, who ruled in the golden age and whose sphere of rule will be associated with that of the unseen master in this interpretation of the play. The association of Caliban with Egypt through his dam, Sycorax, a blue-eyed witch, and her god, Setebos, and Gonzalo's description of a golden age, a commonwealth, are related to this passage.

The collect for Saint John's Day, December 27, petitions that the church "may attain to thy everlasting gifts" (86). The biblical readings prescribed for this day — I John 1, John 21, Revelation 1, 22, and Ecclesiastes 5, 6 (86, 30) — emphasize light and darkness, the invitation to "whosoever will" to "come," recognition of and the forgiveness of sin, the way of peace, the iniquitous and foolish ways of men, and Christ as the light. The iniquitous and foolish ways of men are exampled in some of the court party and Caliban and his confederates. The first Scripture, I John 1, affirms that "God is light" (86), and affirms God's forgiveness for those who acknowledge their sin. The way of "peace" is suggested in the first scene of *The Tempest* and there is "a most auspicious star," light in Prospero's "zenith." The second Scripture, John 21, highlights the individuality of God's dealing with his disciples. In the play Prospero and Ariel deal with the varying characters in a different manner and each has his own revelation or rebuke. Ariel's invitation to "come unto these yellow sands" can be linked to the call in the last chapter of Revelation, for in one way or another "whosoever" is on the island is called and comes to the circle or the cell. Where each goes from there depends upon his defuming, mindset, and will.

Although the festivities celebrated during the period between Innocents' Day and New Year's Day were primarily secular, there were Scriptures and a collect associated with both days and a rite associated with New Year's Day. The collect for Innocents' Day asks God to "mortify and kill all vices in us" (87). The "in us" corresponds to the intended, but uncommitted deeds in the play. The first reading, from Rev. 14, is about the return of the "Lamb" to gather the redeemed, who are "virgins." It speaks of "a voice from heaven as the sound of many waters, and as the voice of a great thunder," "the voice of harpers," and the singing of "a new song" (88). The importance that Prospero lays upon Miranda's remaining a virgin, in light of her figuring as Mary, relates to the biblical text. The variety of voices mentioned in the Scripture corresponds to those heard in the play. Again, Shakespeare's text varies ironically with his source. Instead of "harpers" he uses "harpies."

The second Scripture, Matthew 2 (88), describes the flight into Egypt and Herod's slaying of the children. It, along with another Scripture for the day, Jeremiah 31 (30), emphasizes the dispersal and reunion of families. The dispersal of a family through the treachery of a ruler is described in *The Tempest*: "i th' dead of darkness.../ Me and thy crying self" (1.2.130, 132). It compares with Joseph and Mary's flight into Egypt to avoid Herod's murderous intentions. The dispersal of the "souls" in "troops 'bout the isle" represents division in the human family. These are the examples in *The Tempest* of the "We split, we split" of the first scene. Likewise, there is reunion in *The Tempest* within and adjacent to the magic circle where changes occur in some of the traitors.

Since New Year's Day was the eighth day after Christmas it was the day of the circumcision of Christ. The biblical passages, Romans 4 and Colossians 2, connect the rite of circumcision with its spiritual significance of a *heart* attitude, and purification and *obedience to the intent*, rather than the *letter*, of the law. The collect for the day is a petition for "circumcision of the spirit" and the mortification of "all our members" "from all worldly and carnal lusts" (91). The worldly and carnal lusts of some of the characters in *The Tempest* are mortified and the need for a change in their *intents* stressed. Romans 4 stresses "the righteousness of faith" (91), and the Gospel lesson, taken from Luke 2 (92), describes the angels' message to the shepherds, their visit to the Christ child, and the circumcision and naming of Jesus. It may be that Caliban, Stephano, and Trinculo represent the antithesis of the shepherds, much as Alonso, Sebastian, and Antonio represent the "three wise men." Prospero's direction to Caliban—"Go, sirrah, to my cell;/ Take with you your companions; as you look/ To have my pardon, trim it handsomely" (5.1.291–293)—is significant in light of the likelihood that the "manger" where Christ was born was indeed a cave. There are other examples in religious drama of secularizing or even vulgarizing the sacred, e.g., "The Second Shepherd's Play."

The plot of *The Tempest* and its correlation with the Colossians reading for New Year's Day also provide some justification for the present interpretation of *The Tempest*, for Colossians 2 refers to various rules and ordinances as being "a shadow of things to come" (verses 14–17) and refers to Christ as the "Head" (verse 19) of the body of believers. The reference to shadows and their predictiveness concurs with the figuring of characters in *The Tempest*. The latter reference is significant in this treatise since the Saturn's sphere of the Ptolemaic system is assigned to the unseen master. The Feast of Fools was a Christianized version of Saturnalia, in which the Mass was burlesqued. Saturnalia, the festival of the Roman god Saturn, was celebrated during the month of December, and "the policy of the early Church was to divert the people from their pagan customs by consecrating them, as far as possible, to Christian use."[11] The Saturnine accounted for the nature of much of the secular part of the reveling during the Feast of Fools. In *The Tempest* Caliban "sings drunkenly" (2.2.177) in a brief unholy Feast of Fools:

'Ban, 'Ban CaCaliban
Has a new master:— get a new man.
Freedom, high-day! high-day, freedom! freedom,
high-day, freedom! [2.2.184–186].

Prospero's abandonment of magic in the "ye elves" speech and Gonzalo's
reference to "T'cel the golden age," when tied in with the Christmastide celebration of that golden age as the Saturnalia and the Feast of Fools, take on
more than mortal significance. They can be related directly to Colossians 2,
which was read at Evensong on January 1 (30). That Scripture warns against
"the tradition of men ... the rudiments of this world" and asserts that Christ
has "spoiled principalities and powers ... made a shew of them openly, tri-
umphing over them in it." In Caliban's foolish reveling in finding a false god
Shakespeare makes a show of the rudiments of this world.

In Shakespeare's plays all men, even the best, are subject to folly. There
was a particular significance attached to all the reveling and display of folly in
the medieval and Renaissance eras. It was to encourage recognition of man's
failures and faultiness, effect humility and repentance, and thus bring about
his salvation. In this respect Prospero, who presides over the antics on the isle
as a Lord of Misrule, succeeds in the case of some of the cast.

At the end of the Christmastide festivities, the great house was restored
to the rule of its proper lord. *The Tempest* ends on the literal or political level
with Prospero's having displaced the Lord of Misrule, Antonio, as the duke of
Milan. On the allegorical or figurative level Prospero is the Lord of Misrule
who exposes the follies of man, including his own, on the enchanted isle. His
surrender of magic at the end of the play and his disrobing and his abandonment of staff and book as the historical figure, Moses, signify a surrender to
the true Lord, of humanity, creation and peace, the unseen master.

The first Scripture read on the Sunday after Christmas Day, from Galatians 4, speaks of the "child," who doesn't differ from a servant while he has
tutors and governors, and associates this fact with bondage to the law prior
to the coming of Christ and of Christ's redemption of those who "were bond
unto the law" and "through election" are made "natural sons," and hence "not
a servant, but a son" (89). In harmony with this passage Shakespeare exemplifies Ferdinand and Caliban. Ferdinand is a "servant" in the play and a lost
son, but he ends up as a son, both of "a wond'red father and a wise" and of
Alonso. Caliban, who is still a child, must remain under the law, in Prospero's
charge, until he finds the grace for which he intends to seek.

On Epiphany, January 6, the collect acknowledges "the leading of a star"
(92) in the manifestation to the Gentiles, acknowledged knowing God "by
faith," and makes petition for the future life (92). The Epistle for the day,
Ephesians 3, describes Paul as "a prisoner of Jesus Christ for you heathen"
(93). The Gospel, Matthew 2, tells the story of the visit of the wise men (93–94).

A star influences Prospero. Future life is inferred in Shakespeare's use of "little life," in the vision, and in the example of Ferdinand's receiving the "prize," Miranda, as his bride. It appears that Shakespeare prepared the play to complement both Allhallows and Epiphany celebrations in both church and festival. The emphasis on "faith" in the collect would negate Colin Still's "comparative religion" interpretation.

Three Scriptures read at Evening Prayers in February, Ephesians 4, Ephesians 6, and Galatians 3, provide descriptions of characters and purpose in *The Tempest*.[12] Ephesians 4:17 speaks of "Gentiles [who] walk, in the vanity of their mind," and Ephesians 4:23 advises, "Be renewed in the spirit of your mind." In *The Tempest* vain men think corruptly about acquiring unjust place and exaltation. It is their minds which need defuming. Ephesians 4:19 suggests the "greediness" manifested by Sebastian, Stephano, Trinculo. Ephesians 4:28 advises such as Stephano and Trinculo, who stole the "glistering apparel" (4.1.192–193) "to steal no more" and to work "with [their] hands the thing which is good." After reproving them, Prospero sets them to work decorating his cell. In behavior commended in Ephesians 4:31–32, Prospero puts aside "all bitterness, and wrath, and anger" and forgives his enemies. These Scriptures, read after the celebration of Christ's birth, describe how people should live after the coming of Christ to them.

When Prospero returns to Milan he is equipped with hat and rapier, "the helmet of salvation, and the sword of the Spirit, which is the Word of God" (Ephesians 6:17). According to the Epilogue Prospero will also be "praying" as advised in Ephesians 6:18. Shakespeare creates characters who are living portraits of Scriptural descriptions.

The law is defined as "schoolmaster" in Galatians 3:24, and the duty of the schoolmaster is given: "to bring us to Christ." The careful tutoring of the Prospero-Moses figure has a like purpose, which is fulfilled in the remainder of the play. It is to bring the inhabitants of the isle to the author of forgiveness and mercy. The purpose of the Mystery Plays was similar. Of the Corpus Christi play, Davies wrote:

> Sacred history is treated as contemporary, sublime mysteries are presented through the immediate. God creates man or ponders the Redemption here and now. The Incarnate Son is crucified, rises and ascends in York or Lincoln, and, moreover, gives the impression of speaking the language of ordinary men. That this is his language is, of course, consistent with Scriptural practice, and in the localization of the mystery there is evinced that philosophical understanding, found, for example, in Boethius, of God's "time" as an eternal present in which yesterday is as much today as tomorrow, for He is outside time and knows all always.[13]

Davies named three functions of the Corpus Christi play: didactic, affective, and celebratory. "By its celebratory function," he explained, "I meant that, as a species of both worship and self-realization, it acted out the destiny of mankind under God." Davies stated the intention of the Mystery Plays: "to orientate the will and convert the soul, to draw tears of penitence and to warm the audience into love." He found the plays "inextricably religious and secular at once."[14]

What Shakespeare did in *The Tempest, his* mystery play, compares to what was done in the Mystery Plays, which is evident from the typology, imagery, the dénouement, and Shakespeare's multiple use of the word "now." He incorporates the three functions noted by Davies. The didactic is found in Prospero's teaching. Changes are effected and wrongs acknowledged. Ariel celebrates in a song of freedom, and Prospero, pardoning Caliban, bids him take Stephano and Trinculo and go to his cell and to "trim it handsomely" (5.1.293). The true master of the souls' tempest, he whose law is forgiveness, is the divinity in the play, not Prospero.

Locating words similar to those with their glosses in the Mystery Plays affirms both Shakespeare's sources and the play's sense. The multiple meanings of words used by Shakespeare will be discussed in the next chapter.

Chapter VI

The Language of Belief:
Wordplay in *The Tempest*

"He that thinks with more extent than another will want words of larger meaning." Samuel Johnson, The Idler, *No. 70.*

Wordplay was popular in the sixteenth century, and Shakespeare naturally took advantage of its many forms. Not surprisingly, he also varied those forms to create his own modes of wordplay. Shakespeare's use of novel dramatic structures in *A Midsummer Night's Dream, Measure for Measure, Troilus and Cressida,* and *Antony and Cleopatra,* as well as in *The Tempest,* attest to his deviation from standard usages. He altered events and characters and overrode his sources' time sequences and cultures in order to effect values and meaning. The success he achieved, with this nonadherence to the literal and limited word, validates his creative experimentation. Therefore, a meaningful interpretation of *The Tempest* should focus upon the varied uses Shakespeare makes of words and phrases.

In the playing of *The Tempest* certain words rise above the text just as the notes of a particular instrument in an orchestra may stand out because of their distinct function in a composition. The words may be single notes or phrases, and although they fit well into the immediate context, they may be heard above the action as signals or what Hodge describes as "transparent signifiers."[1] The "signifiers" arouse awareness, bringing to "remembrance" narratives known to members of the audience. They are words used in the Mystery Plays, church ritual, festivals, teachings, and sacraments; in short, they are part of the language of religious belief. This running commentary, along with Shakespeare's insistence on attentiveness in the second scene through Prospero's instructions to Miranda helps expand meaning. It is not Miranda alone that Prospero addresses with, "Dost thou attend me?" "Thou attend'st not!" "Dost thou hear?" "Hear a little further." Miranda's response of "Your tale, sir, would cure deafness" becomes ironic now in light of our loss of hearing. Such comments as "The very minute bids thee ope thine ear./ Obey, and be attentive," "Of any thing the image, ... that/ Hath kept with thy remembrance," "But how that this lives in thy mind?" suggest that not only is Prospero informing Miranda and the audience of past events and preparing her and them for what is to come; Shakespeare is also cuing the audience to listen and associate Prospero's words and phrases with things that live in their minds, even in the "dark backward and abysm" of their minds. These associations will give meaning to the play. There can be no doubt upon a careful analysis of the second scene that Shakespeare intended to bring certain truths into focus. There are happenings that are "far off" and "rather like a dream" for the audience, too, and things that live in their memories.

Recently, literary critics have begun using what they call hypertexts. Hypertexts are texts that contain links to other texts. Two texts may be juxtaposed on a computer screen, affording easy comparison. Long ago Shakespeare created his own form of hypertext. The second scene of *The Tempest* is a prime example. In the second scene, in particular, there are dual references in almost everything that is said: those which apply specifically to Milan history, and those which apply to the history of mankind as recorded in the Judeo-Christian tradition and dramatized in the Mystery Plays prior to 1611.

Some of the notes which Shakespeare sounds act as signifiers and links to other texts and were sure to have echoed in the minds of some of the hearers. Among them are "my heart bleeds ... from my remembrance!," "transported," "neglecting worldly ends," "sinner ... did believe ... out o' th' substitution," and "To have no screen between this part he play'd/ And him he play'd it for." The sinner believes because Christ died in his place for his sins. Images and paintings portrayed Mary and saints with bleeding hearts. The last word group references the biblical account found in Matthew 27:51 when Christ died — "the veil of the temple was rent in twain" — and the commentary made upon the removal of the veil in II Cor. 3:13–16, where the veil put on Moses' face is compared to the veil that remains on the hearts of those whose "minds were blinded." The passage also asserts that the "veil is done away in Christ." The running commentary in the second scene of *The Tempest* continues with "do him homage ... and bend ... yet unbow'd ... To most ignoble stooping," "they durst not,/ So dear the love my people bore me; nor set/ A mark so bloody on the business." It continues: "Under my burthen groan'd," "Providence divine," and "Out of his charity, who being then appointed/ Master of this design." The Gospels attest to the fact that Christ's enemies "feared the people." "Bloody mark," "ignoble stooping," and "Under my burthen groan'd" are phrases associated with the crucifixion. Is Shakespeare not bringing to his audience's remembrance truth about the redemptive sacrifice, the suffering Christ, who made possible the restoration and reconciliation of mankind that are to be exemplified in the play? Is he not linking the *Tempest* text to another?

Such words are not limited to the second scene of the play, but while Prospero, Ariel, and Gonzalo fulfill their roles in the attempts to bring awareness to the ship of souls, the role of the unseen master, his life, and mission are also being documented. The phrase "Put thy sword up," though widely used, becomes significant in this interpretation. The similar phrase, "Put up thy sword," spoken by the New Testament master in the garden of Gethsemane, parallels meaning. The reconciliation in this play, as in the act of redemption, is not to be achieved with swords, but by means of a "spell."

A good place to look for these notes is in the words of Gonzalo, for he reads events well and foresees. The first part of the last sentence that Gonzalo utters in the first scene of the play, after the other passengers have called upon their gods, is a paraphrase of a line of the Lord's prayer. "Thy will be done" in the play becomes "The wills above be done," and it is possible to presume that Gonzalo's commonwealth, which greatly resembles that of the prophet Isaiah's vision (as referred to earlier), is a descriptive account of what he believes would be "Thy Kingdom come. Thy will be done in earth, as it is in heaven" (Matthew 6:10). Gonzalo tells the "troop" with whom he landed that they "have cause ... of joy" and speaks to them of the "miracle" of their preservation. His word is considered "more than the miraculous harp," which raised a city. He is, in fact, rather than building a city, envisioning a state of beings where there are righted relationships, a group of persons among whom equality, purified minds, and peace prevail. He is understood as harping on the miraculous especially in relation to their outer appearance, their garments. The renewal of their garments through immersion is symbolic of baptism, which in turn symbolizes the cleansing of Christ's blood as stated in relation to garments in Revelations 7:14: "These are they which came out of great tribulation, and have washed their robes, and made them white in the blood of the Lamb." The cleansing also forecasts the defuming of minds, which takes place later. It is from inner cleanliness, from a righted mind, that commonwealth will flow. Gonzalo's commonwealth where "nature should produce/Without sweat or endeavor" with "innocent people" (2.1.155–156, 160) suggests Eden before the Fall and restoration to the paradisiacal state. *Innocent people* is descriptive of Adam and Eve; *sweat* is a key memory word since it was used in the curse upon Adam as a result of his disobedience and failure in servanthood. As shown in Chapter V, "sweat" was used in both the "Adam and Eve" and "Cain and Abel" Mystery Plays.

In the character descriptions in Chapter IV attention was called to Gonzalo, who speaks of "a maze trod," which references the treading of the winepress and which is associated in Isaiah 63:1–3 with the shedding of Christ's blood for the remission of sin. That particular passage in Isaiah also contains the phrase "dyed garments," which is echoed in the description of the court party's garments: "new dy'd" (2.1.59, 61).

Alonso's "what strange fish/Hath made his meal on thee?" (2.1.108–109), echoes the Jonah tempest and the New Testament reference to it. Examples of phrases that help to figure characters and provide an ongoing commentary have already been given in earlier chapters. Miranda speaks of "holy innocence" (3.1.82) and later Prospero calls Gonzalo "holy." Even Caliban recalls a biblical story, that of Sisera, with "knock a nail into his head," (3.2.60) and Sebastian's reference to "one tree" and "one phoenix" (3.3.23) are suggestive of the cross and the resurrection. There is to be a resurrection of a son, supposed dead, in this play too. When Trinculo, in response to Ariel's tune, says "O, forgive me my sins!" (3.2.129), Stephano's response is, "He that dies pays all debts" (3.2.130). The word *debts* is used in one version of the Lord's prayer, and there can be little doubt that Shakespeare intended his audience to recognize the wording and the reference to Christ who died for the sins of the human race and thereby paid all debts. There are allusions to the Lord's prayer throughout the play, beginning with Gonzalo's prayer in the first scene and ending, as most prayers do, with "Amen" in the last.

Ariel's discourse in 3.3 to the "three men of sin," who have already been associated with "the three wise men" in this book, depends upon the semantic memory of the audience. The discourse contains the suggestive words "innocent child" and "foul deed" (3.3.72), suggesting Herod's plot to kill the infant Jesus.

The Tempest is syncretically biblical. This running commentary has not been heretofore acknowledged. Failure to discern and include the biblical phrases and allusions in an evaluation of the play have led some critics to conclude that Shakespeare's dénouement is mortal. It appears, however, that to acknowledge solely a mortal ending would divest the play of two-thirds of its meaning and preclude Shakespeare's awareness of man's relationship to two worlds.

Although Shakespeare's propensity for punning has been well established, some of its significance in the interpretation of his works has been lost with the loss of the meanings associated with certain words and phrases. Fernald wrote, "To limit ourselves to the actual present meaning is to defraud ourselves of thousands of years of history; to efface the great background against which the current meaning of words comes out into fullest relief.... By considering words ... [in their background] each word becomes an entity, and language comes to have a perspective."[2] Such consideration of words not only gives language perspective, but affords perspective on earlier cultures. To understand Shakespeare's wordplay it is necessary to be aware of the multiple senses of words available to him, particularly those obsolete senses associated with custom, religious practices and Scripture. If, as this interpretation proposes, *The Tempest* has a biblical plot, fabricated from the Bible, the Mystery Plays, and the *Book of Common Prayer*, then words as well as characters will have biblical overtones, suggesting biblical events, themes and times, all of which will invest the play with meaning.

The mystery dramas not only provide a comparable plot covering all human time, but they also provide a rich source of word senses which have been lost to subsequent centuries. Bethell wrote, "Poetry is especially satisfying because of its 'density' of meaning;... the meaning addresses itself to every level of the mind and, though it may be *apprehended* at times without conscious effort, can be *analyzed* only by a close examination of the words in all their properties."[3] In light of Shakespeare's fertile mind, such an examination is important. In *The Tempest* some words have obsolete layers of meaning; others have mystical qualities as well as precise dictionary definitions.

Although Armstrong[4] started from a different perspective than that pursued in this study, in his examination of word linkages in Shakespeare's plays he reveals the appropriateness of associating word clusters with sixteenth and seventeenth century culture and experience. He found that the same two unusual words appear together in several passages. One word seemed to evoke the other, and the association of the two often could be traced to seventeenth century occurrences. Shakespeare's evident familiarity with biblical texts, occasioned in part by the English church's yearly reading of the same passages, and the omnipresent religious art would give rise to the same phenomena.

Linkages of words and themes in *The Tempest* have been traced to scriptural texts, the texts of the Mystery Plays, and the *Book of Common Prayer* in earlier chapters of this book. Particular linkages of the word *rod* with Mary's proof of virginity, her descent from Jesse, and the rod's flowering, noted in the Mystery Plays, can be found in Scripture and in *The Tempest*. The associations disclose meaning in Ariel's freedom song. In Isaiah 11:1 *branch* and *rod* are used as synonyms and they describe a descendant of Jesse, David's father:

> And there shall come forth a rod out of the stem of Jesse, and a Branch shall grow out of his roots: And the spirit of the Lord shall rest upon him, the spirit of wisdom and understanding, the spirit of counsel and might, the spirit of knowledge and of the fear of the Lord.... With righteousness shall he judge ... and reprove with equity for the meek of the earth.... And in that day there shall be a root of Jesse, which shall stand for an ensign of the people; to it shall the Gentiles seek: and his rest shall be glorious [Isaiah 11:1–10].

Moses' brother, Aaron, had a rod that budded and it was kept in the Ark of the Covenant along with the tables of the law and a pot of manna, evidences of God's spiritual and material provisions for Israel. The budding rods, Aaron's and Jesse's, signify Christ, the unseen master of *The Tempest*. The prophet Zechariah links branch and servant: "behold I will bring forth my servant the BRANCH" (3:8). A further reference describes his rule:

> Behold the man whose name is The BRANCH; and he shall grow up out of his place, and he shall build the temple of the Lord:... and he shall bear the

glory, and shall sit and rule upon his throne: and he shall be a priest upon
his throne; and the counsel of peace shall be between them both [Zech. 6:12,
13].

Both typology and imagery work through the linkages with Scripture
and Mystery Play usage to signify the unseen master in *The Tempest*. The rod
that budded and the branch become the flowering bough in Ariel's freedom
song. Prospero, the schoolmaster, magician, and master of the law, having
dismissed the "weak masters, elves and demi-puppets," promises Ariel, "Thou
shalt ere long be free," whereupon, as the stage directions tell us, "Ariel sings
and helps to attire him":

> Where the bee sucks, there suck I:
> In a cowslip's bell I lie;
> There I couch when owls do cry.
> On the back's bat I do fly
> After summer merrily.
> Merrily, merrily shall I live now,
> Under the blossom that hangs on the bough [5.1.87–94].

Micah prophesied, "But thou, Bethlehem Ephratah, *though* thou be little among the thousands of Judah, *yet* out of thee shall he come forth unto me
that is to be ruler in Israel; whose goings forth *have been* from old, from everlasting" (5:2), and "hear ye the rod, and who hath appointed it" (6:9). There
are within these various Scriptures linkages between rod, branch (bough),
servant, and hearing and the Christ, which also have linkages in the play.
Although *bough* was sometimes used for smaller branches, it also meant main
branch.[5] Ferdinand, a willing servant in *The Tempest*, typifies Christ. The
"bough" in Ariel's song, with its "blossom," has many associations which identify Ariel's new master.

A considerable difference in interpretation of the Epilogue in this study
and others centers around the word "grave" and the meanings assigned to it.
In a discussion of the revels speech in relation to Calvin, R. M. Frye notes that
in Prospero's first appearance he "expresses his faith in 'providence divine'
and in his last appearance vows that 'every third thought shall be my grave.'"[6]
In a discussion of Shakespeare's art he states that "'Happy' endings also char-
acterize the tragicomedies, but are mixed with notes of sadness and thoughts
of mortality.... In *The Tempest*, Prospero even in his moment of triumph
declares of the future that 'every third thought shall be my grave' (5.1.311)."[7]
Frye does not acknowledge any other interpretation of the word "grave" than
the one common to us. It may well have been that one of Prospero's meanings in using the word was that he would remain aware of the limitations of
earthly life, but if so, in what context? Was it because he saw the grave as a
meaningless end and a reminder of his mortality, or could it be that he was

thinking of grave as the rounding-out place of "our little life?" In this interpretation, where multiconsciousness is emphasized, both kinds of grave are inferred. However, one use of grave in Shakespeare's day which has been lost to us was its use indicating "a foreign title" associated with the administrator of an office.[8] Ariel uses the word in that sense when he addresses Prospero: "All hail, great master! grave sir, hail!" (1.2.189). Another meaning of grave was "a steward, a person placed in charge of property."[9] It was also used to describe behaviors and characters.[10] A link between soul and grave, two words weighted with meaning in *The Tempest*, is found in Scripture: "O Lord, thou hast brought up my soul from the grave" (Psalm 30:3). The association of soul and grave, Prospero's assertion that "graves at my command/ Have wak'd their sleepers, op'd, and let 'em forth/ By my so potent Art" (5.1.48–50) and the fact that Prospero has been dealing with the "souls" of those who were on the ship suggests more than mortality. With recovery of the obsolete meanings and the biblical references, the multiple aspects of Prospero's commitment become apparent. In Prospero's last words Shakespeare points to man's dual responsibility and the necessity of a relationship to two worlds: "And thence retire me to my Milan, where every third thought shall be my grave" (5.1.310–311). In the Epilogue he pleads:

> But release me from my bands
> With the help of your good hands:
> . . . .
> And my ending is despair,
> Unless I be reliev'd by prayer,
> Which pierces so, that it assaults
> Mercy itself, and frees all faults [Epilogue 8–10, 15–18].

It is Prospero's intention to keep in mind the responsibility associated with his office as duke of Milan. He intends to be a faithful steward of that to which he was entrusted. He does not intend to neglect his duty as he did formerly, for his trespass as duke of Milan was "neglect of office." On the other hand, he acknowledges his need for mercy, which releases the supplicant from his faults. He also will remember that his soul, like the souls of others, has been "brought up from the grave." Shakespeare focuses on man's part in obtaining mercy (forgiveness of others) and also upon man's duty (service in this world). The grace and mercy of which Caliban and Prospero speak and the "peace of the present" are derivatives of the law of forgiveness. Prospero intends to relate properly to earthly men and society in attending to his "grave" (duty). He also intends to relate to the larger life of man and the unseen master through prayer. Thus in the Epilogue Prospero acknowledges man's proper relationship to both worlds. Prayer may reach beyond petition. It may involve vision, epiphany or revelation, comparable to and surpassing the emotional catharsis that Shakespeare provides for his audiences.

Recovery of meaning through an obsolete definition is not limited to the word grave, although that word's obsolescence has been critical in more than one interpretation. An investigation into the several meanings of the word "sands" greatly extends the sense and wonder of *The Tempest*. It also enhances our appreciation of Shakespeare's wordplay. The first image created in the minds of a twentieth century audience who have just witnessed the wreck of a vessel no doubt would be of warm, peaceful sands of a beach. For an Elizabethan, sand was closely associated with time, for it was often visible in an hourglass. Since yellow was accepted as the color of gold and gold was considered the most precious of metals, "yellow sands" would carry with it a sense of prime or golden time as well as a sense of golden place. But sands in the sixteenth century had still other meanings. Sands also meant sounds.[11] Sands and sound were interchangeable: "sound(e)" is given as one spelling of sand.[12] Interchanging sounds and sands, then, makes possible the idea that the souls also have come to the golden *sounds*, Ariel's music. They are the "sounds and sweet airs" (3.2.134) heard by Caliban. They are the sounds that Ferdinand hears above him — "This music crept by me upon the waters" (1.2.394) — the musical sounds of hope, which are "no mortal business, nor no sound/ That the earth owes" (1.2.409–410). The sounds come from above and are not mortal. It is specifically Ariel who sings, but in the larger sense of the play it is the heavens declaring "the glory of God…. There is no speech nor language where there voice is not heard" (Psalm 19:1, 3), including Shakespeare's isle." Actually, Ariel's song is sung to the "first man that leapt" into the waters, hoping to escape "Hell…/ And all the devils" (1.2.214–215). Ariel's reporting of Ferdinand's behavior may have been a commentary on the behavior of zealous members of religious sects in the sixteenth century, many of whom died in their attempts to purify worship, renew Catholicism, or protect the existing forms and rites of the English church. Ferdinand's enthusiasm and intention to rend Prospero's kingdom from him with a sword reflect the attitudes and spirit of some of the sixteenth century religious groups. However, in the play, violence is not acceptable. Ferdinand's enthusiasm must be augmented and validated with hard work and service.

Caliban can hear the sounds as well as Ferdinand, for "there is no speech nor language, where their voice is not heard" (Psalm 19:3). Caliban hears the sounds but does not have anyone to interpret their meaning until Prospero teaches him. A passage from I Corinthians (14:10, 11) is descriptive of Caliban's situation: "There are … so many kinds of voices in the world, and none of them is without signification. Therefore if I know not the meaning of the voice, I shall be unto him that speaketh a barbarian, and he that speaketh shall be a barbarian unto me." Other obsolete meanings of sands which contribute even more to the Christian sense of *The Tempest* will be discussed in the next chapter.

The words "point," "mark," "print," and "printless" are important in an interpretation of the play. The first question Prospero asks Ariel takes on special significance when Prospero is seen as figuring Moses, the lawmaker: "Hast thou, spirit,/ Perform'd to point *The Tempest* that I bade thee?" (1.2.193–194). In Semitic alphabets point means "any one of the dots, minute strokes, or groups of these, which were placed over, under, or within the letters or consonants to indicate the vowels."[13] Thus Prospero asks the spirit of the law if he has carried out the details of *The Tempest* experience which is afforded souls for their awakening. Later in the play point is associated with words when Prospero commands Ariel "exactly do/ All points of my command." Ariel answers, "To th' syllable" (1.2.503–504). The New Testament is understood by Christians as fulfilling or filling out the Old Testament, the word of God; Ariel, the spirit of the law, supplies the vowels which produce syllables, filling out the words. The vowels soften the harsh consonant sounds, incorporating more feeling, as Ariel does when he tells Prospero, "Your charm so strongly works 'em,/ That if you now beheld them, your affections/ Would become tender" (5.1.17–19). To which Prospero responds, "Hast thou, which art but air, a touch, a feeling/ Of their afflictions, and shall not myself ... be kindlier moved than thou are?" (5.1.21–24). In Shakespeare's day point also meant "a mark indicating a tone or sound; corresponding to the modern 'notes'."[14] Both meanings are appropriate when addressed to the one who represents the spirit of the law and who is the songmaker in the play.

Mark is used seven times. It is used both to call attention to that which is imprinted and to call special attention to a subject or person. In the first scene Gonzalo declares there is "no drowning mark upon" the boatswain (1.1.29). Was that because Shakespeare was associating the boatswain, who cheerily obeys his master, with Noah in one of those Armstrong-like links?[15]In the second scene Prospero interrupts his story several times with instructions to Miranda to mark an element of it. He tells her to "mark his [Antonio's] condition, and th' event," parts of his story which provide both details of Milan happenings and the running biblical commentary. He asks her to evaluate Antonio's brotherhood by his attitude and behavior: "then tell me/ If this might be a brother" (1.2.117–118). "A mark so bloody on the business" (1.2.142), which has already been noted, is a significant part of the biblical commentary on the Milan, and, typically, on the biblical story.

Print can mean simply an identifiable mark or the footprint left by a man or animal. In Shakespeare's day it meant "a symbolic mark, a character; a badge."[16] Thus when all the troops are gathered near Prospero's cell in the final act and Prospero tells the group to "mark but the badges of these men" (Stephano, Trinculo, and Caliban) (5.1.267), he is calling attention to characters. Print also was defined as "an image or character stamped upon the mind or soul, esp. the Divine likeness [in allusion to Genesis 1:27]; a mental impression."[17] Thus Miranda's claim that Caliban will not take "any print of goodness" (1.2.354) infers his lack of divine likeness. He does not shadow or figure the unseen master. In the "Moses" play, *Ludus Coventriae*, Moses says, "print these lawes well in thy mind."[18] In *The Tempest* Prospero attempts to imprint the law in Caliban's mind.

Two other words used by Shakespeare, "line" and "level," and the senses they had in the sixteenth century contribute to meaning. In 4.1 and 5.1 line appears twice with level and three other times. It had various meanings. One meaning of line was "a cord bearing a hook or hooks, used for fishing also fishing line."[19] Ariel baits his line with glistering apparel to catch Stephano and Trinculo. Another meaning of line was "a rope, cord, string; a leash for dogs or for hawks ... or as short for *clothesline*."[20] Ariel's clothesline also acts as a leash to stop Trinculo and Stephano. Still another meaning of line was "rule, canon, precept; standard of life or practice."[21]

One sense having particular significance in this interpretation was "a circle of the terrestrial or celestial sphere," which was used to indicate location.[22] When Stephano takes down the jerkin, he and it are "under the line" (4.1.236), or within the spheres of Providence. Shakespeare uses line in both senses when Ariel informs Prospero that his catch, "all prisoners, sir, [are]/ In the line-grove which weather-fends your cell" (5.1.9–10). They have been caught and are within the providential spheres. In another sense line was used with level: *"by line and level, by rule and line."*[23]

Level was used to indicate "persons or things arriving at their proper place with respect to those around or connected with them."[24] Thus Stephano, Trinculo, and Caliban become prisoners of Prospero, who represents the law, which they have violated by stealing. Level also meant "an instrument which indicates a line parallel to the plane of the horizon, used in determining the position as to the horizontality of a surface to which it is applied."[25] One reference reads: "The deeds of men..are..to be examined by Gods level and line."[26] Trinculo has it backwards when Stephano is his king: "we steal by line and level, an't like your grace" (4.1.240). Their rule and line differs from God's. The statement also carries the sense that Trinculo and Stephano are not yet under grace. Stephano affirms Trinculo's standard of life, "while I am King of this/ country. 'Steal by line and level' is an excellent/ pass of pate" (4.1.242–244). But in spite of their assertions, they are put under "level and line."

The tracing and connection of words and imagery may seem extreme to us, but when one considers everyday word usages that have been lost, Shakespeare's enormous vocabulary, his multiple linkages, and his obvious familiarity with biblical texts, the Mystery Plays and *The Book of Common Prayer*, we should not be surprised at his appropriation, conscious or unconscious, of imagery, illustrations and texts which for us are obscure. Surely, the Bible and the Mystery Plays afforded Shakespeare unparalleled sources of sketches of character types and behaviors, as well as of historical personages.

"Pate," used in the same context as line and level, had meanings as diverse as "cleverness" and "the skin of a calf's head."[27] It is used in 4.1.242 to compliment Trinculo for his clever "pass," but in stopping for Ariel's bait, the would-be usurpers are taking the skin off the "mooncalf's" (Caliban's) head. Wiser than the thieves, Caliban "will have none on't," declaring, "We shall lose our time" (4.1.247). It is impossible to follow all the convolutions of meaning possible in the utterance of a single word. No doubt Shakespeare gloried in the extravagant number of meanings he could imply in the use of one word while audiences gleaned what was familiar to them. We modern audiences, without an in-depth study, lose two-thirds of Shakespeare's meaning as well as an enormous amount of jollity.

While some words are used to identify or locate characters or ridicule man's folly, others trace the sacred meaning of the play. Immediately after Gonzalo pronounces a blessing on Ferdinand and Miranda, calling on the "gods," he adds that "it is you that have chalk'd forth the way/ Which brought us hither" (5.1.203–204). This recognition was undoubtedly part of Shakespeare's method of having Gonzalo as prophet interpret the play and thus affirm the role of the unseen master. Unfortunately, the profound meaning of the passage has been lost by our loss of the full significance of the word "chalk'd." We understand chalk as a marker, and used with "way," it suggests the marking of a clear path. To a twentieth century audience it suggests the marking out of the path by which the shipwrecked come to Prospero's magic circle and hence to reconciliation. However, although it carries that idea, for a Shakespearean audience, it intoned more. In Shakespeare's day chalk was used to list a man's debts.[28] Chalk meant "to write up in chalk (a record, esp of credits given); to score."[29] Accounts of credit given were marked out on doors. The score was entered in chalk, thus a reckoning of debts was kept. When the debt was paid, the debts were chalked out —"To mark *out*, as with chalk" and "to delineate, *esp* by the main features: to outline, sketch *out*, adumbrate."[30] Evidence that such an expression applied to wrongdoing as well as monetary debts is supplied in a quotation under the *Oxford English Dictionary* (OED) definition of chalk: "There's lesse chalk upon you[r] score of sinnes."[31] Consistent with the interpretation of this book is Holy Gonzalo's affirmation that the way has been "chalk'd forth" by the "gods." The unseen master of *The Tempest*, referred to by Gonzalo as "gods," has chalked out the debts as well as having chalked out the way for man to follow. The added meaning strengthens the master-servant theme of the play and is an affirmation of the redemption theme and redemptive time (tempest or highest time). The use of chalk to indicate the marking out of an immortal way is indicated in two references in the OED "God did but (as it were under a dark shadowe) chalk out the..kingdome of his sonne" and "This Book it chaulketh out before thine eyes The man that seeks the everlasting Prize."[32] Shakespeare chalks out the kingdom of the son using the shadows of those who figure him. Yet another meaning of chalk was to blanch or make pale,[33] a meaning which fits with an affirmation in Isaiah, the biblical book from which Shakespeare drew heavily in writing *The Tempest*. Isaiah 1:18 reads, "Though your sins be as scarlet, they shall be as white as snow."

Since those who are "wrack'd" are described as a "ship of souls" rather than men, the multiple meanings of soul expand the meaning of *The Tempest* also. Among the definitions given in the OED are "the spiritual aspect of man considered in its moral aspect or in relation to God and His precepts" and "the spiritual part of man regarded as surviving after death and susceptible to happiness or misery in a future state."[34] Soul is also described as "the principle of thought and action in man, commonly regarded as an entity distinct from the body; the spiritual part of man in contrast to the purely physical."[35] The latter definition disavows a secular humanistic interpretation, for Shakespeare could have used "ship of men" and was probably using "ships of souls" in antithesis to Brant's *Ship of Fools*, a work extant in translation in England in the sixteenth and seventeenth centuries. There are fools in many of Shakespeare's plays and some of the men in *The Tempest* act like fools, but whether fools or not, they have souls that need awakening and minds that need defuming. According to the scriptural tradition man became "a living soul" when God "breathed into his nostrils the breath of life" (Genesis 2:7). Within Prospero's magic circle the "ignorant fumes [vapor or breath] that mantle/ Their [the court party's] clearer reason" (5.1.67–68) are chased away. Thus, they become living souls again, are no longer "dead in trespasses and sins" (Ephesians 2:1).

"Tempest" not only refers to a storm and to the highest time, but is also used figuratively to mean "to disturb violently a person or the mind."[36] The minds of some of those aboard the "ship of souls" are violently disturbed both aboard ship and ashore. The object of the disturbance created by Prospero is to bring them to their senses.

It should be noted with the emphasis given in this treatise on dual time, temporal and eternal, that the biblical texts refer to both the temporal and eternal situation. One of the phrases used by Prospero—"No, not so much perdition as an hair/ Betid to any creature in the vessel" (1.2.30–31)—has been identified as a biblical reference to the preservation of those sharing in the shipwreck experienced by the Apostle Paul. The allusion to that shipwreck appears to have been repeated by Ariel, "Not a hair perished," but those who know Scripture well know that there are four such biblical references. In Luke 21:18 the words of the master are "there shall not an hair of your head perish." This affirmation is associated with "redemption draweth nigh," a dissolution of seen things, and the endurance of the word: "Heaven and earth shall pass away: but my words shall not pass away" (Luke 21:33). In Acts 27:34 the words of Paul are "there shall not an hair fall from the head of any of you," an assurance in a nautical disaster. In I Samuel 14:45, "there shall not one hair of his head fall to the ground" was the declaration of the people to Saul when it was found that his son, Jonathan, had inadvertently fallen under the curse of death by partaking of honey. A fourth reference found in Daniel 3:27, "nor was an hair of their head singed," is associated with the trial of three men's obedience to God rather than to a king and with the presence with them of one "like the Son of God" (Daniel 3:25). Whether or not some members of his audiences made linkages with these Scriptures, it seems they could have been linked in the poet's mind, not only with the outcome of a shipwreck (Paul's rescue) but with the promise of the master (a coming redemption, the enduring word), with the rescue of a king's son from the curse of death, and with the presence in the play of the "Son." The first reference to these biblical passages is preceded by Prospero's assurance to Miranda that there has been "provision in mine art." All the biblical references cited above involve provision in the smallest detail, "hair."

The name of Caliban's dam's god, Setebos, is not found as such in the dictionary, but its components are. Obsolete meanings of "sete" and "bos" are suggestive. Sete is an obsolete form used for city and bos for boss.[37] While boss meant "to be the master or manager of; to manage, control, direct," and to boss it was "to act as master," it was used "in England at first only in workmen's slang, or humourously."[38] If Caliban's god is the boss of the city, the dwelling-place of man's construction, then that god stands in opposition to the god of the isle who is unencumbered with the perishing towers. Although Caliban has known only the isle, his dam, Sycorax, was not of the isle, but was brought there by "th' sailors." Setebos could represent the god of a pagan civilization such as Egypt, a country associated in an earlier chapter with the slavery of the chosen people and hence with Moses. Workmen in Shakespeare's audience who used "bos" as slang might find its use in the play mockery of Caliban's dam's god.

Great compactness of vision is achieved through the richness of association and the natural strata of obsolete word meanings, Shakespeare's use of biblical phrases and imagery, and his shadowing of characters. Not only are the warp and woof of the fabric densely woven together, but the fabric has a nap provided by the running commentary and the layers of word senses, which make it three-dimensional, while word resonances and multiple meanings orchestrate a symphony.

Chapter VII

Shakespeare's Paronomastic Plot

It has generally been conceded that spectacle is more dominant than plot in *The Tempest*, if indeed there is a plot at all. Yet *The Tempest* has not one, but two plots. Earlier, the biblical story of humankind as dramatized in the Mystery Plays was offered as one of Shakespeare's plots for *The Tempest*, one which covers all human time and existence. That plot, which in Chapter V was compared with that of the *Ludus Coventriae* and *Ludus*'s biblical selectivity, is overwhelmingly expansive. It is as expansive as the plots of Milton's final trilogy, *Paradise Lost*, *Paradise Regained*, and *Samson Agonistes*, and its assertions are comparable to those of *Paradise Lost*. Like Milton — but before him — Shakespeare presented "Eternal Providence," which in *The Tempest* Prospero refers to as "Providence divine" and which Ferdinand calls "immortal Providence." "Immortal" expands the time frame of *The Tempest* beyond earth's time, and "divine" expands provision beyond Gonzalo's design. Those who find *The Tempest*'s dénouement humanistic have missed the dual aspect of Shakespeare's vision: man's responsibility and divine provision; man's servanthood and ascent and God's descent to man. Like Milton, Shakespeare writes of man's disobedience and invokes "advent'rous Song" in his greatly condensed version of the loss of innocence and Eden, the "split" in the human family, and "the means to peace."

The second plot, which is more confined, is ordered by convention, juxtaposes the sublime and the ridiculous, and is associated with the English church in a unique way. Shakespeare not only designates the church's seasons and dramatizes its sacraments, but he depicts the order and essence of its service and, although they are not introduced as churchmen, he associates certain characters in a unique way with the English church. Although "the Bermoothes" (1.2.229) are mentioned in the play, the location of the isle appears indefinite since a boat lost in a storm on its way back to Milan from

107

"Afric" (2.1.67) would hardly be expected to reach an isle off the coast of America. Shakespeare makes an extended use of wordplay, locating the isle in a place familiar to seventeenth century English persons. With careful scrutiny (what Bethell calls multiconsciousness) cognizance of Shakespeare's propensity for paronomasia, and the recollection that the Mass was burlesqued in the Feast of Fools, Shakespeare's second plot, the earthly, may be uncovered.[1] That plot is based on the order and essence of the English church service. Aisle was alternately spelled isle.[2] Heard from the stage, isle is indistinguishable from aisle. Again Shakespeare puns. His are no ordinary isles, and those who occupy them when the play begins and those who arrive by shipwreck or royal decree are diverse in nature. A seventeenth century audience, who under command of law was found in St. Paul's on Sundays, would be familiar with the various elements comprising Shakespeare's extended pun. Both aisles represent places apart from "the gorgeous palaces" (4.1.152), the dwelling places of earthly authority. To miss the pun is to miss some of the fun as well as the mystery.

Actually, the church service begins aboard ship when the mariners announce "All lost!" and call, "To prayers, to prayers!" (1.1.51). Gonzalo responds to the call with "the King and Prince at prayers," calls for "mercy," and commits all to a higher power than the boatswain's or the mariners': "The wills above be done!" (1.1.51, 59, 66), a paraphrase of a portion of the Lord's prayer which may have followed the collect of prayers in the English Church. As in seventeenth century England, so in the play: The souls come to the isle/aisle after a baptism of sorts, though they do not seek one. They have come to the aisle under no compunction of their own. Infant baptism was the most common type of baptism practiced and, of course, the infant had no say in its ceremonial presentation. Sebastian and Antonio, irreverent souls, blame the mariners for their predicament. They curse those who are trying to bring them safely to the aisle. (No doubt some persons in seventeenth century England who were forced to attend church against their will likewise expressed displeasure.)

The prayer in the English church *Book of Common Prayer* preceding the ministration of Baptism makes reference to salvaging of eight persons: "Noah and his family in the ark from perishing by water ... [as] figuring ... holy Baptism" and relates it with Christ's baptism and "the mystical washing away of sin."[3] The nine souls in the play come to the aisle via a leaky ark.

After the shipwreck and apparent loss of life, Prospero tells Miranda to "be collected." This, too, is a reminder of the beginning of a service for her — with prayer — with "collect." He tells her there has been provision in his art and encourages her to recollect past providences. He begins with, "Canst thou remember/ A time when we came into this cell?" (1.2.38–39). Within the next thirty lines some form of the word "remembrance" occurs four times. It was customary at particular times in the English church service to recount the providences granted God's people as recorded in Old Testament Scripture. Not only was Noah mentioned in the prayer before a baptism, but reference was made to God's safely leading the children of Israel through the Red Sea.[4] With Prospero figuring as Moses in one of his representations, it is most appropriate for him to recollect.

Words and phrases in Prospero's speech and in what follows in the play would have a familiar ring for a seventeenth century audience who heard them regularly in an English church service as collects and Bible readings, as described in Chapter V.

When they arrive on land, Ariel disperses the souls "in troops ... 'bout the isle." Ariel ushers! "The King's son" is "landed" or seated "by himself,/ ... In an odd angle of the isle, and sitting,/ His arms in this sad knot" (1.2.220–224). Were Ferdinand's arms folded in prayer?

What appears to be an interlude in the play is merely a shift to another part of the aisle.

Both the isle and the aisle were places apart from the ordinary routine of daily life, and yet the profane and secular have entered, crept, into them from afar. Noise and music and disruptive characters were found in the English church aisle as well as in Shakespeare's ocean island whether that was "the Bermoothes," Capri, or some other island on earth. Nor was the English church aisle without the likes of Stephano and Trinculo, who inhabited it, not as supplicants, but as merchants. Both photograph and diary attest to the secular use of the cathedral. When willing and unwilling worshippers arrived in the aisle, they found merchants already established there. Sailors, merchants, and barbarians (such as Caliban, who often were sold or traded) might also be found in the cathedral. Canon Maynard Smith described the St. Paul's cathedral" as "one of the most desecrated churches in Christendom":

> St. Paul's: The grand and spacious nave of the Cathedral obtained the name of Paul's Walk; a name only too suggestive of the profanations of which it became the scene. It was the common lounge of the Idler, the Fops' Alley of the day. It will be remembered that there were two doors exactly opposite each other, piercing the north and south walls, about the middle of the nave; and that there were grand entrances at each of the transepts. These two sets of doors, immediately opposite each other were only too suggestive to the profane of the ease with which a short cut might be made from one side of the churchyard to the other. A common thoroughfare was soon established. Presently men were not satisfied with merely passing through the church. The porter with his heavy burden on his shoulders, the water carrier with his buckets, found it pleasant enough to set down their burdens and rest in the cool shade of the pillars. Nor was this all, for both men and women soon began to bring their wares into the holy place and to buy and sell and get gain ... on ordinary days and still more on festival days, men and women thronged to the holy place with their merchandise. There at their several standing places, just as in the public market, they exposed their wares. Other pollutions took place which revealed themselves not only to the eyes but also to the nostrils of the faithful. Some took delight in throwing stones at the

crows, pigeons and other birds which built their nests about the towers and battlements; whilst some shot at them with arrows and cross bow belts, breaking the pictured windows and even the statues which graced the exterior. Where the merchant might come to sell his wares and talk of exchange, fashionable people came to show themselves off in the large central aisle.[5]

Another historian writes: "The principal gentry, lords, commons and men of all professions not merely merchants, [did] meet in Paul's Church by eleven, and walk in the middle aisle till twelve and after dinner from three to six during which time some discoursed of business, others of news." There must have been continual noise, and in fact one who had often been within wrote that it was "like that of bees, a strange humming or buzz mixed, of walking, tongues and feet: it is a kind of still roar or loud whisper."[6]

Antonio claims he heard "a din to fright a monster's ear,... the roar/ Of a whole herd of lions" (2.1.309–311). Caliban uses "hum" in describing the noises in the isle. His description of the sounds he hears in the isle, "sweet airs," a thousand twangling instruments," and "voices" (3.2.134–136), could be heard in an English church when a service was being conducted. The court party (fashionable people) also walked in Shakespeare's isle and discoursed.

Ariel escorted some of the shipwrecked to the nave, where Antonio and Sebastian attempted to carry out their evil business. The uproar created by Antonio and Sebastian disturbs Adrian and Francisco, who savor the sweetness of the aisle and are in a worshipful mood. The interlude is not a break in the service, but a drowning out of it.

Matthews described John Colet's efforts to reform the cathedral body and notes his failure "to cleanse the Augean stables"— Shakespeare's horsepond?[7]

That such abuses existed in Shakespeare's time is attested by another author who wrote about changes that were made in 1633:

The restoration of the external fabric drew attention to an abuse of long standing. The nave and aisles had from times beyond the memory of men then living been used as places of public resort. Porters carried their burdens across the church as in the open street. Paul's Walk, as the long central aisle (the nave) was called, was the rendezvous of the men of business who had a bargain to drive, and of the loungers whose highest wish was to while away an idle hour in agreeable society.[8]

Paul's Walk, on the next page,[9] with its crowding and dispersion of groups large and small, shows the desecration of the nave.

To the men of the reigns of James I. and Charles I. it was all that the coffeehouses became to the men of the reigns of James II. and Charles II., and all that the clubhouses are to the men of the reign of Victoria. There were to be heard the latest rumours of the day.... There, too, was to be heard the latest scandal.... When the gay world had moved away, children took the place of their elders, making the old arches ring with their merry laughter. The clergy within the choir complained that their voices were drowned by the uproar, and that neither prayers nor sermon reached the ears of the congregations.[10]

Paul's Walk.

St. Paul's was considered "the religious home of the people."[11] But the foregoing descriptions account for the presence of such as Caliban who were, indeed, found in the aisle of St. Paul's, persons brought by merchants as curios to attract attention to their wares or to be used as wares by such as Antonio and Sebastian. Caliban's presence in the aisle is consonant with seventeenth century practice. There is a great deal of noise in Shakespeare's aisle (isle), too, and such a merry maker as Caliban, who drunkenly sings, "Freedom, high day! high-day, freedom! freedom, high-day, freedom!" (2.2.186).

The services held in the English church account for the "sounds and sweet airs, that give delight, and hurt not" (3.2.134). Caliban hears these sounds, but as a natural man from a pre–Christian society, he does not recognize their significance. Ferdinand, too, sitting alone in an "odd angle of the isle" away from the rabble, hears Ariel (the choir) and confesses: "This is no mortal business, nor no sound/ That earth owes: — I hear it now above me" (1.2.409–410).

While Trinculo and Stephano may be easily recognized as merchant types, eager to make money on Caliban, on the other hand Adrian and Francisco find it "of subtle, tender and delicate temperance" where "the air breathes upon us … most sweetly" (Adrian, 2.1.41, 45) and a place of belief in the survival of a son: "I not doubt/ He came alive to land" (Francisco, 2.1.117–118). Prospero, for whom the aisle has become home, and who has a "cell" there, probably figures a church official. He is disturbed by the noisemakers and the desecration of Caliban, Trinculo and Stephano. Ariel's dispersion of the "souls" in troops "bout the isle" is appropriate, for they do not all fit into the same place. As Gonzalo remarked, "All torment, trouble, wonder and amazement/ Inhabits here" (5.1.104–105) — a very brief but accurate description of St. Paul's in Shakespeare's day.

In the English church service the Gospel reading followed the prayers which recalled the specific Old Testament readings of the public baptism service. Ferdinand, after his plunge into the baptismal waters, hears the Gospel invitation. Ariel plays and sings:

> Come unto these yellow sands,
> And then take hands:
> Curtsied when you have and kiss'd
> The wild waves whist:
> Foot it featly here and there,
> And sweet sprites bear
> The burthen. Hark, hark [1.2.377–383].

There is something both mystical and familiar about the song. With careful attention, we may catch the rhythm of the Gospel invitation:

> Come unto me, all ye that labour and are heavy laden, and I will give you rest.
> Take my yoke upon you, and learn of me; for I am meek and lowly in heart;

and ye shall find rest unto your souls.
For my yoke is easy, and my burden is light [Matthew 11:28–30].

Both passages promise release from labor and grief. But we cannot fully appreciate Ariel's invitation until we have considered the other senses of "sands" extant in Shakespeare's day. In the seventeenth century sands not only referred to the sands of a peaceful shore, the sands of time, and the sounds of music; sands also meant invitation, message, present (gift), messenger, and God's dispensation. The OED lists the following definitions: "the action of sending; that which is sent, a message, present; [God's] dispensation or ordinance" "the action of sending for; invitation"; and "a person or body of persons sent on an errand; an envoy, messenger."[12] These uses of sands are also found in the Mystery Plays.[13] Sands had a variety of meanings in *Ludus Coventriae* just as it has in *The Tempest*. In the *Ludus Coventriae*, the meanings are separated. In *The Tempest*, Shakespeare expresses different meanings by punning. In *Ludus* "Abraham and Isaac," the father says to the son, "For we must now sacrifice go make,/ Even after the will of Godes sand," where "sand" is glossed as "sending, envoy."[14] Here the angel is the envoy through whom God sends the message. Later in the same play, Angelus uses sand in another sense: "As sand in the sea does ebb and flow."[15]

Thus Ariel's invitation, as heard by Ferdinand, is an invitation to God's dispensation, and to His messenger to receive His gift of mercy. Ariel's song echoes the words of the invitation of the unseen master of the play.

It is Ferdinand who is ready for that time and the message of hope. Members of the other troop must still be dealt with under the law. The crowing of the cock and the barking of the watchdogs at the end of Ariel's song take on special significance in light of the additional meanings of *sands*. The cock alerts of the dawn of a new day, and the watchdogs bark upon the approach of a messenger. The cock announces the dawn of Miranda's "brave new world," and the dogs proclaim the coming of the messenger of the new dispensation. Mark 13:35–36, which was assigned to be read at morning prayers in mid–February,[16] ties together the coming of the master, cock-crowing, watching, and the sleep awake theme of the play: "Watch ye therefore: for ye know not when the master of the house cometh, at even, or at midnight, or at the cockcrowing, or in the morning: Lest coming suddenly he find you sleeping." As a yearly reading it would be familiar to Shakespeare's audience.

Although "burden" has the sense of bass or low notes, it also means load, which finds correspondence in the Gospel invitation cited above, where the master's "burden is light." The Scripture reading which resembles the invitation to Ferdinand was read on St. Matthias' Day in the English church service.

Ferdinand cannot be sure whether he has followed the music or whether "it hath drawn him," or if it has an earthly or heavenly source, but he associates it with "Some god o' th' island." It allays the fury both without and within:

"This music crept by me upon the waters,/ Allaying both their fury and my passion/ With its sweet air" (1.2.394–396). The sounds which Ferdinand hears are the musical (harmonious) notes of the invitation to the time and place of redemption and resurrection. The messenger is the unseen master. (It is important to note here that although Ferdinand figures that master elsewhere in the play, he is a contemporary person in his own right, the son of Alonso, in keeping with typological usage). Following the coming to this dispensation, time, place, and a response to this invitation, there is to be reuniting of humankind, who are "split" (1.1.60), but who will "*then take hands*" (1.2.378). The perfect timing of the right notes creates melodious symphonic sound, which Wilson, Coleridge, and others attest is heard when *The Tempest* is played.

The "sweet sprites," Ariel, will bear the burden, both Ferdinand's burden (of grief) and the warning notes (bass part of the song) to the men who have come to the island with murderous thoughts. Those men hear something "monstrous, monstrous!" and "the name of Prosper" basing their trespasses (3.3.95, 99). Burden meant the undersong, bass, or accompaniment to the melody. It also meant the chief theme leading idea or prevailing sentiment. The undersong and leading idea of Shakespeare's play is the "best news," the good news of the Gospel. Burden also meant a load of labor, duty, responsibility, blame, sin, and sorrow. The sprite, Ariel, does carry the various kinds of burden.[17]

Ariel's next song comforts Ferdinand in his mourning and assures him that his father is undergoing a sea-change. It promises continuity with change for the better:

> Nothing of him that doth fade,
> But doth suffer a sea-change
> Into something rich and strange.
> Sea-nymphs hourly ring his knell:
> Burthen: Ding-Dong [1.2.402–406].

It is the shriving bell, which was rung hourly, calling men to be shriven of their sins. Alonso is dead in trespasses and sins and must be shriven.

Ferdinand next meets the virgin. At this point in the play, Prospero asserts his authority over both, and Ferdinand finds a duty to perform in the service of love, and his sorrow and sighing flee away. It is probable, as suggested earlier, that Prospero could be seen as officiating at the service in the aisle.

The play moves to another part of the isle (aisle). Attention is focused on another "troop," made up of Gonzalo, Alonso, Sebastian, Antonio, Adrian, and Francisco. Gonzalo recognizes that they have "cause ... of joy" and speaks of "the miracle ... our preservation." He responds positively to the service. Adrian and Francisco, as noted earlier, are men of faith and goodwill. They are true worshippers who respond positively in the aisle. Francisco believes in Ferdinand's survival (resurrection):

he trod the water,
Whose enmity he flung aside, and breasted
The surge most swoln that met him; his bold head
'Bove the contentious waves he kept, and oared Himself
        with his good arms in lusty stroke
To th' shore, that o'er his wave-worn basis bowed,
As stooping to relieve him: I not doubt
He came alive to land [2.1.111–118].

Alonso responds negatively to Francisco's faith, saying, "No, no, he's gone" (2.1.119). Antonio and Sebastian mock Gonzalo and the saints.

Gonzalo, undeterred, describes his "commonwealth," the coming of a more benign society which compares in essence with Isaiah's descriptions in chapters forty-one and forty-two which were read yearly at morning prayers on December twelve and thirteen in the English church. After Gonzalo describes the coming Kingdom, Alonso confesses it has no meaning for him: "thou dost talk nothing to me" (2.1.166). Still in the aisle, the traitors plot murder. Shakespeare was well aware that attendance at the English church, required by law, did not guarantee a worshipful attitude or holy thoughts.

Solemn music (probably familiar church music) is played by Ariel and Gonzalo falls asleep and snores!—in church (2.1.295). It is possible to imagine the laughter this would evoke from an audience who recognized Shakespeare's wordplay on aisle/isle. Sebastian and Antonio encourage Alonso to sleep and promise to guard his person. Upon hearing Alonso's snores, Sebastian and Antonio discuss the unlikelihood of a lineal successor to the throne and plot his and Gonzalo's murders. While Gonzalo hears "humming" which wakes him, the sinners hear "bellowing." This variety of sounds compares with those described earlier in accounts of St. Paul's Cathedral.

When Shakespeare reintroduces the royal party, which consists of believers and unbelievers, they have not discovered the son whom they seek. Sitting down to rest (3.3.6) (people stand for some parts of the church service), they hear *"Solemn and strange music"* and see *"several strange Shapes, bringing in a banquet"* (3.3.17). While old Gonzalo responds to the "marvellous sweet music!" (3.3.19), Sebastian and Antonio, still harboring treasonous thoughts, are so impressed by the strange shapes that they are willing to believe in "one tree, the phoenix' throne, and one phoenix/ At this hour reigning" (3.3.22–23). Their minds, which formerly were closed to Gonzalo's prophesy of miracle, are being changed as the church service proceeds.

In his response, Alonso describes a trope:

Such shapes, such gesture, and such sound, expressing —
Although they want the use of tongue — a kind
Of excellent dumb discourse [3.3.37–39].

The strange shapes who "dance about" in a "dumb discourse" actually present a trope. *Sound* here can be interpreted not only as audible voice, but as one of its other meanings, the expressing of an invitation. Here the invitation in a church service would be to the Lord's Supper.

When the shapes vanish, Sebastian and Alonso prepare to "feed." The Scripture advises those who are hungry to eat at home: "If any man hunger, let him eat at home; that ye come not together unto condemnation" (I Cor. 11:34). This is not an ordinary meal. The banquet is removed. When Ariel addresses Sebastian, Antonio, and Alonso, we find out why. They are "three men of sin." They are not ready to partake of communion. They are in danger in so doing of "lingering perdition."[18] "Ling'ring perdition" in connection with the "table" with "the banquet [which] vanishes" (77) is a reminder of the sacrament of the Lord's Supper where "he that eateth and drinketh unworthily, eateth and drinketh damnation to himself, not discerning the Lord's body" (I Cor. 11:29). The eleventh chapter of I Corinthians is part of the epistle read on the Thursday before Easter.[19] The Prayer Book used in 1611 describes these men as unworthy: "For otherwise the receiving of the Holy Communion doth nothing else but increase your damnation. And because it is requisite that no man should come to the Holy Communion but with a full trust in God's mercy, and with a quiet conscience."[20] These men do not have quiet consciences, nor are they trusting in God and believing the Son is alive. The "men of sin" are saved not by their own restraint, but by the removal of the banquet from them. Since the outcome of this play is to be good cheer and peace, no one is allowed to partake unworthily of the table.

There is a way out: "nothing but heart's sorrow,/ And a clear life ensuing" (3.3.81–82). The sacredness of the banquet is emphasized further when Gonzalo asks Alonso, "I'th'name of something holy, sir, why stand you/ In this strange stare?" Alonso's response is an acknowledgment that his sin is responsible for his loss of a son: "it did bass my trespass./ Therefor my son i'th' ooze is bedded; and / I'll seek him deeper than e'er plummet sounded,/ And with him there lie mudded" (3.3.94–95, 99–102). He is determined to die for his trespass. Since Ferdinand, in addition to being Alonso's son, also figures another Son, Alonso is acknowledging his sins as the cause of both deaths. As Ariel sang to Ferdinand earlier, Alonso is undergoing a change.

Meanwhile Ferdinand, as a supplicant, is granted a vision of provision enacted by Roman gods and goddesses. It is a "corollary" which parallels the Judeo-Christian providence displayed throughout the play. It might be associated with the homily or sermon which would expand the meaning of biblical readings. Ferdinand's response simulates the Psalmist's: "I will dwell in the house of the Lord forever" (Psalm 23). It is "Let me live here ever!/ So rare a wondered father and a wise/ Makes this place Paradise." He acknowledges a father greater than his own and a restoration that changes man's understanding of his environment. The experience is mystical, seeing whole, through all time, even beyond the dissolution of earth, as Prospero intimates with a description which extends the sense of providence to include "a new heavens and a new earth," echoing the prophesies of II Peter 3:11–13 and a passage from the Wakefield play. Churchgoers who worship and respond positively to the service may also have a vision of eternal providence.

Trinculo and Stephano are both representative of the profane persons found in St. Paul's walk, but they also belong to the expansive plot and are symbolic of the journey through the wilderness. Caliban is uncultured and an unwilling slave to Prospero, the law, who tried in vain to instruct him. Although he does not respond kindly to servitude, he delights in what he hears in the aisle: "sweet airs." There is a curious relationship between what Caliban perceives and the audience's perception of him, which can be found in Scripture:

> There are ... so many kinds of voices in the world, and none of them is without signification. Therefore if I know not the meaning of the voice, I shall be unto him that speaketh a barbarian, and he that speaketh shall be a barbarian unto me [I Cor. 14:10–11].

Not only do Prospero and the audience consider Caliban a barbarian, but from Caliban's point of view — because Prospero took over the isle that was his and gives him instruction that has no meaning for him — Prospero is alien to him.

Through Ariel, Prospero-Moses has the enemies of the law "all knit up in their distractions," their own wrong intentions. The law brings conviction of wrongdoing and sin snares the sinner, even as the Gospel "nets" sinners. Gonzalo, the interpreter of events, recognizes that the "three men o' sin" "are desperate" because of "their great guilt."

In a significant submission to a higher authority, Prospero abjures "rough magic" in the "ye elves" speech and requires "some heavenly music." The wayward are escorted to the circle which Prospero has made: Gonzalo brings Alonso, and Adrian and Francisco bring Sebastian and Antonio. They "there stand charmed." Since Prospero has only made the circle and has just previously abandoned his spellmaking magic, we may assume that the members of the royal party are now under a different spell — God's spell, or that of the Gospel.

The circle becomes one of confirmation for holy Gonzalo, "a loyal sir/ To him thou follow'st," which on one level of the play refers to Alonso the king, on another to God. For Antonio and Sebastian, who stand adjacent to the circle, it becomes a place of "clearer reason" and forgiveness, if not obedience to a higher calling.

Ariel next sings of his freedom from the law's (Prospero-Moses') demands and rejoices that he may "live now,/ Under the blossom that hangs on the bough," an affirmation of his new master, who also promised "to set the prisoners free."

Having previously confessed his sin in the death of a son, Alonso now asks forgiveness of Prospero, resigns the dukedom of Antonio, and is confirmed. Sebastian, too, undergoes a change after having a vision of the resurrected son. He who scoffed at miracles now declares, "A most high miracle." For those who are sure Ferdinand "i'th' ooze is bedded," the vision amounts to as genuine a resurrection as the coming to life of the Hermione statue in *The Winter's Tale*.

The sacrament of matrimony ensues.

In pronouncing a benediction Gonzalo, the interpreter of events, calls for rejoicing, "beyond a common joy!" (5.1.207). He declares the "lost" found: "In a poor isle,... all of us ourselves/ When no man was his own" (5.1.211, 212–213) and ends the service with "Be it so! Amen" (5.1.215). Thus Shakespeare presented an English church service with a collection of prayers aboard ship, followed by a mock baptism, a recounting of God's providences, a Gospel invitation, a banquet and trope, a homily, confirmation, a wedding, and a benediction, all of which are representative of observances that take place in an English church while people are found in its aisle.

The master and boatswain enter prepared to take the souls — upon whose minds the law, the prophet, and the Gospel have operated, and whose true selves have been revealed or recovered — back to their duties and places in society.

Lest the untutored or secular three — Stephano, Trinculo, and Caliban, who would replace Prospero's law and order with rioting and licentious freedom — remain a threat (however ridiculous), they come to see their foolishness. Prospero forgives them and lets them participate in the celebration by trimming his cell handsomely.

Many concerns may be traced in *The Tempest*, for human ways are varied. Political, societal, and even ecclesiastical pressures may affect people negatively. Shakespeare rises above the ecclesiastical and ritual controversies of the time and gets to the heart of the matter. Whatever the theological controversies, humankind had available the means of reconciliation. In the English church service humans heard the "bass" notes of the law, the joyful sounds of the prophet, and the drawing and merciful sounds of the Gospel. A change of mind and way of life were possible. In the midst of the complexity, a simplicity evolves. *The Tempest* presents the biblical story of humankind, transgression, alienation —"We split, we split, we split!" (1.1.59) — law, miracle, and mystery. It also simplifies man's way: forgive, seek forgiveness, and accept one's task on earth, as Prospero intends when he declares, "Every third thought shall be my grave" and in the Epilogue says, "I ... pardoned the deceiver,... [and will] be relieved by prayer." The simplicity of this formula and the resolution of the play concur with a statement in the 1559 Prayer Book in the section titled, "Of Ceremonies, Why Some Be Abolished and Some Retained":

And besides this, Christ's gospel is not a ceremonial law, as much of Moses' law was, but it is a religion to serve God, not in bondage of the figure or shadow, but in the freedom of spirit, being content only with those ceremonies which do serve to a decent order and godly discipline, and such as be apt to stir up the dull mind of man to the remembrance of his duty to God by some notable and special signification whereby he might be edified.[21]

In *The Tempest* the Prospero-Moses figure relinquishes his authority over both Ariel and the characters after performing those ceremonies which serve to bring decent order and discipline and which stir up the minds, bringing remembrance to duty and to God.

In Shakespeare's aisle it is not the ministry of Papist, Puritan, or English prelate that the playwright exalts, but the author of salvation and His law which makes possible hope, good cheer, and the way of peace and grace. The mariners, ordinary men, do their best to bring the "ship of souls" to the aisle. They call to prayers and are "left asleep" (1.2.232), while the minds of the "fraughting souls" are left to the effective sounds in the aisle. In one sense they figure those officials who were responsible to see that church attendance was enforced. "'Bout the isle" the law, administered by Prospero, who figures Moses, operates on the minds of the recalcitrant, bringing conviction of sin; Gonzalo, the prophet, describes the coming kingdom; and the Gospel brings comfort to those who mourn and allays the fury within and without. Ariel, the spirit of the law, old and new, operates on the minds of all of the occupants of the aisle. He comforts those who mourn and convicts those who err. The Gospel and the law of a greater master than the Prospero-Moses figure, the law of forgiveness and reconciliation, are celebrated in the aisle. The Gospel invitation is given, some of the occupants of the aisle confess their wrongs, and a blessing is pronounced. Shakespeare dramatized the salient elements of the English church service in bringing release from bondage, displayed in a hidden and artful way the sacraments, and suggested the washing of the church's tides.

The prime movers in the church service depicted in *The Tempest* are not ministers, priests, or other ecclesiastics, but the stars in the Judeo-Christian tradition represented in Shakespeare's transposition of the celestial spheres from the gods and goddesses of the Ptolemaic system of planets.

Chapter VIII

"All the Tuned Spheres": A Cosmological Framework

"Earth changes, soul and God stand sure." Browning

Shakespeare's characters, their behaviors, and their typological identities, related to particular times, fit well into a space-time continuum which gives the play a unified structure. *The Tempest's* shape is consonant with its use of sound, music, time, space, its master theme and its imagery.

Overlooking the Bible, the Mystery Plays, and the English church as sources, and disregarding Shakespeare's many references to the heavens, critics have made various attempts to identify Shakespeare's plan or story source for *The Tempest*—something they felt would give it a plot and a unified structure. Several critics have proposed a pattern, design, or shape for the play. Waller found in Shakespeare's romances "exquisite variations on the basically similar pattern of reconciliation growing out of tragedy." He acknowledged that "the relationship between time and Providence, a dominant intellectual preoccupation in so many of his [Shakespeare's] earlier plays, is given a further dimension in both *The Winter's Tale* and *The Tempest*." He found "radical structural juxtapositions," and a "showing how the passing of time may work towards a mysterious and apparently miraculous triumph of the most extreme human optimism and idealism."[1] However, he did not give shape to the pattern or structure to time; nor did he identify Shakespeare's juxtapositions or transpositions in a space-time continuum.

Knight claimed an all-encompassing pattern in the play: "*The Tempest* is Shakespeare's instinctive imaginative genius mapped into a universal pattern; not neglecting, but enclosing and transcending, all his past themes of loss and restoration, tempest and music."[2] Yet he did not map out his pattern or specify the boundaries of the play.

121

Tillyard claimed, "Prospero is the agent of his own regeneration, the parent and tutor of Miranda; and through her and through his own words he changes the minds of his enemies. It was by this play centring of motives in Prospero as well as by subordinating the theme of destruction, that Shakespeare gave *The Tempest* its unified structure."[3] As the giver of the law, which brings awareness of sin, the Prospero-Moses figure brings the changes noted by Tillyard, but according to my study Prospero is not the center or focus of the play. He is only one of the operatives in it. Tillyard also found a motive in *The Tempest* which he described as "planes of reality" "in terms of colour": "the colours are broken into a brilliant pattern, very complicated, yet not confused, a pattern consisting of large bold contrasts, of small subtle contrasts, and of delicate transitions. Nor is the sense of planes of reality fitful; it permeates the entire play and is, indeed, its main motive."[4]

He found Shakespeare expressing "his sense of different worlds" in the play and in the fourth act, "the most complicated display of different worlds."[5] Although Tillyard, like Peter Brook, found the play to be about reality and acknowledged Shakespeare's different worlds were arranged in a pattern, he arranged those worlds in a visionary rather than a visible model, and he did not associate them with specific historical characters who belonged to differing time periods.

Two of those who have attempted to find a shape for the play are Levin and Rose. Levin gave *The Tempest* a pyramidal shape, which indicated various levels of action in the play. His structure reached "its apex in the third act, where the lovers plight their troth while the spirits confound both royal party and the clownish plotters." He found, "The rest of the play has the falling cadence of resolution, recognition, reconciliation, and celebration."[6] There are levels in Levin's structure, but they differ from Tillyard's levels in that they are based on the action rather than on the different worlds. Levin's focus on a romantic plot emphasizes the human rather than the eternal and divine. It does not provide for an explanation of Shakespearean imagery, typology and time.

Unlike the critics who found no plot, structure, or design, Rose found *The Tempest* to be "one of the most disciplined, most severely controlled plays in the canon." He assigned three arches to the play. He proposed that Shakespeare's basic dramatic unit was the scene, and that "Shakespeare's scene divisions generally define units of meaning as well as units of narrative." He averred that the unity of the scene is thematic rather than narrative and that the central scene of the play which is overarched by three spans "provides the crucial emblematic tableau."[7]

Thus both Levin and Rose focused on the central scene, one as an apex of a pyramid and the other as the focal point of arches. Although Rose's arches suggest the arcs of the spheres of the structure proposed in this book, they do not represent those spheres. Rose's design differs from this study in that his arches relate to the appearances on stage of the characters in the play and are not associated with a model which carries with it themes and personages with established characteristics, areas of influence, and historical time periods.

The frame identified in this book emerged from due consideration of certain words and their resonances; from an awareness of the cosmological dispositions of the sixteenth century; and from a sense of Shakespeare's use of biblical plot and time and its adoption in the Mystery Plays.

Shakespeare not only incorporated two plots in *The Tempest*, but he appears to have stretched his fabric over a model which provided a space-time continuum for his vision. The frame conforms to Sypher's definition of plot as "a synoptic vision of the entire action, bringing the episodes into simultaneous focus," of which he wrote: "the events [in the plot] cohere in a static pattern or design, preordaining the meaning and scaling the incidents against each other as if one had foreknowledge of the outcome." Sypher stated that "if Gothic art is a linear narrative, Renaissance art is a labyrinthine plan. Plot, as different from narrative, is a juxtaposition that is spatial as well as temporal, and is demonstrative, much as a Euclidean proposition being worked through is demonstrative." Sypher found that "Renaissance art was dramatic because it coordinated episodes into a more static vision, making time subordinate to spatial relationships."[8] Frye concurred with Sypher. Writing of Shakespearean romance, he claimed, "When it is all over, it assumes a quite different appearance. Now we see it as a simultaneous unity, something that has not so much a beginning and middle and end as a center and a periphery."[9]

The model suggested in this study has a center and a periphery and the play can be justifiably called labyrinthian. It provides a graphic display of Tillyard's "planes of reality," Sypher's "static vision," and Frye's "simultaneous unity." Shakespeare suggests both circularity and the labyrinth with the word "coil" and the phrase "all knit up/ In their distractions" (3.3.89–90). There is, in fact, both expansion and closure in *The Tempest*, for all time narrows down to "now," and as the characters are "drawn," to the music they "meander," "mope," or follow it to Prospero's cell or his magic circle, which are small enclosures upon a small isle, where one law brings "good cheer," freedom from the elements, and the "peace of the present." The plot of *The Tempest*, then, is the closure of "immortal Providence" upon individuals in the play who are representative members of the human race who can be associated with divergent cultures or differing responses to life. The expansion and closure in *The Tempest* can be equated to Frye's center and periphery and to the characteristics of "synoptic vision" and "focus" in Sypher's definition of plot. However, time in *The Tempest* does not become subordinate to spatial relationship, but becomes one with it.

As one considers the figurings of various characters, the biblical time periods associated with those figures, the description of other characters, and the corollary, a framework emerges that would have been familiar to some members of the Renaissance audience. It originated with Greek astronomy, was associated with Greek and Roman mythology, and later was adapted by the medieval church to conform with its beliefs by replacing gods and goddesses with a hierarchy of angels. Correspondences between the layers of the earlier frameworks and Shakespeare's provide a means of resurrecting concepts and ideas related to the meaning of *The Tempest*. The ways in which Shakespeare differentiated between the two frameworks attests to the uniqueness of his artistry. Moreover his creative genius provided not only a unique framework for the play, but a new cosmology for a society that had lost one through scientific discovery. His framework was both a re-creation and a reaffirmation. It transferred belief from an assumed physical framework of the universe to the unseen but nevertheless real framework of an eternal providence working through history (time). It restored man to the central position in the universe and made him the object of divine providence.

Some critics have pointed to the similarities between *A Midsummer Night's Dream* and *The Tempest*. The structures of the two plays are similar, for there are concentric spheres of action in each play and the shapes of both plots are determined by the arrangement of the heavenly bodies in the Ptolemaic system. Tillyard observed, "In *A Midsummer Night's Dream* Shakespeare approximated his sprites and his human beings; in *The Tempest* he keeps them to their own worlds."[10] In the earlier play Shakespeare localized the inhabitants of the celestial spheres, giving them "a local habitation and a name" (5.1.17), whereas in the latter he distanced them, making some of his characters figure historical personages. In *A Midsummer Night's Dream* the supernatural is represented by sometimes quarrelsome fairies and a bumbling messenger. The diurnal motion, alternating day and night, influences the characters. The night action takes place within the moon's sphere, which represents mutability and change and also corresponds to the confusion of dream. In *A Midsummer Night's Dream* the fairies and Puck's bumbling bring persons to self-knowledge and the fantastic supernatural. Thus self-knowledge is accomplished largely by accident. *The Tempest*, on the other hand, reveals the purposeful and providential plan to bring awareness by law and grace. Although the nature of the earth and moon spheres are similar in the two plays, the larger spheres contrast radically. In *The Tempest* the larger spheres have historical, biblical, and providential significance; Shakespeare appears to be equating the planetary orbits to the prime influences in the Judeo-Christian tradition. Thus *The Tempest* is a play of wider scope than *A Midsummer Night's Dream*. In *The Tempest* the replacement for the Ptolemaic system provides a "synoptic vision" of action from the dawn of human time. It not only preordains the meaning, but it scales the incidents and actions against eternal time.

Young noted:

The four groups into which the characters of *A Midsummmer Night's Dream* fall present us with another spatial aspect of construction. Each set of characters has its own set of experiences. Since we know that these are occurring simultaneously, we are conscious of the location of each group.... This consciousness is essentially spatial.[11]

Young found that "Shakespeare achieves unity, partly through ... a spatial organization which is almost geometrical in its order."[12] The Ptolemaic system provided Shakespeare with a geometrical order. Although the Copernican system of planetary motion was available to Shakespeare, being generally unpeopled except for Earth, it was culturally cold and unadaptable by a playwright for whom the warmth of human blood figured most meaningfully.

Consider Figure 1 and Figure 2. In Figure 1, a two-dimensional projection of the concentric spheres of the planets shows the spheres occupied by mythologic gods and goddesses bearing the same name as the planets. Figure 2 represents the spheres of influence occupied by the characters of *The Tempest*. Shakespeare fills the upper spheres with a spirit and persons who figure in biblical history. Thus *The Tempest* does provide what Sypher claims of Renaissance drama, "a kind of retrospective view on the part of author, hero, and audience."[13] Shakespeare uses spatial time with zones of time represented by the beings reigning in those zones. The action of *The Tempest*, described in the episodic plot in Chapter VI, is the impact of those time zones upon men in the present.

Shakespeare placed humans back at the center of a group of concentric spheres, where they could hear the music of those spheres. In the episodic plot persons with differing needs appear as the focus of divine intervention in an effort, as in the Mystery Plays, to bring them to awareness of the provisions of the beneficial, to hope and to repentance.

Each of the critiques of design, pattern, and structure cited earlier contributes something to the understanding of the play, but none is as inclusive as the nested spheres structure adopted in this study. That Shakespeare consciously used this model can be deduced from his designation of the masque in which the gods and goddesses appear as a "corollary," a parallel that functions as a confirmation of structure, as subplots do in some of Shakespeare's other plays. Recognizing the function of the masque, Traversi wrote, "The rather perfunctory masque ... belongs more to the structural unity of the play than to its intimate poetic sensibility."[14] Shakespeare's model brings awareness of some of the echoes and resonances which might be created in the minds of Shakespeare's earliest audiences for whom the model was still a living, if not a rational, cosmos.

Returning to figures 1 and 2, we can see Shakespeare's vision of "Providence Divine," a fabric stretched over the space-time continuum, with its focus on the objects of that providence, playing to them the music of the spheres and catching them in its coils. Figure 1 represents the Ptolemaic system

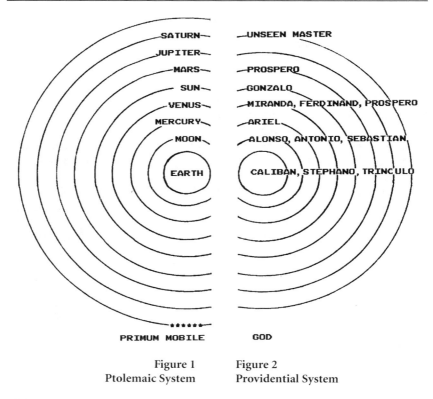

Figure 1	Figure 2
Ptolemaic System	Providential System

of the planets and Figure 2 Shakespeare's transposition to represent, not the planetary gods, but the characters in his providential design.

"Providence divine" indicates the range of the concentric spheres and the nature of their influence. All but one of the spheres are associated with characters in the play who fit or "figure" in providence, either as its instrument or as its recipient. The two lower spheres are occupied by the more sinful, changeable, and earthy or bestial characters of the play. Prospero's figuring of Moses places Prospero in one of Shakespeare's concentric historical spheres.

Recognizing Prospero's control in the play, James compared him to Jupiter, a god in the Ptolemaic system,[15] but he forgot the greater depth Shakespeare gave to the play in Gonzalo's "design" in providing Prospero's escape from his enemies.

Gonzalo, who figures as Isaiah and who is the preserver of Miranda and Prospero, influencing their possibility for action, belongs in a sphere of influence which encompasses theirs: the sun's sphere. He sees with clarity from the start and is a major figure in the heavens who throws light on the whole. As Prospero declares, he is the "appointed/ Master of this design" (1.2.162–163), a design that goes beyond that of Prospero-Moses. It is highly possible that

Shakespeare meant the latter reference to document not only Gonzalo's place in the play, but the sun's position of mastery over the celestial array of the planets as it controlled them in the new Copernican model of the heavens. The newer system replaced the old in science, though not necessarily in the beliefs of the audiences. It was characteristic of Shakespeare's genius not only to transform an old system of belief (the Ptolemaic), but to adapt a new concept (from the Copernican model) for use in his art. Such inclusiveness was appropriate in a society where Rationalism, with its unidirectional mode of thinking, had not yet taken root.

Ariel, who is subject to Prospero, belongs within Prospero's sphere of influence. The mythologic god associated with the planet Mercury in the Ptolemaic system of the universe was, of course, Mercury, the wing-helmeted, wing-footed messenger. Ariel, as Prospero's messenger, the messenger of the law, who invites, protects, and wreaks vengeance — which, although it alarms, does no injury — fits well into a sphere comparable to Mercury's. Prospero refers to Ariel as "Spirit." Sixteenth century chemists called the element mercury "spirit." It was one of five principals separable from a mixture by fire. Moreover, mercury was considered to be one of the three elements in water. In the conversation between Ariel and Prospero where "mighty Neptune," the god of water, is mentioned, there are confirming references — "sulphurous" and "brine" (1.2.204, 211) — to the other two elements considered to be in water, i.e., sulphur and salt. Thus for sixteenth and seventeenth century audiences Shakespeare provided multiple references that would affirm Ariel's association.

Shakespeare makes it quite plain with several references that the "three men of sin" (3.3.53) belong in the moon's sphere. The latter sphere was considered in the medieval order of things as the sphere of change and mutability. Just as the moon is inconstant, so are the "men of sin." Gonzalo associates them with a sphere, changeableness, and the moon with "you would lift the moon out of her sphere, if she would continue in it five weeks without changing" (2.1.177–179). Two other references in the same scene attest to the changeableness of the three: the indecision indicated by Sebastian's remark, "I am standing water" (217), and Antonio's reference to "ebbing men" (221). Antonio declares, "The Man i' th' moon's too slow" (244), which emphasizes his impatience. The words, spoken by Antonio with reference to the intended usurpation of power, follow the comment that "Claribel ... can have no note, unless the sun were post" (240, 243). Thus Antonio's remarks compare not only the speed of the lesser and greater lights, but their revealing power. Both lights, the sun and moon, are mentioned, and men of both spheres are interacting in this scene, although by the time of the utterance cited, the greater (Gonzalo) has gone to sleep; thus the sun has set, leaving the affairs of earth to the men of the moon. However, they do not rule over darkness as do the fairies in *A Midsummer Night's Dream,* for in this play the ultimate control is in the light that appears in Prospero's zenith, which Prospero acknowledges and yields to, instead of giving way to his vengeful feelings

Caliban, Stephano, and Trinculo belong to the circle of the Earth, the lowest. Shakespeare designates Caliban as a "savage" and "deformed" slave. Miranda calls him "abhorred slave" and "savage," "Which any print of goodness wilt not take,/ Being capable of all ill!" (1.2.353–355, 357). Prospero addresses him as "thou earth" (1.2.316) which places him on earth, the innermost sphere in the Ptolemaic system, and hence in the lowest position of characters in the play. Caliban asks his new "god," Stephano, "Hast thou not dropp'd from heaven?" and Stephano affirms his present position by claiming, "I was the Man i' th' Moon, when time was" (2.2.137–139). In the now of the play, he, too, is "earth." Stephano calls Caliban a "moon-calf" after calling him "man-monster," indicating changeableness, immaturity, and something less than human (3.2.11, 20). Animals as well as man inhabited the earth, and animals occupied the link in the chain next lower than man. According to Caliban's own admission Prospero has endeavored to teach him what is above him, teaching him to name the "greater" and "lesser" lights. Stephano and Trinculo, however, encourage Caliban to move down the chain of being and behave more like an animal, which to all appearances he is when Stephano finds Caliban and Trinculo together under Caliban's garment. Forthwith Trinculo addresses Caliban as "monster."

Miranda and Ferdinand, with their association with providence and love, belong in the sphere associated with Venus, the goddess of love in the Ptolemaic system. Prospero belongs with them, or, at the times of his "vexation," in the planetary sphere above, that of the god Mars, who represents vengeance and war. In the end Prospero chooses to align himself with love and virtue rather than warring vengeance, blesses the union of Miranda and Ferdinand, and sets his messenger free. In terms of his association with Moses and the law, his final stance is to surrender to the "most auspicious star," to accept his earthly duty, and to free the spirit of the law.

Ariel informs Prospero, "In troops I have dispers'd them 'bout the isle" (1.2.220), which indicates that the characters are in groups and in different places. The use of '*bout* in reference to their placement is suggestive of a circle. In fact, the present action of the play has one less dimension than the history aspect, which is represented by three-dimensional spheres. The play takes place within Prospero's magic circle and upon the circle of the isle, which because of its indefinition of place may be extended to be "the circle of the earth" (Isaiah 40:22). Although Jan Kott acknowledged that "on Prospero's island, Shakespeare's history of the world is played out, in an abbreviated form," he did not recognize the heavenly spheres or associate *The Tempest* with the Mystery Plays. He claimed that "Shakespearian dramas are constructed not on the principle of unity of action, but on the principle of analogy, comprising a double, treble, or quadruple plot, which repeats the same basic theme;

they are a system of mirrors, as it were, both concave and convex, which reflect, magnify and parody the same situation."[16] The principle that unifies this drama and is reflected in all the spheres, as well as in the vision Prospero presents for Ferdinand and Miranda, is divine providence. Divine providence encompasses the experiences of the various characters who come by different routes to self-knowledge and forgiveness.

It was Knight who suggested that a true interpretation of Shakespearean drama could be achieved only as one was "prepared to see the whole play in space as well as in time."[17] After noting that there are sets of "thickly-scattered correspondences in a small view of the whole" in Shakespeare's plays, relating to each other independently of the "time-sequence" which is the story, he suggested that "if we are prepared to see the whole play laid out ... as an area, being simultaneously aware of these ... thickly-scattered correspondences in a single view of the whole, we possess the unique quality of the play in a new sense." From this perspective he finds that "the Shakespearean person is intimately fused with this atmospheric quality; he obeys a spatial as well as a temporal necessity."[18] Although Knight did not intimate the kind of substantive framework that is proposed in this chapter, he found that "the 'spatial' approach is implicit in our imaginative pleasure to a greater or a less degree always," and that an interpretation that would translate our reaction to great literature in a "positive and dynamic" spirit "should regard each play as a visionary whole, close-knit in personification, atmospheric suggestion, and direct poetic-symbolism." The identification in this book of the spatial framework of the play which ties to it the persons, the time, and the symbolism helps to provide the kind of perspective Knight recommended. Just as Knight found "the spatial, that is the spiritual quality" using "the temporal, that is, the story," this study finds Shakespeare using a framework that is spatial and has spiritual meaning.[19] Although it is more substantial than Knight's "atmospheric" or "spiritual quality" it does not detract from that quality, but substantiates it, widening vision and unity by drawing together personifications, time-frames, and space.

Knight found that "each incident, each turn of thought, each suggestive symbol throughout *Macbeth* or *Lear* radiates inwards from the play's circumference to the burning central core without knowledge of which we shall miss their relevance and necessity: they relate primarily, not directly to each other, nor to the normal appearances of human life, but to the central reality alone."[20] There is in the spatial array for *The Tempest* presented in this chapter a corresponding inwardness, for each sphere encompasses those within it, and providence works inwardly through each to the central globe, the earth, to the isle, upon it the magic circle within the isle, and inwardly to the "soul" of the man who stands inside that circle or adjacent to it.

Manifold circular and spherical images in *The Tempest* confirm the shape and integrate the play. Sycorax "was grown into a hoop" (1.2.259). Ariel was commanded to be "invisible/ To every eyeball else" (1.2.303–304). "Cell" (5.1.291) suggests a cubicle. Eyes become "pearls" (1.2.401). The island is "an apple" (2.1.87). The moon moves in a "sphere" (2.1.178). The sun is globular. The earth is "the great globe itself" (4.1.53). "Our little life/ Is rounded with a sleep" (4.1.153, 157–158), and men are "all knit up/ In their distractions" (3.3.89–90).

Obsolete meanings of the word "coil" are significant in an interpretation of *The Tempest*. Coil meant to select, choose (cull), to beat and to thrash. There is culling, beating, and thrashing in the play. Coil also meant hurly-burly, noisy disturbance, confusion, and tumult, all of which quite clearly describe the initial tempest as well as the behavior of Caliban, Trinculo, and Stephano. Another sixteenth century definition of coil affirms the structure of the play: "the laying up of a cable in concentric rings so that one ring lies within or above another." Other definitions were to "enwrap within coils, to enfold in a coil, ensnare, to twist or wind round." With Ariel's help Prospero ensnares his enemies. The most suggestive definition found in *The Oxford English Dictionary* is "A series of concentric circles or rings in which a pliant body has been disposed."[21] The structure of the play described in this chapter fits precisely with the latter definition. Thus when Prospero asks Ariel, after the latter's account of *The Tempest* he has raised, "Who was so firm, so constant, that this coil/ Would not infect his reason?" (1.2.207–208), he speaks not only of the hubbub caused by the induced fire and storm, but forecasts his intention to ensnare the souls — to encase them in the concentric circles of providential design — as well as to affect the reason of those thus encased. The coil of the concentric rings of providence differs from the coil in *Hamlet* (3.1.67), which is "mortal" and which does not offer hope. Shakespeare keeps the idea of spheres and circles before us with his imagery. That Shakespeare is concerned with the lights of the heavens is apparent from the many references to them.

In his study of time, Waller cited one of the main issues with which he was concerned as "the question of the relationship between time and an eternal, transcendental Providence." He found after reading "sixteenth-century treatises, tracts, and sermons" that "Battenhouse's claim that 'the doctrine of Providence was the chief apologetic interest' of the age" was viable, and that "the traditional Christian doctrine, which saw God as creating and directing time towards a foreordained goal, still dominated most sixteenth-century thought." Walker went on: "In particular, the Calvinist doctrine of Providence, which considerably tightened the relationship between divine Providence and time, was extraordinarily influential upon late sixteenth-century thought when the nature of God's providential control over time became a widespread and even explosive intellectual issue." Waller showed that "Shakespeare and his contemporaries responded and in some sense contributed" to "a wide-ranging debate" "provoked" by the Calvinist doctrine of providence.[22]

The transposed Ptolemaic framework in this treatise relating character, providence, and time provides a unity appropriate for the sixteenth century.

The vision of the gods and goddesses which Prospero presents as a "corollary" both affirms Shakespeare's use of the Ptolemaic system and provides an additional account of providence or provision. The meaning of corollary which precedes the quotation from *The Tempest* is "something additional or beyond the ordinary measure; a surplus; a supernumerary."[23] It, like the entire play, is a vision of provision. It is a vision of the goddesses of nature's provision for the physical needs of humankind. The vision of the whole play predicates provision for the minds and souls. In other plays Shakespeare used a masque or a play within a play to parallel and affirm meaning. In *The Tempest* he used a vision within a vision. Another obsolete meaning of corollary is "Something added to a speech or writing over and above what is usual or what was originally intended; an appendix; a finishing or crowning part, the conclusion."[24] Prospero's vision crowns meaning.

Beyond Saturn in the Ptolemaic system was the sphere of the fixed stars, and beyond that the primum mobile, which controlled the motion of all the spheres. Within the sphere of the unseen master lies the sphere of the prophet, and within the prophet's sphere that of the law and the miracles of nature. At the core of all the unseen master's spheres are found the men and the miracles of grace.

Closely tied in with the structure of the play are two of its major themes other than time and providence. There is music in the air in *The Tempest,* and hearing and sound play an important part throughout the play. A contemporary of Shakespeare, Tycho Brahe, was a Danish astronomer who spent a great deal of time studying the positions of the stars and planets. His pupil, Johannes Kepler, turned to the ancient Pythagorean notion of the music of the spheres and attempted to discover the celestial harmonies by associating the pitch of the note supposedly sung by the planet with its velocity. Although he did not succeed harmonically, he had revived a notion which apparently had aesthetic appeal, for Shakespeare mentioned the "music of the spheres" in Pericles (5.1.230), and according to this author's structure for *The Tempest,* he exemplified it in this play, for Ferdinand acknowledges Ariel's song "is no mortal business, nor no sound/ That the earth owes: — I hear it now above me" (1.2.409–410).

Rastall referred to a paper by John Stevens, who "was able to show that the [Mystery] plays used music largely symbolically to represent certain types of character in the drama."[25] He discussed the representational and structural functions of music in the Chester plays. One of the representational functions he noted was the "depiction of Heaven," characterized by singers, instruments, and harmony, which accords with pictorial representations of heaven. Other uses of music were "representation of Divine Order," "restoration of Divine Order" by minstrels' playing, and angelic music which represented the "active intervention by God through his messengers, the angels, in the affairs of men." Persons who sang were considered to be "chosen instruments of God's Will." Singing was also considered to have an influence on behavior. In *The Tempest* Ariel's music is the instrument of God's will, and that music, melodic or base, intervenes in the affairs of humans and influences their behavior. Ferdinand hears music with "its sweet air" (1.2.396). The bell with which the "*Sea nymphs hourly ring his* [Alonso's] *knell*" (1.2.405), however, would likely be heard as the shriving bell, as was pointed out earlier, although in its forgiveness of wrong it could be likened to the bells of nativity and resurrection of the Mystery Plays, for some characters' minds are reborn when they are defumed and their true selves are resurrected. Loud music was representative of a king, earthly authority, as in *The Tempest*.[26] Examining the use of music in the Mystery Plays, Rose observed that "God and the angels are characterized by harmony; Satan and his rout by cacophony."[27]

Rastall pointed out several structural functions of music in the Chester plays. Music could cover movement of characters about the acting area; announce entrances and exits; symbolize the passage of time; and draw attention to a new location.[28] Music was used rather than "academic scene division to cover exits."[29]

Shakespeare uses music in many of the respects cited by Rastall. In *The Tempest* music changes with the kind of scene. The characters hearing of different sounds, varies both with their attention and intention. Base characters hear base or hollow (meaningless) sounds. Alonso, a king, hears a loud sound, the thunder, "bass" his "trespass" (3.3.99), whereas Ferdinand is attuned to the music of the spheres and the airy assurances of transformations of the "sea-swallowed" earthy. It is "destiny, —/ That hath to instrument this lower world" (3.3.53–54) to which the "men of sin" belong, whereas Ariel, "a spirit too delicate/ To act her [Sycorax's] earthy and abhorr'd commands" (1.2.272–273), comforts Ferdinand with his songs.

Other themes closely related to the plot and its hierarchical levels are the master and authority themes. Prospero is a many-sided master. As temporary master of Caliban he is master of the instincts and the bestial in man. He is master of a greater magic than that of Sycorax, Caliban's dam, and of her god, Setebos, representatives of pagan powers. As master of the law he directs the work of the spirit of the law until, relinquishing his control, he frees the spirit who chooses to live under the new master and the new law. As schoolmaster both of Miranda and of the recalcitrant characters of the play, Prospero is the teacher who brings them to the knowledge of themselves and truth. "By Providence divine," Gonzalo is the "appointed/ Master of this design" (1.2.159, 162–163), of the preservation of the life of and the provisions for the nurturing of the banished lawmaker and his descendant and thus for their continuance as the chosen remnant. The qualifying adjective "appointed" indicates that Gonzalo is subject to an authority greater than himself.

Tillyard wrote, "In *The Tempest* ... man is distanced into a more generally cosmic setting. The heavens are actively alive. It was by Providence divine that Prospero and Miranda survived in the boat." He asserted, "Prospero is at the apex of humanity with his magic power and his decision to spend what remains of his life in contemplation."[30] The heavens are alive, but Prospero doesn't stand at the apex of humanity in his magic power, which he surrenders. Nor does he spend the rest of his life in contemplation, but acknowledges his dual responsibility: earthly duty as duke, and heavenly servanthood through his need of prayer. In the latter he is on a level with all humankind, not above them.

The structure assumed in this study provides for a sphere of operation which may be attributed to deity and thus avoids the error some critics have made in deifying Prospero. In Prospero's "zenith," "a most auspicious star" has appeared (1.2.182, 181). Indeed, beyond Ariel's, Prospero's, and Gonzalo's sphere, and beyond the sphere of that of any god or goddess associated with the Ptolemaic spheres of the planets thus far discussed or of the any of the gods or goddesses mentioned by name in the play (Juno, Jupiter, Iris, Ceres, Mercury, Venus, Dis, Mars, and Neptune), lies the outermost planetary sphere known to the Renaissance era (Uranus having not been discovered until 1781), that of Saturn. Now Saturn was the father of Jupiter, Juno, Ceres, Dis, and Neptune, the first four of whom appear in the "majestic vision" presented to Ferdinand and Miranda. He reigned in the Golden Age. His was a reign of happiness, peace, serenity, and contentment. Moreover, it was a time of equality, for during his reign slaves and masters ate at the same table. The master of the outermost sphere of influence in the play which corresponds to the sphere of Saturn in the Ptolemaic system has been designated in Figure 2 as belonging to the unseen master. The unseen master in *The Tempest* is not Prospero, although, in his oversight of Miranda and Ferdinand, he is at times invisible to them. It is the unseen master's kingdom that Gonzalo envisions in his commonwealth.

A planet was often referred to by early astronomers as a wandering star, because of its rapid movement through the night sky. The star's position in the zenith, according to the zodiacal scheme, indicated that the star was in control of the affairs of earth at the time of the play. It is the unseen master and his law of forgiveness that control the outcome of the play; Prospero's action and Gonzalo's prophecy are only his precedents. As Hirst wrote, "[Prospero's] project begins and ends with Miranda." Prospero's "time has run out" But Miranda will not be, as Hirst suggested, "a ruler without paragon."[31] She figures as the mother of the true master to whom Prospero surrenders. As in biblical writ Moses prefigured Christ, so Prospero prefigures the unseen master. The real master of *The Tempest* is not found amongst the human beings in the play who are masters or who pretend to mastery. The master is exalted and invisible, except as he is manifested in the imagery and typology of the play. He is represented by the "most auspicious star" (1.2.182), the "*blossom that hangs on the bough*" (5.1.94), and in the craft that was "split" and is found at the end of the play "tight and yare" (5.1.223–224); He is figured by Ferdinand, the prince; Prospero, the lawmaker; and Gonzalo, the counselor.

The theme of master dominates, and in his examination of various masters, their capabilities, their areas of effectiveness, and their limitations, Shakespeare diminishes the earthly and elevates the unseen master who both provides the center of unity of the play and determines its periphery. With his model Shakespeare not only integrated space and time, but provided a new cosmology, based in belief rather than in scientific discovery, for a generation that had lost one. With his cosmology Shakespeare restored man to his central position in the universe.

In terms of the characterization used in this treatise, figuration, the light from that star casts shadows. Prospero is one of those shadows; he shadows Moses, who is a figure of the unseen master according to Scripture: "Nevertheless death reigned from Adam to Moses,... who is the figure of him that was to come" (Romans 5:14). Whereas Macbeth has light at its still center, in *The Tempest* Shakespeare evokes the light from above, and this star in its ascent to its zenith casts shadows. When the light is directly overhead, the shadows disappear, a fact consistent with the surrender of Prospero's spell-wielding instruments to the higher authority and his resumption of his earthly authority as duke. The light is the highest authority or master in the play, who, though unseen, nevertheless is omnipresent, manifesting in the shadows, the time of the play, the themes, imagery, and the law of forgiveness, which determine the outcome of the play. Prospero also figures the unseen master, controller of tempest, bearer of the guilt of others, but he is not absolute; he only *figures* or shadows the unseen master and in the end surrenders to his greater mastery.

All of the heavenly "figures" exert a kind of mastery in the play, whereas the "earthy" creatures only pretend to mastery. Not only do Prospero and his agent, Ariel, perform the mastery of the teacher and Gonzalo the mastery of design, but Ferdinand and Miranda are masters of Alonso's and Sebastian's mind changes when the latter two observe the couple playing chess. Alonso sees a resurrected son, Sebastian "a most high miracle." Ferdinand, the prince, easily controls kings (on a chess board), as does the unseen prince of peace, whom Ferdinand figures.

The modern audience does not very often think in terms of masters except in a deprecatory sense, since today's society emphasizes equality. Yet, equality is also a prime concern of Shakespeare's in *The Tempest*. It will be considered in the next chapter.

Chapter IX

Weaving the Tapestry:
Themes, Focus, and Design

The artistic unity of *The Tempest* is not in question whether the play is heard as a great symphony or viewed as the fabric of a vision. In fact, *The Tempest* is hailed as the most artistic of Shakespeare's plays. Its music is written in so many voices that it is tempting just to catch its mood. Interpretation, however, remains an important part of art, particularly musical and literary art. One is presented through a vocal or instrumental medium that involves one or more interpreters. In the other, literary art, much is lost if there is no one to gloss obsolete words and classical and historical events referenced or portrayed in the work. Both forms of art evoke a response in the listener or reader, a response that is not necessarily confined to mood, but may be expressed as heightened awareness or consciousness, which if sufficiently heightened may effect not only a mood, but an epiphany.

A variety of soundmakers play in *The Tempest*'s orchestra. They are as diverse as "roarers," "thunder," a "master's whistle," "sweet sprites," "a thousand twangling instruments," "watch-dogs," "strutting chanticleer," "mighty Neptune," "the wind," "Sea nymphs ... bell," and wayward men. After a turbulent overture with its thunderous notes, roaring sea and "howling" men "who are louder than the weather," the orchestra plays the tender notes from a "piteous heart" and the voice of a loving father whose lengthy story lulls a child and, possibly, an audience to sleep. After a pastoral interlude, near the sandy shore a soloist, Ariel, sings a song of invitation which is interrupted with the bark of watchdogs and the "cock-a-diddle-dow" of a "strutting chanticleer" (1.2.376–380). The sweet airs continue, followed by the ringing of a bell, "Ding-dong." The orchestra soon plays the contrasting notes of joyous prophesy and raucous scorn. Its "solemn music" (2.1.179) brings sleep to the old and royal. The sound of snoring, accompanied by the strident voices of would-be murderers, is interrupted by "a hollow burst of

135

bellowing/Like bulls, or rather lions," indeed "a whole herd of lions" (2.1.306–307, 311). Softer music, interrupted with occasional outbursts of harsh voices, is played until near the close solemn music is played, a song of freedom is sung, and the symphony closes in a peaceful mood.

When *The Tempest* is considered as a fabric, such an intricately woven warp and woof appears that it is difficult to separate the many themes. It is almost impossible to follow one thread without picking up another. The threads of master-servant-slave-authority themes intertwine with those of equality. The threads outlining paths to self-knowledge change color and become threads of repentance and reconciliation. Familial and political threads intertwine with themes of duty, change, and relationship. The threads of preservation, masters, and providence are interwoven. Time and music are intricate parts of the master theme. Hearing and sound themes are closely related to sleep/awake, dream, and awareness themes. The threads of sound are interwoven with those of time and mind.

The interweaving of various themes corresponds to a similar association of those themes in biblical writ, the Mystery Plays and *The Book of Common Prayer*, as was pointed out in Chapter V. An example is the awake/sleep–"high time" series of threads which occurs both in the play and in Romans 13:11. In the Scripture "high time" is related to the "now" of the play and its awake/sleep theme: "knowing the time, that now it is high time to awake out of sleep." Yet another biblical text relates the time of the play to the "hearing" theme and to Israel's journey in the wilderness following its exodus from Egypt: "Today if ye will hear his voice, harden not your hearts, as in the provocation. For some, when they had heard, did provoke: howbeit not all that came out of Egypt by Moses" (Hebrews 3:15, 16). Stephano, Trinculo, and Caliban not only provoke Prospero in their folly, but experience the miry fen (wilderness) and are in bondage to their own lower natures. Antonio, too, is still in bondage when the play ends.

The density of the fabric's weave has been responsible in part for the great variety of main themes that different readers claim to have found in the play. Brower stated that "the key metaphor of the play is 'change' ... and 'change' is the analogy common to all of the continuities ... not forgetting that they also are expressive of many other relationships, or that Shakespeare is often playing with two or three metaphors at once, as in the various figures of 'sea-swallowing.' But all are at least expressive of change, or changeableness."[1] Brower finds it hard to pull one thread from the fabric without dislodging others.

Knight claimed that "tempest and music are ... our main themes here."[2] Hirst claimed the central theme is "the conflict of nature and art,"[3] a claim incompatible with the present interpretation.

Traversi acknowledged that providence was at work in the play: "the events we are witnessing — which, we remember yet again, constitute a 'play,' a proposed pattern of reconciliation—have a dimension that can be called 'providential,' a meaning in relation to some conception of justice conceived as operative and valid."[4]

A great variety of themes are present, and the intricacy of the weave has led to attempts to focus on scenes as a means of identifying a central theme. Rose and Traversi attempted to relate theme and "design" in *The Tempest*. (Design is used in two different ways: as the plan or structure of the play or as a pattern or picture woven into its fabric.) In considering the design (structure) of Shakespeare's play, Mark Rose found that scene 3.1 "provides the crucial emblematic tableau, the picture of Ferdinand joyfully carrying logs, laboring to win Miranda, while Prospero, who has set the task to discipline the youth 'lest too light winning/ Make the prize light' (1.2.453–454) looks benevolently on unseen."[5]

From his design Rose read discipline as the central theme of the play.[6] Rose focused on the requirement rather than the purpose, spirit, and result of Ferdinand's behavior. Ferdinand's discipline has a purpose. It is service: "The very instant that I saw you, did/ My heart fly to your service" (3.1.64–65). The restrictions imposed upon Ferdinand in order that he may have his vision of perfection are gladly accepted. The theme of discipline does not relate directly to the other themes of the play. It does not go far enough. Moreover, although Rose acknowledged the other part of the central "tableau"—the unseen observer, Prospero—he did not interpret that aspect of it and thus missed the dual focus of the central scene: the obedient son and Prospero, the unseen father. Traversi, too, focused on the central scene. He differed from Rose as to theme, claiming, "The problem of liberty is set at the centre of the play."[7] Liberty is the result of discipline and service, that of both Ferdinand and Ariel. Liberty relates more directly than discipline to other themes in the play.

The image of the play as a fabric apparently proved useful for Dowden, who averred, "A thought which seems to run through the whole of *The Tempest*, appearing here and there like a coloured thread in some web, is the thought that the true freedom of man consists in service."[8] The central scene with Ferdinand carrying logs is an event typifying Christ's serving and carrying the cross to set humankind free. The freedom for humankind achieved through the son's obedience to the father, typified in the central scene, was also typified in "Abraham and Isaac" of the Mystery Plays.

Linking two other themes, "forgiveness and freedom"—which he called the "keynotes of the play"—Dowden united the themes of freedom, service and the forgiveness that made meaningful change possible.[9] The law, which is a form of discipline, does help to set at liberty those who are bound or enslaved by bringing them to the author of the new law of "liberty" (Galatians 5:1). By accepting the duties prescribed by Prospero, Ferdinand not only has a daily vision of Miranda, but in the end, he wins a bride.

Others characters in the play accept service or find freedom too. Caliban, Trinculo and Stephano escape from the fen and trim Prospero's cell (5.1.291–293). In the play Shakespeare makes it clear that liberty and freedom are not functions of physical space, for Ferdinand cries, "All corners else o'th' earth/ Let liberty make use of; space enough/ Have I in such a prison" (1.2.494–496). Shakespeare affirms here that "space" is not a matter of the physical, for he is giving his generation an alternative view of the space whose physical structure had been decimated by the Copernican theory. Also implied is that individual men are imprisoned by their own mindsets, their desire to be in a position of authority, unlike Ferdinand, who finds joy and meaning in serving.

Rose and Traversi used the differing structures they assigned the play to locate the central theme. Both felt that one particular scene — the same scene — reveals the main theme of the play. It contains a tableau that depicts not only Ferdinand, but Prospero, behind and unseen. The invisible master in the end grants full liberty and the prize, complete fulfillment of that for which the son hoped and worked. Yet Rose and Traversi ignored the theme of unseen master in this central scene.

Although Rose declared that "in matters of structure Shakespeare is more the calculating architect than the inspired singer carried away by the beauty of his song,"[10] he did not recognize the frame from which Shakespeare derives his architecture for *The Tempest,* which provides for the primum mobile, represented in the central scene by Prospero, the invisible father. Rose's arches do not provide for the peripheral. He finds only closure, and thus he loses part of the meaning, even though he notes "the inseparability of form and meaning in Renaissance art generally."[11] On the other hand, the structure identified in this treatise provides a framework for a dual meaning. There are two kinds of closure in the central scene. The kind not mentioned by Rose and Traversi is closure on Ferdinand as the key typological feature where "so rare a wonder'd father and a wise/ Makes this place Paradise" (4.1.123–124).

Not only are the themes interwoven in the play, but the structure assumes the nature of one of the themes, providence. Design is a particularly appropriate term to apply to *The Tempest* since Shakespeare, through Prospero, speaks of a "design" in the play as well as a "fabric" of "vision," and a fabric may have a design. Rose's use of design, however, is limited to one aspect of it in the play. The preservation of Miranda and Prospero is Gonzalo's design, and their preservation on a larger scale is the design of providence for the good of souls who come to the isle and for the good of the ones who were there already. The answer to the question raised twice in the first scene of the play — "Where is the Master?" — is answered in the central scene with Shakespeare's inclusion of Prospero in that scene. In the larger dimension of the play, too, the ultimate master of the "ship of souls" is looking on unseen.

Design as used in *The Tempest* is not limited to the picture presented in one scene, for many pictures appear on the fabric. From a fabric one may be able to discern both an overall pattern and a specific focus. Design is formed from the many tableaux that appear on the fabric after it has been woven. It is not one framed picture, although the central picture most clearly reveals the major themes: the unseen watchful master and the one who serves out of love in hope of winning the prize and knowing complete fulfillment. The type of fabric and design conceptualized in this book do not preclude one or more foci. In fact, the larger design of the play shows the way in which providence provides life-changing visions for various characters in the play. Provision and vision harmonize with individual need. When a central theme or themes are discovered at foci, they should relate in some way to all the other themes in the play.

In the second scene of a play, Shakespeare often sets limits upon the considerations of the first scene or clarifies or modifies his earlier assertions. Sometimes, as in *Measure for Measure*, he achieves this through the worldly wisdom or the practical sagacity (horse sense) of corrupt men. In other plays the folly of fools illustrates a wisdom that surpasses that of the wise. In *The Tempest* Shakespeare chooses to furnish the background for the action of this delightful, but overwhelmingly meaningful play through a schoolmaster who has been "preserved." It is in the second scene that the idea of design and the masters of design is presented. There are, in fact, two masters of design: the mortal master, Gonzalo, and the immortal, providence, or the creator (primum mobile) who provides for human needs. One operates during his own lifetime and is the vehicle of the other, which operates throughout history. Likewise the liberty and master-servant themes and the time and perfection themes have dual aspects and dual resolutions and are closely related to the design.

For an integrated design or pattern all other themes of the work must lead into or radiate from the central theme or themes. Traversi's theme of liberty fits better with the themes of master, servant, and slave. Freedom is won through submission and service. Submission not only affords a vision of perfection, but enables one to attain it. Ferdinand counts all things but loss: "My father's loss, the weakness which I feel,/ The wrack of all my friends, nor this man's threats,/ To whom I am subdued" (1.2.490–492) that he may "once a day/ Behold this maid" (493–494). The way to freedom of the spirit or mind and to a vision of purity, beauty, and provision is through servanthood by submission to a master both demanding and benevolent. Ferdinand's "spirits" may be "as in a dream,... all bound up" (1.2.489), but he can see, and eventually he wins the prize. There is a vision of the prize as well as a gaining of it, which in the larger setting of the play implies the eternal fulfillment of the serving soul.

Because of their dominance in the play, spectacle and vision have been mistakenly taken as a substitute for the plot or structure of *The Tempest*, for the play is so well integrated that it is difficult to separate the parts. Vision is as dominant in the play as hearing, and the play's structure is Shakespeare's vision of souls "enwrap'd" in the concentric circles of eternal providence. As has already been shown, this is not a baseless vision. One vision in the play, that of the gods and goddesses shown to Ferdinand and Miranda, is called "baseless," which may be interpreted to mean it has no foundation or actuality, for the gods and goddesses are not real. It may have been Shakespeare's way of distinguishing between the Judeo-Christian concept of provision and that of a pagan culture which had provided the basis for a structural system of the cosmos proved false by scientific discovery. The masque of gods and goddesses with its vision of provision is interrupted by "that foul conspiracy/ Of the beast Caliban and his confederates" (4.1.139–140). There is no provision in that vision for the spiritual needs of such as Caliban, but in the whole vision of the play Shakespeare supersedes the masque with a providential reality which encompasses the needs of *all* humans; there is "grace" even Caliban can seek.

The irony evident in Shakespeare's substitution of "three men of sin" for "three wise men" is repeated when Caliban, after hiccuping on his own name, proclaims the "high-day" and "freedom" drunkenly in his song. "High-day" emphasizes the importance of time in the play, while "freedom" announces the purpose. Both express major themes of the play. Moreover, "high-day" was a solemn or festal day, the day kept to honor the conception of Jesus by the Virgin Mary. For the would-be violator of Miranda's virginity to be celebrating high-day is ironic.

Vision is also a major theme in the play. Beside the vision of eternal providence that Shakespeare offers his audience and readers, there are visions granted to different characters. Almost everyone in the play has a vision suited to his character, need, or condition. Ferdinand has a vision of beauty, purity, and innocence, and of "a wond'red father and a wise" (4.1.123)—reasons to continue living in the face of the assumed loss of his own earthly father and supposed friends. For him, vision spatializes place: "space enough/ Have I in such a prison" (1.2.494–495). Miranda, who before had seen only her aging father and a demi-devil, has a vision of youth and regal man that expands her hope for humankind. Alonso, who has been an unimportunable authority and a treacherous ruler, has a vision of the equality of persons, especially of male and female members of the human race when he sees a true prince and princess in control of kings in a chess game. Stephano's and Trinculo's vision of "glistering apparel," although wrongfully acquired, distracts them from usurpation of a false authority. Glistering is a word used only twice in Scripture, once in the Old Testament to describe stones David had gathered for the temple that his son, Solomon, was to build, and once in the New Testament to describe Christ's raiment as it appeared to his chosen disciples on the Mount of Transfiguration. In the description of that occasion in the Gospel of Luke there is shadowing, "a voice out of a cloud," and sleepers who awake and recognize one of the men who has joined their master as Moses. The authority of the sleepers' master is established by a voice from heaven declaring, "This is my beloved Son: hear him" (Luke 9:35). It is notable that this biblical passage combines major themes of the play, sleep/awake, hearing ("I hear it now above me" [1.2.410]), and master. Two of the masters identified in this treatise, Moses and the unseen master, are linked in this biblical scene. Since glistering is not a word commonly used in the literature of Shakespeare's time, it functions in the play as a signifier. In the Hebrew Scriptures it describes stones to be used in the building of the temple, and in the play it is used just before Caliban, Trinculo, and Stephano are sent to decorate Prospero's cell; thus it is suggestive of one of those Armstrong-like connections often seen in Shakespeare's plays. As a distinct and seldom sounded note it invokes biblical overtones and specific references affirming character representation and meaning.

Sebastian and Antonio, would-be murderers, have a vision of a banquet other than that of the blood of their victims. Prospero, who found an earthly dukedom boring and who invokes "weak masters," has a vision of the dissolution of earth's manmade towers, the seat of man's dukedoms, and catches sight of a star above him. Caliban, who would be king of the isle or own a drunken master, has a vision of the dignity of an earthly duke when he sees Prospero in his hat and rapier.

Not only is awareness created by the waking visions of the characters in the play, but dreams bring awareness, too. Caliban, waking and made to sleep again by the humming of "a thousand twangling instruments" or "voices," sees the clouds opening and "riches/ Ready to drop upon" him (3.2.135–140). His pain in awaking from such a vision is expressed in "I cried to dream again" (141). This pain can be compared with the pain of Prospero's "beating mind" induced by his waking from a daytime vision to the actuality of Caliban's waking plot. Vision and dream in *The Tempest* substantiate that resources beyond man's making are available to him. Even as Miranda's past existence is "rather like a dream" (1.2.45), so is man's "little life" "such stuff/ As dreams are made on." When that life is "rounded with a sleep," (4.1.157, 156–158) there is the waking to the larger life of the immortal. (Rounding carries with it the sense of removing corners and shaping into the perfection of the circular form.) Alonso would choose to shut out his son's supposed death with sleep: "I wish mine eyes/ Would, with themselves, shut up my thoughts" (2.1.186–187). Sebastian and Antonio, the would-be murderers, are not disposed to sleep to escape from contemporary events. Their minds are not alive to the greater reality. Plotting in passing time is all they can do on their own. For them sleep and death are equivalent since they have no hope beyond the grave:

> Here lies your brother,
> No better than the earth he lies upon,

If he were that which now he's like, that's dead;
Whom I, with this obedient steel, three inches of it,
Can lay to bed for ever... [2.1.275–279].

In the spell-stopping "And as morning steals upon the night" (5.1.65), with its awakening, the fumes rise and the clouds open to reveal and bring "clearer reason" (68). It is not logic or scientific reason that is subsequently revealed, but Isaiah's kind of reason: "Come now, and let us *reason* together, saith the Lord: though your sins be as scarlet, they shall be as white as snow; though they be red like crimson, they shall be as wool" (Isaiah 1:18). Isaiah's kind of reason was prophetic of the law of forgiveness of the unseen master.

In Chapter VIII, the structure of *The Tempest* was depicted and described as a transposition from an outmoded planetary system with planets and a sun rotating around the earth to the concept of providence operating through real representatives in real historical time upon a variety of individuals. Shakespeare moves from a physical, material system of the universe to a divine with human agents, and the focus of that system was not the planetary body, earth, but the souls of humankind who ride upon it. In the play's design, there are many pictures illustrating how providence acts. The plot itself is based on the experientially real but invisible frame of providence. Even as Ferdinand finds a kind of liberty in submission or servanthood, so do others in the play. Prospero finds freedom from a beating mind through the virtue of forgiveness. Caliban acknowledges the path to grace through submission to the schoolmaster.

R. M. Frye, looking at the end of the play, saw a humanistic dénouement.[12] However, at the end, too, there are two components in man's living on earth: a horizontal component — "reasonable service," attention to his "grave" or office — and the vertical component of prayer. The dénouement, as well as the rest of the play, focuses on man's relationship to two worlds. The overseeing by Prospero of Ferdinand's service is symbolic of the unseen master's or prime mover's observance of humankind's fulfillment of duties.

The whole design in this study provides a comprehensive vision uniting the eternal and the timely, God's ways and man's. Providence provides the overall pattern, whereas the earthly focus, at the center of the play and in man's location in the Ptolemaic system, is service. Moreover, central themes of service and providence fit better with the questions about master and the more inclusive concerns of master-servant-slave themes in the play. It is, of course, true that self-discipline is a requisite of effective service and the result is freedom. Ariel, the servant and spirit of the law, is set free, too, after performing his required service to Prospero.

Ferdinand, who is to be the bridegroom, is seen as serving the bride to be, just as the unseen master "made himself of no reputation, and took upon him the form of a servant" (Phil. 2:7). Prospero serves as schoolmaster in the play in the figure of Moses, who "was faithful in all his house, as a servant" (Hebrews 3:5). After the schoolmaster comes the "Son," who on earth is the servant, but is "the Master in heaven." In the unseen master of the play, servanthood and mastery are united and given an image in Ferdinand, the son, the prince and future king.

In examining the play, which has been declared biblical in this work and which works toward reconciliation, it is important to remember that there are two parts to the New Testament interpretation of the law. One part concerns the master in heaven, and the other concerns human relationships. Taken together they provide a summary of the Old Testament law. "Thou shalt love the Lord thy God with all thy heart, and with all thy soul, and with all thy mind. This is the first and great commandment. And the second is like unto it, Thou shalt love thy neighbour as thyself. On these two commandments hang all the law and the prophets" (Matthew 22:37–39). These are restatements of Deut. 6:5, "Thou shalt love the Lord thy God with all thine heart, and with all thy soul, and with all thy might," and Leviticus 19:18, "Thou shalt love thy neighbour as thyself." The various authorities acknowledged by men in the first scene and throughout the play are made subject to the unseen master, whose attributes are represented in several characters. Prospero, as the unseen spell-maker, evokes the aspect of invisibility of the creator, although later in the play Prospero is manifest to the occupants of the "ship of souls" and becomes their lawgiver and schoolmaster. Ferdinand as the grieving son who carries wood and treads the maze is an image of sacrifice and service. Miranda, in her innocence and virginity and in her care for the "souls," is an image of purity and mercy. Gonzalo, as a "holy" man and a master of earthly provision in providing the craft in which Prospero and Miranda reached the isle, offers an image of heavenly perfection and providence.

Although the emphatic uses of time, masters, music, spheres, and sound have been pointed out, there are other major themes in the play, two of which are change and relationship, as Brower claimed. As may well be expected, these two are interwoven with each other as well as with the other themes. Although forms of the word "change" occur only four times in the play, it is so often seen in image or example and its synonyms so often used that it is indeed a major concern. To begin with, there is an abrupt change from a raging tempest to the yellow sands of the isle. Prospero recounts his undergoing a kind of change when he was "transported/ And rapt in secret studies," after which Antonio "new created/ The creatures that were [his] ... or chang'd 'em" (1.2.76–77, 81–82). Prospero changes his garments as he changes his identity. Ariel changes his appearance and song as he "ministers" to the shipwrecked. Caliban changes his master often. The sounds in the play change from "dreadful thunderclaps" to "sweet airs," from clapping of harpy wings to soft music, from the singing of Juno and Ceres to "a strange, hollow, and confused noise," from a recitation of man's magical achievements to "solemn music." Gonzalo observes changes in his troop's garments, interchanges names of historical cities, and proposes a change in "plantation" of the isle, his commonwealth. He notes the moon's changing. Antonio and Sebastian plot change, as do Caliban, Trinculo, and Stephano. The monster, Caliban, changes shape when Trinculo takes cover under Caliban's "gabardine." Whether ridiculous, elevated, magical, mystical, or profound, changes continually take place. Shapes and spirits appear and vanish. Eventually minds, values, and relationships are changed. Alonso undergoes a sea-change and a change in parental attitude. He is no longer a domineering father, but one who "Must ask ... [his] child forgiveness!" (5.1.198). Ferdinand changes from servant to equal partner. There is a change from the inconsiderate to the considerate in the treatment of a daughter by an earthly father, Alonso, as shown through Claribel and Miranda. Sebastian changes his tune from that of a self-centered opportunist, who would have seized a crown through murder, to the vision of Ferdinand alive with "a most high miracle!" (5.1.177). Whereas the "ship of souls" was "split," it is in the end united and the craft itself renewed.

There are many changes in relationship in the play. Early in *The Tempest* Gonzalo expounds his ideal relationship among human beings with "all things in common," which is a biblical phrase found in the book of Acts (2:44). That text also refers to baptism, wonders and signs done by the apostles, and the union and sharing of all who believed. Gonzalo's ideal, an aspect of the perfection theme, is for a commonwealth (common wealth). The play begins with a scene of equality. As far as the men and their souls are concerned, their lot is common, for the welfare of all those on board the ship is equally threatened by both the physical and the supernatural tempest. Prospero and Miranda, too, were threatened by both the raging sea and tempestuous man before they found harbor in the isle. Persons in Gonzalo's commonwealth are to be equal in their relationship with one another and with their access to resources. However, they are not to be equal with God, but submissive to his laws.

Although in his dramas Shakespeare explores almost all possibilities in human relationships, he works toward an ideal of equality and mutuality. In a play like *The Tempest,* which abounds with references to authority, masters, and slaves and in which serving is a part of love, it is at first amazing to find how far Shakespeare has carried the theme of equality. He has indeed been true, however, to the equality phrase, "as thyself," of the unseen master's second commandment.

The common predicament of man is mistaken identity, changeableness, and substitution. These are displayed in the amusing but very significant scene where Stephano and Trinculo discover Caliban and take refuge with him from the elements under the "gabardine." To the recalcitrant who think only in terms of controlling and not in terms of peace, equality is "nothing." They do not understand that someone greater than man rules in the commonwealth which Gonzalo describes and would found. Men's many "inventions" which "they have sought out" (Eccl. 7:29)—"sword, pike, knife, gun," which such as Antonio and Sebastian rely on—Gonzalo would not have in his commonwealth, which is "t'excel the golden age" (2.1.157, 164). Thus Gonzalo points to a kind of reign which is to be greater than the greatest era known to man, the golden age of Saturn when slaves sat at the king's table. If it is to be a greater reign than the Saturnine, it follows that it must have a greater master than Saturn.

By the time Alonso has his vision of his lost son and Miranda playing chess, the "name of King" has dwindled to a piece manipulated on a chess board, and the question asked in the first scene—"What care these roarers for the name of king?"—has been answered. Two French emblems illustrating the proverb "The end makes us all equal," use "a very appropriate and curious device from the game of chess."[13] The chess game used in the final scene of *The Tempest*, then, is a symbol of the equality of men and women, for the vision that Alonso has of Ferdinand and Miranda, the romantic pair moving pieces around a gameboard, attests to their equality in a world of right and loving relationship. The control which Alonso exerted over his daughter in marrying her off in Tunis effected a distancing of family, and ended in a splitting, not only of the craft which bore the souls, but of his control over them. In Miranda and Ferdinand's freedom of choice, families are united. The theme of equality is further emphasized in the law of forgiveness, which necessitates Prospero's confession of guilt and his need for repentance, as well as forgiveness of those who wronged him. All souls are subject to the tempest, inner and outer; all are in need of grace and are subject to the condition inherent in the law of forgiveness. Through repentance and choice of virtue—"heart's sorrow, And a clear life ensuing," or in Caliban's case submission to the law which brings to Christ—all persons become potential recipients of the grace of God.

Gonzalo, who envisions the ultimate good, acknowledges the unseen master, "the wills above," in the opening scene. In the final scene his utterances are acknowledgments of reunion, the overall way of providence, and of the specific servant example of the unseen master, who has "chalk'd out" the debt and pointed the way of forgiveness: "For it is you that have chalk'd forth the way/ Which brought us hither" (5.1.203–204). He calls for rejoicing. The rejoicing is not alone for a holy man, but for all humankind: natural man, Caliban, Trinculo and Stephano—civilized men who reject authority both human and heavenly and follow the flesh, for they are employed in decorating Prospero's cell. As the shepherds, men of nature, and foreign kings came to a manger (cave), so do the occupants of the isle.

There is a centricity about the play and two major themes to be found in the central scene. However, without Prospero's vision of dissolution and the "ye elves" speech, the play would lose much of its emotional impact. They, too, are central to its meaning and will be discussed in a later chapter.

Chapter X

Golden Hours, Yellow Sands:
Time and Place in *The Tempest*

"Not of an age, but for all time." Jonson
"Mind is its own place." Milton, Paradise Lost *I, 254*

Many authors have attempted to deal with the concepts of time as they appear in Renaissance literature. Their works are informative, giving various historical approaches to time and showing their contributions to the developing concepts. They acknowledge the impact of cultural, religious, and societal changes and astronomical and navigational discoveries. Those authors refer to specific Renaissance works, distinguishing and relating the various concepts of time. On the other hand, many critics whose research does not focus on time but on *The Tempest* seem content to limit their evaluation of time in *The Tempest* to the quality of unity.

In a particularly insightful examination of Shakespeare's use of time in various plays, Wylie Sypher uses such descriptive terms as *linear, geometric,* and *durative*.[1] His primary focus is on the qualities of time pervading in the plays that he examines. His critiques are distillations that describe the atmosphere of each play, rather than particularized investigations of the time references in the plays.

No critic has heretofore been concerned with a detailed examination of all the specific references to time in *The Tempest*. Yet such an examination might well contribute to an expanded vision of the play, for time references in *The Tempest* are not limited to the hours of its duration.

Time references in *The Tempest* are varied, manifold, and both imagistic and numeric, and it is necessary to scrutinize them carefully in order to establish their relation to the themes and their role in determining the central focus of the play. Since this book avers a Judeo-Christian structure for

The Tempest, the time concepts of that tradition and some of those of *The Tempest* should be compatible. Moreover, since "the three men of sin" are addressed as men of "destiny," Ariel assumes the role of a Greek minister of fate, and the Greek goddess of the rainbow, Iris, appears in the vision, one might expect Greek concepts of time to surface in the play also. The fact that Augustinian and Calvinistic concepts of time were the dominant influences in Shakespeare's day and their differences the subject of "a wideranging debate to which ... Shakespeare and his contemporaries responded and in some sense contributed"[2] should also be weighed as an interpretation of Shakespearean time in *The Tempest* is made.

Before proceeding with the detailed examination of time references in *The Tempest*, however, it might be profitable to glean some facts from the generalizations of some of the aforementioned authors. Sypher and Turner deal with time as it is manifest in Shakespearean drama, whereas Quinones and Waller present a broader historical approach to the concepts of time but refer to some of Shakespeare's plays in drawing their conclusions. Turner generalizes about Shakespeare's *Tempest* time: "The destroyer, devourer, and tyrant of the Sonnets has become a more mysterious but less malignant force." After quoting the revels passage, Turner concludes, "Time is no longer a problem for a poet who could write such lines of acceptance of transience."[3]

Quinones finds that in *The Tempest*, "Unlike Spenser or Donne, Shakespeare does not turn his back on the new age of reason." He describes Shakespeare's "achievements" further, stating, "Rich, mythic patterns closely linked with the human life cycle and man's more creatural nature persist and even predominate within a changing universe." He sees a new vision emerging "after suffering and through sheer length of time ... in the last plays that represents a reconciliation of the demands of the histories and the desires of love, of the remarkable human capacity for continuity and the pressing realities of time and change."[4] He writes,

> Prospero shows the very aspirations of his mind, seeking to lend permanence and continuance to the passing things of this world. Generational continuity and married love are granted extension in his remarkable vision of bounty and grace — Shakespeare's "Prayer for a Daughter." The songs of Juno and Ceres bring an abiding spirit into the earth:... This bountiful sense of life, of fruitfulness and growth, naturally involves Prospero in intimations of immortality.... But ... Prospero's art is interrupted by the rude entrance of history. He had momentarily overlooked Caliban and his plot.... The persistence of his unregenerate nature suggests a vast universe, similar to that of Petrarch's *Triumph of Time*, which dwarfs all man's efforts and renders vain all his desires. Prospero's vision of bounty was a baseless fabric, his theatre an insubstantial pageant. Such constructs of human ideality count for little in a universe that will dissolve not only man's more solid cultural achievements but the great globe itself. Nihilistic conclusions approaching those of Jacques and even of Macbeth are Prospero's.[5]

There is an integration of the temporal and the eternal in *The Tempest* as implied in Quinones's linking of the "human cycle" with "mythic patterns," but Quinones seems to be overwhelmed by Caliban, Trinculo, and Stephano, whereas Prospero and Shakespeare are not. Hence he draws a humanistic conclusion.

Quinones's evaluation differs from this author's in the interpretation of Prospero's vision and the expanse of influence he allows for in the persistence of Caliban's unregeneracy. Quinones does not take into consideration Caliban's acknowledgment, finally, of Prospero as his master and his determination to "seek for grace." For this author the vision Prospero offers Ferdinand and Miranda is not a "construct of human ideals," but a parallel to the biblical providential vision which unfolds both in the Mystery Plays and in the main body of *The Tempest*. Prospero's vision of bounty serves the same purpose as the masques and plays within Shakespeare's other plays. The fabric of Prospero's vision is baseless and his pageant insubstantial in that it is fabricated with gods and goddesses. It is ahistorical. In contrast, the play itself, which is a vision, is substantive since the characters figure real persons in the Judeo-Christian tradition.

Quinones' interpretation of Prospero's conclusions as nihilistic is short-sighted. Prospero's statement about a dissolving globe is a commentary on his eternal vision of providence. It is a statement of belief in the limits, not only of the plans of "fools," but of the constructs of civilized man. It reaches in scope even further, to the sense that earth is not man's final home. As such it parallels the Isaiah-Moses-Christ tradition. Prospero needs time to be alone after such a flight, for it is always difficult for the visionary to come down from the mountaintop to deal practically with the foolishness and plotting of wayward men. When Moses, descending from Mount Sinai after meeting with God and receiving the Ten Commandments, found the Israelites worshipping a golden calf, he became angry and broke the tables of stone upon which the commandments were written by the finger of God.[6] In comparison with the golden calf which incurred Moses' anger stands Caliban, "moon-calf" (3.2.20), who incurs Prospero's wrath when he interrupts the vision Prospero prepared for Ferdinand and Miranda.

Waller's evaluation of *The Tempest* extends beyond Quinones's but does not go as far as this author's in its interpretation of Shakespeare's perspective on time. Waller observes:

> Prospero's island is a realm both in and out of the world: paradoxically the play's strict unities of place and time have the effect of making the island appear to be outside the demands of time and space but mysteriously related to them.... Central to the intellectual structure of the play is [Shakespeare's] ... concern with Time and Providence.... Prospero, according to some critics, embodies the traditional Christian view of Providence.... This view ... is certainly maintained in the play by Gonzalo, but it is obvious that Prospero

cannot embody providential power in any way related to the traditional Christian sense.... Time and its opportunities are crucial to Prospero's success. The action Prospero is directing occurs in a crucial [period] that "must ... be spent most preciously." In this time the nature of the future and the meaningfulness of his past exile will be established.... The magical island, isolated in time, is nevertheless one where the importance of time is strongly realized.[7]

Waller does not grasp or take into consideration the greater working of providence in the historic intimations that go beyond Prospero as former duke. His finding that "Prospero cannot embody providential power in any way related to the traditional Christian sense" is consistent with the figuring of Prospero as Moses of this treatise, for Moses was pre–Christian and can only bring men *to* Christ. His humanist conclusion that "the responsibility for meaning in time is found not in relating events to a non-temporal, transcendent eternal Providence, but rather in celebrating the possibilities in human responses to time's opportunities"[8] differs from this interpretation, which argues that time's opportunities are the opportunities to respond to provision. However, the findings in Waller's detailed, extensive historical tracings of time concepts applied to the action, dénouement, and numerous textual time references in *The Tempest* affirm the conclusions of the present interpretation. What Shakespeare celebrates is the death and resurrection of Christ and the opportunities given humans to respond to the invitation to the grace of forgiveness, a response to eternal providence — now.

According to Plato and Aristotle the first cause and ultimate meaning of time, the prime mover, existed outside of time, and true reality existed beyond time and history. The prime mover (primum mobile) was pictured in the Ptolemaic cosmological array of gods and goddesses, the framework whose structure was adopted by the medieval church and has been adopted for this book as the framework used and transposed by Shakespeare in *The Tempest*. The medieval church placed God in the position of prime mover.

Writing in terms of the soul, Shakespeare's concern in *The Tempest*, Plotinus asked, "Would ... [it] be sound to define Time as the Life of the Soul in movement as it passes from one stage or act of experience to another?"[9] Plotinus's answer was "Yes." He described eternity as "life in repose, unchanging, self-identical, always endlessly complete."[10] Prospero's "spell-stopping" of the "souls" within the magic circle could be considered an expression of the eternal where the souls' wanderings cease and self-identity is revealed. The resolution proposed in the first scene, "the peace of the present," suggests "life in repose," man at peace with himself, others, and the universe. According to Plotinus, "Time ... is not to be conceived as outside of Soul; Eternity is not outside of the Authentic Existent: nor is it to be taken as a sequence or succession to Soul, any more than Eternity is to the Divine. It is a thing seen *upon Soul*, inherent, coeval to it"[11] (emphasis added). According to the framework used in this study, eternity is co-existent with the "fraughting souls" and works upon them.

Waller contrasted "the Greek *chronos*, the measurement of duration, and the Judeo-Christian *kairos*, the moment of opportunity." The opportunities were known "as a 'series of "times-with-contents" sent by God for his own purposes, and demanding certain appropriate responses from his people.'" Furthermore, Waller claimed that the "New Testament writers transform the Jewish concept of *a* time of opportunity to *the* time, the *kairos* the advent of Jesus of Nazareth in whom the time is fulfilled." He claimed, "The commencement of a new *aion* or era was proclaimed, in which men were called to live eschatologically, in a new pattern of living in which the quality of eternal life is revealed in time."[12] Miranda's "brave new world" echoes the proclamation of such a new age. Certainly the time on the island is represented in *The Tempest* as moments of opportunity. In the minds of Antonio and Sebastian it is the moment to seize a kingdom. In the minds of Caliban, Trinculo, and Stephano it is the time to take over the island. For Prospero it is the moment of opportunity, as a man, to wreak vengeance upon his enemies or to forgive them, and as a providential schoolmaster and lawmaker, to bring them to the awareness of kairos, redemptive time.

Like Moses in the Mystery Plays, as pointed out in Chapter V, Prospero is the "schoolmaster" who submits to the greater master whose law is forgiveness. That master is represented in *The Tempest* figuratively by Ferdinand. But in scene 3.1, where Prospero watches as Miranda discloses to Ferdinand "the bigger bulk" and in an "aside" prays, "Heavens rain grace/ On that which breeds between 'em!" (3.1.81, 75–76), he figures as the prime mover.

According to Waller with the concept of kairos, "time was thus given a positive meaning, centred on the Incarnation and looking towards the parousia, which was to be prepared for not by escaping from time but by transforming it."[13] Prospero, with Ariel's help, becomes an agent in the transformation of the time of the recalcitrant, who claim time is "theirs." Antonio sees time as an opportunity "to perform an act/ Whereof what's past is prologue; what to come,/ In yours and my discharge" (2.1.247–249). When Stephano and Trinculo attempt to acquire a wardrobe, Caliban declares, "We shall lose our time" (4.1.247). In bringing Stephano and Trinculo to awareness, Prospero appeals to their acquisitive natures. He prevents Antonio from "o'er stepping" the present by "basing his trespass." In the end, the actors do lose their time — plotted time — but are made aware of a more important time, *now*, which in fact is the only time available to humankind.

In discussing the Mystery Plays, Meyers wrote:

> Supposing, then, that there is a "unified" view of time in the plays, how would it be shown? The first evidence of it ought to be a radical restructuring of time itself. In the definition of restructuring of time should be included all

attempts to bring the past or future into the present, the first through a recounting of the actions of Providence, the second through prophecies of what is to come.

The second evidence of a different view of time is parallel structure, in any of several planes. Through the breakdown of what modern man would think of as the immutable sequence of time, all events, at whatever time they occur, become contemporaneous.[14]

The spherical structure proposed in Chapter VIII provides for the impact of past events on the lives of the characters. It provides the type of parallel contemporaneous structure suggested by Meyers.

There is compounded evidence in the play of the triumph of good over evil. Ferdinand has a vision in the midst of loss of a reason to serve. He is willing to serve if he may but see, i.e., have a vision of love and perfection. Good Gonzalo prays for the dropping of a "blessed crown" on Ferdinand and Miranda. Alonso is twice blessed. He recovers a son and gains a daughter. The three revelers, Caliban, Trinculo, and Stephano, participate in the celebration of reconciliation and restoration of proper rule and order by trimming Prospero's cell. Caliban recognizes Prospero as his true master and declares his good intent — to "seek for grace." Sebastian has a mind change from "no hope" to "a most high miracle," although he reverts to his mercenary ways again upon the appearance of Caliban: "Ha, ha!/ What things are these, my Lord Antonio?/ Will money buy 'em?" (5.1.262–264). Only Antonio appears to be unaffected in character. However, he is under the jurisdiction of Alonso, who has relieved him of his dukedom. Shakspeare's "now" in *The Tempest* is comparable to Augustine's "present" time: "The present time of past things is our memory; the present time of present things is our sight; the present time of future things our expectation."[15] Both authors encompass the past in memory, the present, and the future in "foreknowing" or expectation.

Time in *The Tempest* as in Augustine's Confessions is related chiefly to the impressions made on mind as time passes, since there is little action in the play.[16] In other words time is measured by what happens to the mind. Certainly in *The Tempest*, for Prospero, the past survives in memory and the future in anticipation of bringing his enemies to awareness and his offspring to fulfillment in holy matrimony. In fact there is little fulfilled activity on the island. Most of the action in the play takes place in the minds of the characters. Activity is stopped, or nearly so, as impressions are made upon the minds of persons by the isle's atmosphere and by Ariel in his different forms. In Prospero's spell-stopping, humans "catch at a beam of light from that ever-fixed eternity, to compare it with the times which are never fixed, that [they] thereby may perceive how there is no comparison between them."[17]

Time in *The Tempest*, as for Augustine, is the medium through which the eternal is transmitted to man and the medium in which the soul is saved or damned. In *The Tempest* Prospero uses time "most preciously," making impressions through Ariel upon the minds of men in the isle in its *now* through song and sound.

The Tempest, like the Mystery Plays, covers all human time. Human time in the Mystery Plays begins after the creation and the fall of Satan with the fall of man in the garden. All three events are recorded in the play called "Creation and Fall."[18] The other extreme of human time is portrayed in the Mystery Plays as doomsday, when the obedient and disobedient are respectively rewarded and punished. There was an earlier biblical doomsday for all but eight members of the human race — the Flood. In the Wakefield Play "Processus Noe Cum Filiis,"[19] Noe says:

> Behold to the heuen! The cateractes all,
> Thai ar open full euen, grete and small,
> And the planettys seuen left has thare stall.
> Thise thoners and levyn downe gar fall
> Full stout
> Both halles and bowers,
> Castels and towres.
> Full sharp ar thise showers
> That renys aboute.[20]

Shakespeare's "dissolution" passage, cited by critics as coming from II Peter 3:10–14, follows the Noe text more closely than the biblical, as a comparison of the three texts reveals, suggesting that the Wakefield play was Shakespeare's source for that passage rather than the Bible.

> …be cheerful, sir.
> Our revels now are ended. These our actors
> (As I foretold you) were all spirits, and
> Are melted into air, into thin air,
> And like the baseless fabric of this vision,
> The cloud-capp'd tow'rs, the gorgeous palaces,
> The solemn temples, the great globe itself,
> Yea, all which it inherit, shall dissolve,
> And like this insubstantial pageant faded
> Leave not a rack behind [4.1.147–156].

The Flood *prefigures* the second (final) destruction of the world at the last judgment to which the biblical passage and Shakespeare's "revels" (4.1.148–158) speech refer.

> But the day of the Lord will come as a thief in the night; in the which the heavens shall pass away with a great noise, and the elements shall melt with fervent heat, the earth also, and the works that are therein shall be burned up. Seeing then that all these things shall be dissolved, what manner of persons ought ye to be in all holy conversation and godliness. Looking for and hasting unto the coming of the day of God, wherein the heavens being on

fire shall be dissolved, and the elements shall melt with fervent heat?...
Wherefore, beloved, seeing that ye look for such things, be diligent that ye
may be found of him in peace... [II Peter 3:10–12, 14].

The passages in the Wakefield manuscript and *The Tempest* mention towers; the Wakefield text also uses "Castels" and Shakespeare "palaces." The
Scripture does not designate any of the three structures. The similar usage by
Wakefield and Shakespeare may be attributed either to Shakespeare's use of
the Wakefield manuscript or to the practice by both cycle editors and Shakespeare of incorporating the contemporary and the specific in the vision. Both
the Mystery Plays and *The Tempest* are anachronistic, in that they included
some nonbiblical elements and join unlikely places, custom, and costumes.

However, the similarities in *The Tempest* and the Wakefield play suggest
the latter as Shakespeare's source rather than the biblical passage. Moreover,
the Wakefield passage is associated with a boat and a storm, as is Shakespeare's
opening scene in *The Tempest*. The number of passengers on the two ships
approximate one another. May we assume that Shakespeare's "ship of souls"
was a salvaging craft of Noah's type? An audience familiar with the Mystery
Plays would know from them and probably from other sources that Noah's
ark, a wooden vessel, "typically" looked forward to the wooden cross which
was the vehicle of salvation for the human race. In the Mystery Plays Old Testament events as well as characters were typologically directed toward the
Christ and salvation history. Similarly in *The Tempest* Prospero's recollection
of past events serves as a backdrop for the restoration of proper relationships
through forgiveness and clearer reason in the isle. Since Prospero's observation comes after the preservation of the "souls" on *The Tempest* ship, it looks
forward to the second doomsday. However, the use of the Noe play, which
involves a salvage of souls, corresponds in outcome with *The Tempest*. Thus
Shakespeare incorporates a rescue within time, but also predicts the end of
parousia, a concept contained in Prospero's "I find my zenith doth depend
upon/ A most auspicious star, whose influence/ If now I court not, but omit,
my fortunes/ Will ever after droop" (1.2.181–184).

Although the structure of *The Tempest* is similar to that of *A Midsummer Night's Dream*, its time frame is different and has not aroused as much
interest as the time of the earlier play. Time and action in the earlier play is
determined by the diurnal rotation of the spheres. The circular motion is
reflected in the pursuits of the characters. However, time in *The Tempest* is of
great importance.

Time is variously described in *The Tempest*. It is *highest* (Temp-est). It
is *golden*: Gonzalo speaks of a time "T' excel the golden age" (2.1.164). It is
good: "In good time" (2.1.91), the isle will be exchanged for the Eden apple[21]
of offense and the sowing of its "kernels" will bring forth more places of resolution. The "past is prologue" (2.1.247) to the present, which it truly is in

the play as exhibited in the ages of Adam, Noah, Moses, Jesse, and the kings and prophets. It is not that past to which Antonio refers. Although Antonio thinks he is in control of the future, the audience knows Prospero is in control of the island at this point. That the past is prologue to the present is true in terms of the meaning of the play, for Old Testament characters figure the one who is manifest in the play as the true master of events. As in the Mystery Plays, past events are only prologue to the present happenings, which lead to the new master's forgiveness. The past is dark and backward, buried in the abysm, and survives only in memory (1.2.49–50). Time "goes upright in his carriage" (5.1.3). The play begins at noon. Time becomes a theme in the play and is related to the sound-hearing theme of the play where timing is often the distinguishing factor between noise and music. The beating of Prospero's mind occurs when Caliban's noneternal plotting *in time* counters the eternal time of the vision. After the discord in his mind has been allayed through virtuous choice, he can advise Alonso, "Do not infest your mind with beating on/ The strangeness of this business" and promise to "resolve" him (5.1.246–248), which includes separating the cacophonous sounds of time from the eternal melodies. The differences in sound between the cacophonic disturbances and the "silent Christ" of the Mystery Plays is portrayed by Shakespeare throughout the play until the resolution is reached, the time of parousia for most of the wayward characters.

Shakespeare's *now* in *The Tempest* is biblical full time, the day of salvation, in which man is potentially restored through the law of forgiveness, enabling him to be free from the curse of sin and from bondage to the cycle or wheel of fortune, which is repetitious linear time. Only a volume or three-dimensional space can be visualized as full, for a linear sequence can mark events, but not contain them. Thus in *The Tempest* Shakespeare has made time three-dimensional and one with space.

Time is full in the sense that it is filled with opportunity, meaning, and significant change. An amazing number of happenings take place in a very limited time. The exploded moment, now, of the present in *The Tempest* is the eternal moment of literature, raised to a spiritual level, of self-knowledge, proper relationship, and of awareness of the truth. Now or the eternal moment is the present filled with meaning. It is the static or still center where men are "spell-stopp'd." It compares with T.S. Eliot's still center of the moving world. In *The Tempest* the now of time crystallizes out of all that is past. The image suggested by "the dark backward and abysm of time" is of a globular *now* formed out of the chaos or ravages of time much as the earth has been described as taking shape "in the beginning," out of the void. Past time is no longer a linear sequence of events, but a vast space of voided time out of which the present emerges as full time. The only significant historical time in the play, preserved in the memories of both Prospero and the audience, is that of providence, which is eternal (as is evidenced in the structure of the play and exhibited in the visions). The linear time of happenings in Milan and Naples is dispensed with. The only significance of those events is in their contribution to present relationships and needs. It is true that the recalcitrant characters try to develop a linear time sequence of their own on the island, but they are "spell-stopp'd" on the enchanted isle. While players move inward to a smaller and smaller circle of place where frictional relationships must intensify or be resolved, the importance of momentary happenings explodes so that present time, now, fills space. Full time is an expression used in the biblical text to refer to the time of Christ's coming to earth to redeem humankind: "But when the fulness of the time was come, God sent forth his Son, made of a woman, made under the law" (Galatians 4:4). As pointed out in Chapter V, the master in the New Testament was characterized in the Mystery Plays by his "silence," as "blossom," and by his law of forgiveness. The New Testament master, designated in this study as the unseen master, declared his purpose: "Think not that I am come to destroy the law, or the prophets; I am not come to destroy, but to fulfil. For verily I say unto you, Till heaven and earth pass one jot or one tittle shall in no wise pass from the law, till all be fulfilled" (Matthew 5:17–18). Thus full time is associated with the law. Time and the law are filled out just as the Old Testament figures become full of meaning with the advent of the true master.

Shakespeare's specification of Miranda's age when she and Prospero were "heaved thence" (three years old) and the length of time they have been on the isle when the "ship of souls" arrives (twelve years) suggests Shakespeare is alluding to the seven ages of the world. In *Ludus Coventriae* Noah identifies with the second of the seven: "In me, Noah, the second age/ In deed beginneth as I you say/ After Adam, withouten language,/ The second father am I, in fay."[22] Both stories offer an example of the condition of man in the second age (of seven) and still part of the first age of man (of three), the time before Moses. It is the period of time to which Caliban belongs when *The Tempest* opens, for Caliban's first exposure to law takes place after Prospero's arrival on the island.

Various times in the history of man have been considered golden. Some concepts of a golden age suggest primitive societies; some, pastoral scenes. In *As You Like It* young gentlemen flock to the forest of Arden to join the banished duke and his many merry men to "fleet the time carelessly as they did in the golden world" (1.1.126–127). In Roman mythology the golden age was associated with the god of harvest, Saturn. Elements from Saturnalia, Saturn's festival, continued to be celebrated in Renaissance England. During the original festival, work ceased, gifts were exchanged, and slaves were freed to do as they pleased. It was a time of equality. The Old Testament golden age figured as the time of the reign of Solomon. Old Testament prophets, particularly Isaiah, predicted a time of peace, which has been associated by Christians with the coming of the Messiah and the establishment of his kingdom. Gonzalo, who figures Isaiah, describes the Messiah's kingdom and its surpassing of other golden ages described by man when he declares that his commonwealth will "excel the Golden Age" (2.1.164), the golden age of pagan lore.

In *As You Like It* Duke Senior calls "the seasons' difference" "the penalty of Adam" (2.1.6, 5). Levin pointed out that "to exist without seasons is to be suspended in a state of timelessness, which is humanly inconceivable except in an earthly paradise"[23]— or in C. S. Lewis' *Perelandra*! Levin called the golden age a "myth" which he regarded as "an attempt at transcending the limits of history" and concluded that "the truth is,... the golden age resides within us, like the kingdom of heaven, so far as we have any contact with either."[24] The changes take place within the characters of *The Tempest*. Timelessness or lack of cyclic time corresponds to and is eternal time. Although the play offers images of several kinds and uses of time, its prime time is not cyclic time, but golden time, the time of salvation, rescue, redemption, which restores man to a spiritual state of timelessness. On the isle, the limits of history are transcended, for the operations of earthly governments are suspended in the timeless now.

Although man can be inwardly aware of the age of gold, while earthbound he finds himself exposed to the seasons' difference. There is a sense in the Judeo-Christian tradition, associated with the rotation of the seasons, of hope for recurrence. As in the Mystery Plays, the tradition encompasses an earthly paradise, its loss, years of bondage, and a trek through a wilderness to a promised land, all of which can be interpreted in terms of the soul, as states of being. Although *The Tempest* begins in a lost paradise, there is in it bondage, a trek through a fen, and places of restoration: the sea, Prospero's circle, and the isle, which becomes paradise for Ferdinand.

The concept of recurrence of the age of gold, celebrated in the tides of the church year, is found in Edmund Sears's nineteenth-century Christmas carol "It Came Upon the Midnight Clear," which speaks of a prophesied time "when with the evercircling years/ Comes round the age of gold" and promises that "glad and golden hours/ Come swiftly on the wing." Although Sears antedates Shakespeare, he echoes earlier beliefs. This present interpretation of *The Tempest* proposes that the need for these tides in effecting change in the recalcitrant is forecast in the first scene.

Shakespeare is never so emphatic about time as in *The Tempest*. Both the name of the play, *Temp-est*, and "high-day," as well as "Zenith," suggest prime time. Although Caliban's proclamation of a "high-day" is made when he sings drunkenly, he associates high-day with the finding of a new master and with freedom from earthly chores. Even his song carries a major theme of the play and the means of resolution: finding a new master. The particular master that he has found when he sings of freedom is not a better one, for Caliban has chosen the wrong means to true freedom, i.e., strong drink and irresponsibility. Shakespeare shows the quagmire into which those negative concepts of freedom lead. Caliban's celebration, however, is an example of Shakespeare's use of antithesis in making a point in the play. It is worth noting that people in the Middle Ages freely borrowed religious music for secular songs, even songs that celebrated profane topics such as drinking.[25]

The time of restoration comes to individuals in the play through changes in their minds, allegiance, and behavior. Shakespeare invokes specific Scriptural times, events, and potentialities through the mouths and characters of Prospero, Ariel, and even Caliban.

The most used time reference in the play, "now," appears seventy-nine times. However, although the emphasis is on now, there are other time references in the play that inform, and images of others appear. Several specific times are mentioned in the play other than the time of duration of the play. One of these has already been mentioned in reference to Prospero's identity.

The significance of Miranda's age upon her arrival on the island and upon the arrival of the ship of souls has been variously interpreted. Wagner, one critic who examined some of the time references in *The Tempest*, found some of the periods of time related to historical periods in religious history rather than biblical story. She declared that Shakespeare equated a year to a hundred, giving Prospero's twelve-year period of his banishment a span of twelve centuries. Likewise, Miranda's age upon arriving at the island, "three years," represents to Wagner three centuries. For Wagner these periods of time and the time of Ariel's confinement in the cloven pine represent significant times of duration in the history of Christianity and pagan influence. Wagner begins the time periods of Prospero's recounting history with 900 B.C., when the influence of paganism began to decline — a period represented, Wagner says, by banishment of Sycorax. The first twelve-year period of Sycorax's banishment carries through to the Council of Nicaea in A.D. 325. Wagner accounts for the discrepancy of twenty to thirty years by suggesting that "the Christianity as taught and promulgated by Jesus dates not from his birth, as does supposedly the Christian era, but from his ministry, presumably about A.D. 30."[26] Wagner compared Miranda's age at the time of her banishment, century-wise, with the period before the confession formulated and decreed at Nicaea. Thus Wagner relates Miranda, who for her is "the symbol of the Christian ideal," with the early Christians and their simple adherence to the teachings, uncodified, of Jesus. Three centuries of noninstitutionalized or primitive Christianity could be represented by Miranda's age and the following twelve centuries by the period of Miranda and Prospero's banishment. Wagner's twelve-year/twelve-century period from the date of the Nicaea Council in 325 takes her to the time of the Reformation, which she believes is the subject of Shakespeare's play.[27] A better representation of Miranda than Wagner's, one which would fit her time periods, is Miranda figuring the bride of Christ, his church, who has been kept pure and undefiled. The attempts made by persons during the period of the Reformation to rid Christianity of nonessential additives whether pagan, ecclesiastical, or institutional make Wagner's association of Prospero's final time period of history consistent with the spirit of the Reformation.

Wagner's dates are consistent with her thesis, and there seems to be no doubt that certain aspects of the Reformation are evident in the play, just as the references to paganism noted and accumulated in Colin Still's work are too persistent to ignore. However, direct or indirect acknowledgment of the facts of history or the recorded experiences of man does not necessarily prove their centricity in the play. To idealize the Reformation and its pronouncements would, in the same sense as Wagner sees the Council of Nicaea doing, tend to draw attention away from the heart of Christianity, the biblical fabric, and Shakespeare's focus on divine providence, grace, and the law of forgiveness.

With the typological relationship between Prospero and Moses a different multiple of a twelve-year period can be shown to relate to other historical events. It is consistent with Shakespeare's usage to allow for multiple inferences in his references. The time of Israel's enslavement in Egypt was less than a dozen centuries; however, the length of time from the beginning of Israel's oppression by Egypt and her entrance into the promised land, Canaan, is another multiple of twelve years. That period of time was one hundred and twenty years (ten times twelve). The description of Sycorax's "age and envy/ [which] Was grown into a hoop," Ariel's servitude to Sycorax, and his imprisonment by her "a dozen years" because he refused "to act her earthy and abhorr'd commands," being "a spirit too delicate," (1.2.258–259, 279, 273, 272) suggest aspects of Israel's bondage in Egypt and continued bondage in the wilderness on the way to Canaan. The fen of the play is a miniature wilderness through which men in bondage to their own unredeemed and perverted natures pass. Sycorax's age would suggest Egypt's age. In *Antony and Cleopatra*, Cleopatra, who represents Egypt, is "wrinkled deep in time" (1.5.29). Sycorax's "envy" can also be associated with Egypt's resentment of the Israelites, whose rapid population increase occasioned the murder of newborns and the hiding of Moses in the bulrushes. The association of a multiple of a twelve-year time period with Israel's bondage relates to the master-slave and freedom themes of the play, and such an association is warranted in an interpretation where Prospero figures Moses, the deliverer of Israel and the one whose purpose, according to New Testament Scriptures, is to bring persons to the new master, the master of the law of forgiveness. The "hoop" suggesting encircling confinement corresponds to the entrapment of the spirit of the Israelites by the Egyptians who would not let them go into the wilderness (Exodus 7:16) to worship their God and to "hold a feast" (Exodus 5:1).

According to Kolve:

> the figural pattern, found at the core of all the English cycle plays, was derived from the teaching of the medieval Church Fathers and in particular from a

scheme of favorite iconographical subjects known as the seven Ages of the World. This scheme, repeatedly illustrated in stained-glass windows, stone carvings, and other mediums, depicts the first three ages of the world as the time of natural law.... The fourth and fifth ages, devoted to Moses and the prophets, are the time of written law. The sixth age, the time of grace, extends from Christ's birth to the present.[28]

Miranda came to the isle with Prospero when she was three. According to Prospero they have been on the isle twelve years. Natural law prevailed for three centuries and the written law for twelve centuries, which brings the time of the play up to the time of "grace." The play continually acknowledges its time as the present with its emphasis on "now."

One hundred and twenty is an oft-occurring number in biblical history, associated both with God's providence and God's limits on earthly chronicle. Any or all of these associations may have been in Shakespeare's mature mind. Since Shakespeare is talking about a "ship of souls" that survives a tempest, and since Iris, goddess of the rainbow, appears in the play, it may be that Shakespeare alludes to the one hundred and twenty years associated with the limit put on man's earthly years following the time eight souls were preserved in Noah's ark. The allusive density of the text is everywhere overwhelming. Even in earlier plays Armstrong traced unusual linkages in Shakespeare's thinking.

Since Shakespeare uses both expansion and closure in the play, both for time and place, there is the possibility of "a dozen years" expanding into one hundred and twenty years or into twelve centuries. Alternately, twelve years may narrow to twelve days, which along with the suggestiveness of the designation of "three men of sin" could intone for a hearing audience the twelve days associated with Epiphany, which began on Christmas Day and ended twelve days later and was associated with the coming of the Gentiles (the three wise men) to the Christ Child. The three wise men, who in response to a heavenly light journeyed on camels to bring rich gifts to a King, contrast ironically with the court party in the play, "belch'd up" by the "never surfeited sea," who are "mourning a lost son" and plotting a usurpation.

It is notable that time on the isle ends in a celebration in a cell. Prospero's cell on the isle was probably a cave; in St. Paul's aisle, the priest's cubicle. The cave may have suggested the Nativity to Shakespeare's audience, since mangers often were located in caves.

Just as Shakespeare portrays typologically the biblical story in three hours, so he portrays the three ages of man. Caliban progresses from the first to the second and promises to seek the third in three hours time. As we first see him Caliban is natural man following his instincts and responding to the delights of nature. He comes under law when he is subjected to the lawgiver-magician, the Prospero-Moses figure. Near the end of the play he announces that he will "seek for grace." Thus Shakespeare exemplifies in Caliban progress from natural man, to man under the law, to man under grace.

However, to concentrate on time past is to miss the continual emphasis Shakespeare lays upon the present. The play is rightly named tempest, not only because of the storm in the first scene, nor that within the breasts of the men of sin, but because the time of the play is the highest time in the history of Christianity. It is the highest time in the providential history of the world and the highest time in the lives of individuals. It is related to the New Testament concept of *kairos* and the time of the act of redemption as well as its fulfillment in the life of the individual, *parousia*.

Prospero's disclosure to Miranda brings him to the present and to the appearance directly above him in the sky of "a most auspicious star, whose influence/ If now I court not, but omit, my fortunes/ Will ever after droop" (1.2.182–184). These words certainly echo those of Isaiah: "Arise, shine; for thy light is come, and the glory of the Lord is risen upon thee" (60:1). Other verses in the sixtieth chapter of Isaiah describe events similar to those which take place on Prospero's isle, for "thy sons shall come from far, and thy daughters shall be nursed at thy side.... The abundance of the sea shall be converted unto thee, the forces of the Gentiles shall come unto thee" (4, 5). Prospero's son-to-be comes from far, his daughter is nursed at his side, and the "forces of the Gentiles"— the usurping duke and the king and their holy and profane escorts — come to Prospero. The ship of souls, which is purposely shipwrecked, does provide an "abundance from the sea."

Prospero's response to the star in his zenith means bringing those found on the isle to the healing ministry outlined in Isaiah for the coming Messiah: "to bind up the brokenhearted," Ferdinand: "to proclaim liberty to the captives," Trinculo, Stephano, Caliban, captives of their own appetites, and Antonio and Sebastian, captives of their own evil intentions; "to proclaim the acceptable year of the Lord," high-day, "and the day of vengeance of our God," when all will be dissolved — Prospero's doomsday; and "to comfort all that mourn," Ferdinand, Alonso, Gonzalo (61:1, 2). There are captives to be set free, mourners to be comforted, a day of vengeance to be proclaimed, and an acceptable time, *now*, declared in the play.

As Prospero says, "'Tis time." "The hour's now come;/ The very minute bids thee ope thine ear;/ Obey, and be attentive" (1.2.22, 36–38). Thus Shakespeare narrows down the time of the action of the play to *now* and emphasizes the importance of careful listening that his audiences may not miss the overtones, for Shakespeare has more to say about the time. Prospero says it is "past the mid season./ At least two glasses" (1.2.239–240). Prospero does not say how far past "the mid season" or mention the work that has not been completed when he speaks those words. Later, Prospero reminds Ariel that there is much to be done "before the time is out," or in terms of hourglass measure, by the time the sands measuring the third hour have run through the hourglass — the "time 'twixt six and now" (1.2.240). The time of the play is moving toward the time of redemption of the souls on the isle. As the sands flow through the hourglass, some of the characters have their individual times of parousia. Time is moving on in the play toward the process of redemption. There are things for Ariel to do "before the time is out," before the sands measuring the third hour have flowed through the hourglass. The time of the play and of the time represented by "six to nine" must be spent at great cost, "most preciously," for that is the time of the act of redemption. "Now from the sixth hour there was darkness over all the land unto the ninth hour. And about the ninth hour ... Jesus, when he had cried again with a loud voice, yielded up the ghost" (Matthew 27:45, 50). The time of the play's duration, during which men are normalized, corresponds in length to the duration of the suffering of Christ on the cross. There are men of sin in the play who "have turned every one to his own way; and the Lord hath laid on Him the iniquity of us all" (Isaiah 53:6), but the suffering is not futile, for the Lord's pleasant purpose will prosper, as Prospero's magic and law do in bringing persons to new awareness. Because "thou shalt make his soul an offering for sin, he shall see his seed, he shall prolong his days, and the pleasure of the Lord shall *prosper* in his hand" (Isaiah 53:10, emphasis added). It is "by his knowledge," not by man's reason, that the "righteous servant" justifies many; "for he shall bear their iniquities" (Isaiah 53:11). It is the knowledge that C.S. Lewis so aptly describes in *The Lion, the Witch and the Wardrobe* as "Deeper Magic from Before the Dawn of Time." It is the magic that operates "when a willing victim who had committed no treachery was killed in a traitor's stead." Then the "Table [of the law] would crack and Death itself would start working backwards."[29] The acceptable time for man is now: "Behold, now is the accepted time; behold, now is the day of salvation" (II Cor. 6:2). That Scripture was read at evening prayers in the English church in February.[30] The exact time in which the process of redemption takes place in the play is affirmed by the boatswain: "The best news is, that we have safely found/ Our King, and company; the next, our ship —/ Which, but three glasses since, we gave out split —/ Is tight and yare and bravely rigg'd, as when/ We first put out to sea" (5.1.220–224).

Throughout the play Shakespeare continues to use specific Scriptural times, events, and potentialities through the mouths and characters of Prospero and Ariel. As Prospero appears in his magic robes at the beginning of the last scene of the play, he is reminded by Ariel that it was "on the sixth hour" that he promised "our work should cease" (5.1.4, 5), the work of the master of the weak masters of nature and of the book of the law, whose purpose is to bring the inhabitants of the isle to the master of a new dispensation.

"'Twixt six and now" (1.2.240) involves two aspects of the time of redemption. Not only was six the hour of the crucifixion of Jesus, but *now* is the time available to the individual for his salvation. The time of redemption extends, according to Shakespeare as expressed in Prospero's words, from the time of the act of redemption to the present.

There is one time reference which seems inconsistent with the three-hour time of the play, but which in terms of Ariel as the messenger of the law is significant. It is Prospero's promise to free Ariel "after two days" (1.2.298), rather than after three hours. This would be the time of Christ's stay in the tomb, which is suggested by the sleep of the boatswain, mariners, and the ship's master, who wake to find their craft newly outfitted and afloat before Ariel is granted his freedom, for the "Son of man must be delivered into the hands of sinful men, and be crucified, and the third day rise again" (Luke 24:7). "After two days," the messenger of the law would be free, for the risen Christ made possible man's redemption, a way of escape from the justice of the law, and the holy spirit was given to do the office work of the law. Ariel's song of "liberty" suggests this when he sings of living "under the blossom that hangs on the bough" (5.1.94). As was pointed out in Chapter V, the *Ludus Coventriae* referred to Christ as the "that fair fresh flower," "flower of flowers," and "Maidenes flower." It hangs on Shakespeare's bough."[31]

Since in *The Tempest* the *now* dominates and time sequences are relegated to the abysm, the spatial elements are particularly effective. In fact time becomes spatial, absorbing all sequences into its effulgence. Thus the highest time, temp-est, assumes the spherical shape of the play's structure and absorbs all linear time, for it is the unseen master's eternal time.

Prospero's spell-stopping may be thought of as arresting the actions of men on the wheel of fortune, which represents man's experience in the world after the Fall. The Fall was, in fact, a fall from three-dimensional time (the eternal) to two-dimensional time (the temporal) of the birth-death cycle. It was a fall from eternal time and eternal life to cyclical fortune and misfortune, chance and mischance, and was brought on by man's own disobedience. The destruction of the ship carrying souls is the mischance of "the hour." Through the manifestation of the eternal in the appointed servant, the God-man, who fills full the figures which have provided an outline of him and his sacrificial obedience and forgiveness, many are made righteous, restored to normality, redeemed from fortune's cycle to become obedient or dutiful servants in this world and participants in an eternal kingdom. The cycle of man's "little life" on the surface of the earth has been changed by those who have become aware of full time to a cyclical remembrance of "time now full," through the seasons of the church year, of the rending of the veil between the eternal and the temporal. Thus it is that Shakespeare predicts, through Gonzalo in the opening scene of the play, that the untutored will be subject to "the washing of ten tides!" (1.1.57).

The purpose of spell-stopping is to round out man's little life, give it a third dimension, and bring man to awareness of the eternal. The storm in *The Tempest* is not lasting. At least it is stopped on the isle where the human family is reunited. It goes beyond the experience Marina describes in *Pericles* when she declares, "Born in a tempest when my mother died,/ This world to me is a lasting storm,/ Whirring me from my friends" (4.1.18–20). Ariel's first song predicted the end of a storm, not a lasting one, and rather than separation through tempest, the joining of hands after the tempest.

Shakespeare achieves some of the unity of the themes of the play through his references to time. It is to the "yellow sands" that the "ship of souls" has come, to the golden time of Christianity, the highest time, the time of redemption. It is a time like, but excelling, the golden age of mythology, ruled by Cronus (Saturn); it is a time of serenity, peace, and equality. Shakespeare does not look backward to a golden time in the life of primitive man, for he has buried the past in an abysm. Nor does he look forward to a mechanistic, humanistic, or rational utopia. Rather, he transposes the mythologic golden time of Saturn and plays it in the key of the master, unseen, but imaged and figured in the play.

It may appear from the mixed references in the play that place is not important, yet it does have great significance. Agreement on the specific location of the enchanted isle is as difficult for Shakespeare's audiences and readers as agreement on the isle's attributes or deficiencies is for the characters of the play upon their arrival there. For a seventeenth century audience "the Bermoothes" would have called to mind the exotic descriptions of savage and monstrous creatures purported to have been seen on explorations — creatures perhaps resembling Caliban. On the other hand, for a vessel voyaging from Naples to Milan to be blown to Bermuda would be preposterous. The isle of Capri, with its proximity to Naples and its grottos and sea caves, would provide a more likely location for the isle. We may assume either that the references prey upon the audiences' ignorance of geographical distances and provide humor for the few who were knowledgeable, or that they broaden the scope of place to include the whole earth. More likely, both assumptions are true. Shakespeare invokes multiconsciousness through indeterminacy of place, introduction of time past, and amalgamation of custom and costume, characteristics shared with the Mystery Plays. The combinations of places that occur in the play are inconsequential when one is thinking of earth as core in a hierarchy of spheres.

That the action takes place somewhere on earth, however, we can be sure, for we have a good sampling of the kinds of persons to be found on our planet. That the nature of place is dependent upon each person's experience of it is obvious from the varied descriptions. Shakespeare gives many good examples of the relationship of man's mind to his environment of which Milton wrote:

> The mind is its own place, and in itself
> Can make a Heav'n of Hell, a Hell of Heav'n.
> What matter where, if I be still the same [*Paradise Lost* I.254–256].

Gonzalo sees the isle as a kind of Eden, a place which is contrary to (contrasts with) the existing world. For him it portends to be a place where there is no labor, division, or sovereignty, and where there exists "everything advantageous to life." Miranda, who values people, sees it, upon the appearance of Alonso and Sebastian, as a "brave new world." Ferdinand sees it as a place where "so rare a wond'red father and a wise/ Makes this place Paradise" (4.1.123–24). It is in submission to a new father and acceptance of servanthood that he understands and senses the return of paradise. Antonio sees it as a stage: "We all were sea-swallow'd, though some cast again,/ And by that destiny, to perform an act" (2.1.246–247). This affirmation and his failure to repent remind us of Macbeth's view of life. Unlike Prospero and Gonzalo, whose personhoods and lives are enhanced by the historic persons they shadow, Antonio's life is but "a walking shadow, a poor player/ That struts and frets his hour upon the stage,/ And then is heard no more; it is a tale/ Told by an idiot, full of sound and fury,/ Signifying nothing" (*Macbeth* 5.5.24–28). He is not a celestial luminary, a planet in the Ptolemaic system as are Prospero and Gonzalo, but a short-lived manmade light, a "brief candle." As Shakespeare declared earlier, "All the world's a stage" (*As You Like It*: 2.7.139), and according to Prospero's vision that stage will be dissolved.

For Antonio there is no now (present). His existence is in the past and the future, like that of Macbeth. Unlike Macbeth he is spell-stopped. He is made aware of his sins by the master of the law, Prospero, but shows no signs of repentance. He is divested of his illegitimate dukedom by Alonso. Although the last words Antonio and Sebastian speak identify them as traders, Sebastian at least admitted earlier to having seen a miracle. Caliban, Stephano, and Trinculo intend to capture the king of the isle and appropriate the isle's bounty for their earthly wants. They see the isle as a means to gratify their basic instincts and their desires to control. Adrian notices that "the air breathes upon us here most sweetly" (2.1.45). He is sensitive to the pleasantness of the isle. Sebastian finds the island breathes as if it had "rotten" "lungs" and Antonio find it breathes "as 'twere perfum'd by a fen" (2.1.46–47). Their own minds pollute the air, for their minds sink to low purposes. The comments may also be associated with their location in the aisle of St. Paul's.

The truth about the isle is that although the players (and the audience) may be unaware of it, they are being acted *upon*. They eventually do come to the reign of the law of the unseen master which draws them together into the closeness of the magic circle drawn on the "yellow sands," in golden time, where the minds of some are cleared of the "fumes" of a mixed knowledge, passed on to them through Adam's partaking of the Edenic tree of the knowledge of good and evil.

Just as time expands in the play to include all time and then narrows down to now, so place, anywhere on earth, narrows down to the circle on the "yellow sands," the time of the dispensation of the true master and the individual. Shakespeare expresses this idea not only through Prospero's enclosure, the magic circle where persons are resolved, but through Miranda's words to

Ferdinand: "There's nothing ill can dwell in such a temple./ If the ill spirit have so fair a house,/ Good things will strive to dwell with't" (1.2.460–462). The dwelling place of good is further emphasized when Antonio says of "conscience," "I feel not/ This deity in my bosom" (2.1.272–273).

However the island appears to those who arrive there, whether "lush" or desert-like, it is a place apart from "the cloud-capp'd towers, the gorgeous palaces,/ The solemn temples" (4.1.152–153) which man has built. The structures (pagan temples, prison towers and palaces) of men and even the intents of those who control them vanish on this isle just as surely as Prospero claims those of "the great Globe" will. Its only place of refuge seems to be a cell or cave, a natural formation. The isle is a place where some men come to their proper selves through the clearing of their minds.

The chapter in Hebrews that names heroes of the faith describes Moses at greater length than any of the other Old Testament characters. It mentions that the heroes "wandered in ... dens and caves of the earth" (11:23–29). (It is interesting to note that neither the Mystery Plays nor Shakespeare follows the selectivity of that chapter.)

The emphasis that Shakespeare placed on the mind in this play and that Milton placed on knowledge in his final trilogy, *Paradise Lost*, *Paradise Regained*, and *Samson Agonistes*, is not amiss, for the Genesis tree was not hung with either apples or phallic symbols, nor was the immediate consequence of man's imbibing the forbidden fruit gastrointestinal disorders or sexual perversion, but the distortion of the mind. The result of man's eating the fruit of the "forbidden tree" was a mixed knowledge, the "knowledge of good and evil." In zeroing in on man's reason, then, Shakespeare is not, as Wagner suggested,[32] ratifying the new scientific knowledge (whose emphasis on reason has led to the fragmented vision), but focusing on the healing of the mind of man which had been polluted in the Fall. Man who until his disobedience had only partaken of the knowledge of good, thereafter knew both good and evil. As Prospero observes the men within the magic circle, the fumes clear, and man's mind rises from its grave. The "understanding" of each man within the circle "begins to swell; and the approaching tide/... shortly fill[s] the reasonable shore,/ That now lies foul and muddy" (5.1.79, 81–82). The use of tide could be a pun, referencing the time of shriving and cleansing, the Lenten season of the church year.

Whereas the now of the play explodes into time now full, for the characters it narrows to a moment. The play narrows in on the place in the wheel of fortune where each man is found, and upon his faults. As the players move inward to a smaller and smaller circle of place, their bad relationships must intensify or be resolved. Misfortune or mischance becomes the occasion for chance, the operation of grace in man's life. Prospero expresses the closure of time with "the very hour, the minute bid thee." Thus time diminishes in circumference along with place so that it is no longer three hours, but now. In earlier plays lost and found involved the restoration of human relationships through the intersection of the linear times of two or more persons. The meeting place in *The Tempest* is circular, the projection on earth of heaven's sphere.

In *The Tempest* some persons not only are restored to one another and find the identity of the others, but find their own identities in relationship to the universal times now and the sixth hour as exemplified in Prospero's submission to the law of forgiveness of the new master. According to the Mystery Plays, the type of response each makes determines the destination that will be prescribed for him on doomsday.

Since the arrival of the ship at the island, no one has carried out a treacherous deed. To be sure, the men have behaved ridiculously and spoken foolishly, but the real treachery was in their minds, the evil intent in their hearts and their wills. The men, who are brought to awareness of their sin through the law and its messenger, will differently. Stephano, who would seize control of the island and be god on it, chooses now to "shift for all the rest, and let no man take care for himself" (5.1.256–257). He is given the task of decorating another master's cell. Sebastian, who has appropriated the "glistering apparel," acknowledges he has stolen it. Alonso, like Egeus in *A Midsummer Night's Dream*, not only attempted to force his daughter to perform his bidding in accepting marriage against her will, but he did enforce her marriage. Alonso would not be "importun'd otherwise,"/ even by "the fair soul herself," who "weigh'd, between loathness and obedience, at/ Which end o' th' beam should bow." (2.1.124–127). Claribel was forced to perform Alonso's bidding in marriage. *Now*, however, Alonso has a vision of the equality of man and woman when he observes Ferdinand and Miranda at chess, and he sees a young lady who not only has chosen for herself, but who proposed to her lover. The relationship between the chess game and equality was established in Chapter VIII. In contrast to Alonso and to Egeus in *A Midsummer Night's Dream*, Prospero uses his fatherly authority to instruct and to ensure responsibility and appreciation. For Alonso, the sight of Miranda and Ferdinand at chess has the quality of a vision in that it is a revelation involving, for him, the resurrection of a son as well as the concept of the equality of men and women. But the game of chess intones more than that. This couple move kings and queens, around symbolizing the authority which encompasses all earthly authority. In figuring Christ, Ferdinand is seen as the mover of earthly kings in the chess game, along with Miranda who figures Mary. Armstrong's linking and Burgess's proposal that Shakespeare had so absorbed Scripture that he "breathed" it into his work are manifest here, for Ferdinand, who figures Christ, appears imagistically in the chess game as "the prince of the kings of the earth" (Rev. 1:5).

Within Prospero's magic circle on the isle another sphere exists. It is the soul of a man who arrived on the ship. Thus Shakespeare moves through the all-encompassing spheres of the heavens to the sphere of the soul, the sphere changed in the beginning by the breath of God from dust of the earth to a living soul. In *The Tempest* that soul, the seat of the rational, emotional, and volitional faculties of man is "rounded out," made whole. The prime awakening of the play takes place in man's mind. When it is defumed, he can see clearly his own shortcomings and is free to acknowledge his fault, make restitution and accept a new master. As Gonzalo declares, "in one voyage … [we]/ Did … find … all of us ourselves" (5.1.208–212). It is as Vyvyan says: "Shakespeare pictures the soul as a kingdom (potentially the kingdom of heaven) wherein man's true self should be enthroned."[33] Eternal or providential time in *The Tempest* is represented by nested spheres whose core sphere is now; that is *when* the change takes place. Space or place is represented by nested spheres whose core is the soul of man; that is *where* the change takes place.

It is on the golden time of Christianity, the time of redemption of man from the Fall, that Shakespeare focuses; it is that time to which he brings the "ship of souls." But there are disturbances brought by men to this golden time, and they must be resolved before reconciliation and perfect harmony can be restored and the "split" in the human family mended. The sounds of Caliban and his confederates do not harmonize with the vision of providence; rather they produce the "beating" associated with unsynchronized vibrations. It is an example in musical terms of "time out of joint." The difference in beat between Caliban's "our time" and that of the unseen master must be "resolved." Time must be synchronized with the eternal. Man must "lose" his time. On the other hand, he must assume his proper place as do the characters in the play. Caliban must accept his place under the law, which is his schoolmaster. Prospero, as the Moses figure, must submit to a greater master, and as a man, he must return to rule as the proper duke of Milan.

The isle is a place away from civilization, from the rule and misrule of men, where king and duke alike are subject to powers outside their realm, for the isle is ruled by heavenly spheres, whether of law, prophecy, or grace. It is a place where political authority is subordinated to spiritual authority. Man's cyclic or fortunate time is swallowed up in the eternal now. Civilizations with their institutions, their appointed authorities, and their manmade towers and castles — strongholds of man's rule — dissolve in a sense on the island just as they do in the vision. Passions and inward storms fade before law and divine grace. As Sypher points out, the "task of redeeming time is in many plays deeply related to the dilemma of reconciling the moral and political orders, and with taking arms against a sea of troubles."[34] On the enchanted isle men escape from the dominance of political order and are engulfed by eternal providence and a spell.

Chapter XI

Beyond This "Little Life": A Vision

The Tempest is true to its sources, the Bible, the Mystery Plays and the 1959 *Book of Common Prayer*. Shakespeare did not, as in other plays, revise his sources to emphasize different values and create new meanings. Using his sources, Shakespeare orchestrated a symphony and wove a complex fabric, portraying the follies, fears, and hope of humanity in a vision of providence. *The Tempest* vision is not "baseless" like the vision Prospero grants Ferdinand and Miranda. It reaches beyond this "little life" to the stars. It must be heard and felt, for it is not "a series of messages" but "a series of impulses that can produce many understandings."[1] It sets up resonances, which have not ceased to intone new relationships with Scripture and new levels of meaning.

In spite of its brevity, *The Tempest* portrays the history of all humankind and presents the providential solution to the "mischance of the hour," whether that "mischance" is political, conspiratorial, ecclesiastical, familial, or personal. Shakespeare separates the ship of souls from its everyday worlds, exposing its passengers to eternal verities. However, he does not take away the souls' knowledge of their worlds or free them from their commitment to responsible behavior in religion, government, and family relationship.

The Tempest is overwhelmingly expansive and inclusive. It not only takes into account the status of Christianity in the world in Shakespeare's day, but also gives it in its historical perspective, including its Judaistic beginnings, its absorption of paganism, and in its deeper roots of "In the beginning God" of Genesis. It sorts out the simplicity of the truth amidst the many misconceptions about Christianity and the movements toward ecclesiasticism and reform in the institutions arising out of or around persons who claim to be committed to Christianity. Shakespeare handles the massive amount of material and detail by sounding certain fundamentals, depicting scenes with biblical correspondences (and differences), engaging old and new concepts of the heavens, displaying nature and magic, figuring characters, and playing on word meanings.

Shakespeare's chief concern was not with the church, although he does not ignore its rites and rituals. Neither is his chief concern with kings, as in the histories and tragedies, although a king is among those rescued by an enchantment and a banished duke regains his dukedom. Nor is his chief concern with the follies of humankind, though he parades them. Shakespeare is concerned with the means to peace and freedom for "fraughting souls" (1.2.13) and distorted minds in their predicament which is common to all humankind. "The King and Prince [are seen] at prayers!... our case is as theirs" (1.1.53–54). Even a king must ask a son's forgiveness. In the end Prospero, too, must bow to a greater law than his, which includes the forgiveness of enemies, and to a greater master, one who "took upon him[self] the form of a servant" (Phil. 2:7), who could renew the mind of man, and save a ship of souls from eternal disaster. "Shakespeare's genius illuminated human life. In the broadest sense he wrote neither comedy nor tragedy, but interpreted men and women whose dealings with earth and time resulted in one or other or both."[2] Shakespeare deals with the specific frame of the individual mind of those who come to an isle (aisle)—Prospero's, the Globe's, and that of the English church. He reveals that a mastership that exceeds human authority is needed.

As pointed out in Chapter I, although Shakespeare incorporates gods and goddesses in his drama, he does not prescribe pagan rites as a means to peace for errant souls. Even Alonso, who according to Colin Still experiences the initiating experiences of the elements, declares "there is in this business more than nature/ Was ever conduct of: some oracle/ Must rectify our knowledge" (5.1.243–245). Nor are the gods and goddesses of the corollary able to arrest the threat of such as Caliban. Prospero uses the elements of nature to get the attention of the "fraughting souls," but the elements of nature are insufficient in bringing relief to humankind. They are only tools to make humans aware of their predicament, as Prospero attests when he drowns his magic book and his staff.

Although Prospero uses a tempest to get the attention of the souls aboard the ship and to bring them to their senses and to their need for an effective master, one of the purposes of the play as stated in the first scene is "to command these elements to silence." The wayward men experience the ineffectiveness of the "elements,/ Of whom ... [their] swords are temper'd" (3.3.61–62) against the greater power represented by Prospero, the lawgiver, and his helper, Ariel, the spirit and messenger of the law. In the "ye elves" speech Prospero acknowledges that the representatives of the elements of nature are weak. Whether the elements exist as fire, water, or earth (Caliban) or in the inventions of man (swords) or as creatures of nature ("elves," "demi-puppets," and "printless" footed ones), Shakespeare finds them limited. Nor is the law sufficient in meeting all human needs.

Shakespeare uses superlatives in the mouth of Gonzalo to indicate the transcendence of Christianity over magic, pagan rites, and Moses' law and subordinates all human authorities to the master whose law of forgiveness makes possible reconciliation of members of the human race. Gonzalo identifies the unseen master's reign as one "t'excel the golden age." He summons those gathered at Prospero's circle to "rejoice/Beyond a common joy! and set it down/ With gold on lasting pillars" (5.1.206–208) that the prince, considered drowned, is alive, has found his bride (with her typological implications), and "all" have found themselves "when no man was his own" (5.1.213).

After the history plays with their hegemonic problems, the comedies sporting the follies, limitations and misunderstandings of human beings, and the tragedies with the awfulness of sin, *The Tempest* provides a resolution to the human dilemma. Humankind is not left uncared for and unprotected, on one of many swirling planets in an uncentered and rationalized universe. Rather, they are encircled by providential spheres where individuals are the focus of divine grace. Although still under the law, learning the nature of sin and the way to community, they can celebrate, decorate the cell, and find hope in "a most high miracle." The magical is o'ertopped by mystery, the law by grace, the kings of earth by the prince of peace, and the crowns of earth's kings by a "blessed crown."

Hankins wrote of Shakespeare, "His weariness of strife and hypocrisy, his longing for peace and simplicity, reflect the perennial desire of all mankind found in an even greater message: 'Peace on earth, good will toward men.'"[3] Hankins' assertion of peace and good will is compatible with the present interpretation, which takes the stance that *The Tempest* is, in fact, a dramatic presentation of the Gospel. However, this author does *not* find *The Tempest* an expression of "weariness," but a vision of eternal provision for man amidst tragedy and woe and an affirmation of faith and hope for humankind, whether the human is an untutored Caliban, a once unrelenting king, an ardent reformer, or a human being "rapt in secret studies." It is Shakespeare's answer to the problems of the city's institutions examined in *Measure for Measure*, the problems arising out of imperfect authority in the history plays, and the means to reuniting the family of man. It is the "way" Shakespeare has "chalk'd forth" to the "peace of the present," both for England and for whoever watches or reads *The Tempest*. It is a way of good cheer.

Bethell noted, "It is significant that in the last fully Shakespearean play the planes of reality appear with the most complexity." He cites Tillyard's observation: "'On the actual stage, ... the masque is executed by players pretending to be spirits, pretending to be real actors, pretending to be supposed goddesses and rustics.'"[4] The structure of the play is reinforced by the repetition of its pattern. A group of concentric circles comparable to those of the spheres could be drawn for the arrangement of the actors. Likewise, a series of concentric spheres representing various spells could be drawn. The sense of "coil" persists in all aspects of the structure of the play.

Prospero's spell is not the only one in the play. At first the audience is only made aware of the spells Prospero casts, but as Prospero says in the Epilogue, he has been held on the "bare island" by the audience's spell. The innermost circle in the design would represent the spell of the corollary, which enthralls Ferdinand. Next in circumference would be Prospero's spell-stopping; the next, Shakespeare's; the next, the audience's; and beyond that is God's spell, the Gospel. One of the early spellings of gospel was "Godspell." Shakespeare's audiences' association of the use of "spell" in the play with God's spell would be more immediate than ours. The magical spells in *The Tempest* and the vision of provision in the corollary are o'ertopped by God's spell and eternal providence.

In another sense, the audience has been "spell-stopp'd" by Shakespeare's presentation of the play. The audience, too, has stopped its "chronicle of day by day" while under Shakespeare's enchantment. The high points of that enchantment do not coincide with the central or reasonable part of the play, but are experienced in the emotional turning points of *The Tempest*: the dissolution and "ye elves" speeches.

Whereas Prospero's spells close in on the individual characters, identifying their faults and bringing a new awakening, the speeches expand to the periphery of the play, pointing to man's larger life, "immortal providence" (5.1.189), and "a most high miracle" (5.1.177). They have seldom been correlated with an expanded and eternal vision. The dissolution speech has been associated with the end of man's existence, and the "ye elves" speech with an abandonment of the supernatural and a return to the mundane. The dissolution speech was particularly à propos for Shakespeare's sixteenth century audience, for they had already experienced a heavenly dissolution, the dissolution of the crystal spheres inhabited by a hierarchy of gods and goddesses or angels. Not only had there been a dissolution, but the earth had been moved out of its central place. Shakespeare made it central again, though not as the physical center of a dissolving universe; instead, he placed the earth and its inhabitants in the center of an eternal providence.

> The cloud-capp'd towers, the gorgeous palaces,
> The solemn temples, the great globe itself,
> Yea, all which it inherit, shall dissolve,
> And, like this insubstantial pageant faded,
> Leave not a rack behind. We are such stuff
> As dreams are made on; and our little life
> Is rounded with a sleep [4.1.152–158].

Bethell noted, "The solidity of the first plane of reality, the plane of our terrestrial life, is seen to be illusory."[5] In the words of one who is at the "core" of humanity, caught in the coils of celestial providence, Bottom: "The eye of man hath not heard, the ear of man hath not seen, man's hand is not able to taste, his tongue to conceive, nor his heart to report, what my dream was" (*A Midsummer Night's Dream* 4.1.207–210).[6] There is more for humankind than a "little life/ ... rounded with a sleep" (4.1.157–158). Bottom's dream has "no bottom," but he "will sing it in the latter end of a play." Likewise Prospero's vision of dissolution has no base part, for it penetrates the clouds that shroud earth's highest towers, and outshines earth's richest palaces. In the interpretation of the "dissolution," Shakespeare's audiences may choose to align themselves with Sebastian's early stance of "no hope," or with his later declaration of "a most high miracle." In *The Tempest*, it is not a fairy's love as in *A Midsummer Night's Dream*, but in a love "that neither death, nor life, nor angels, nor principalities, nor powers, nor things present, nor things to come, nor height, nor depth, nor any other creature, shall be able to separate us from" (Romans 8:38, 39). Humans may attempt to live by tactics — plotting in measured time — and fantasy; or they may choose to live by belief and vision, something greater than the self, and commit to prayer and duty, as Prospero does in the Epilogue.

A careful analysis of the "ye elves" speech reveals, both by Prospero's call for solemn music and by inference, a substitution of one kind of supernatural for another — not an abandonment of the supernatural as critics have read into Prospero's resumption of his dukedom. In his speech Prospero "abjures" as rough magic "demi-puppets," figures who are intermediate in size and themselves not autonomous, but representational subjects of another; "elves," tiny creatures with magical powers; and those "with printless foot." With their dismissal one might expect the wonder to depart. But in their places he finds necessary "some heavenly music," the music of the spheres, played in a providential key.

Prospero not only acknowledges his dual responsibilities as he heads back to Milan, but prepares for them. He dons a hat and takes a rapier, a pointed two-edged sword. The hat and rapier he takes symbolize not only the office of duke, but his equipment to carry on under his new master: "For the word of God is quick, and powerful, and sharper than any two-edged sword ... and is a discerner of the thoughts and intents of the heart" (Hebrews 4:12). Prospero, who has abandoned the elements and creatures of nature, now takes "the helmet of salvation and the sword of the spirit" (Ephesians 6:17). He is not just ducally equipped for earth's tasks, but takes on the dual role as a New Testament figure just as he performed a dual role as an Old Testament figure. He will be "praying always ... and ... mak[ing] known the mystery of the gospel" (Ephesians 6:18–19). The apparent return to the mundane is, instead, evidence of the humility of one who has accepted the task of bringing children (Caliban) "up in the nurture and admonition of the Lord" (Ephesians 6:4) and in recognizing the equality of servants and masters under the master in heaven.

In the vision of the corollary Ferdinand experiences an epiphany: "So rare a wonder'd father and a wise/ Makes this place Paradise" (4.1.123–124). Those who read or hear Prospero's "ye elves" speech also may experience an epiphany, centered around the mystical "printless." It radiates energy and is fringed with joy. Printless is defined as leaving no print or trace, having no symbolic mark. Its opposite, print, means "an image or character stamped upon the mind or soul, especially the divine likeness."[7] Neither Caliban nor the fantastic creatures of nature bear the mark of any aspect of divinity. Nor do the magical creatures leave any permanent mark on the sands of time, for their feet are "printless." But the unseen master bears the image of divine likeness, and his feet bear the mark of the print of the nails.

Just before Prospero's "ye elves" speech, Ariel says it is "the sixth hour; at which time, my lord,/ You said our work should cease" (5.1.4, 5). "Now from the sixth hour there was darkness over all the land unto the ninth hour" (Matthew 27:45), the time of the crucifixion. The redemptive sacrifice began at the sixth hour. Prospero, as one who figures Moses, surrenders his reign of law and magic to the master of the third age of man. The supernatural no longer resides in weak masters but in the power of one who has the imprint of the divine nature and who bears the print of the nails in his feet. It is he whose sacrifice brings freedom from bondage, renewed minds, joy "beyond a common joy," and hope of immortality, for "as we have borne the image of the earthly, we shall also bear the image of the heavenly" (I Cor. 15:49).

The play's circularity, believed to be perfection of shape, provides complete provision for humanity. Its numeration, three, believed to be a perfect number, references full time, the time of third man: "This/ Is the third man that e'er I [Miranda] saw" (1.2.447–448); "This man is a thing divine; for nothing natural/ I ever saw so noble" (1.2.421). Is Prospero, as one who figures Moses, not surrendering his reign of law and magic, to the "third man," to receive "power," not from fantastic creatures, but from on high by yielding to the "most auspicious star"?

The supernatural in *The Tempest* is beneficial. It does not entice or threaten man's welfare, nor does it have the tincture of the occult found in *Hamlet* and *Macbeth*. Prospero's magic is harmless. It progresses from white magic, which arrests the actions of the errant; to law, which brings awareness of sin; to grace, which provides forgiveness and restoration. It moves from magic to miracle, from Prospero's spell to God's spell (Gospel), from letter to syllable, from law to grace, from "a chronicle of day by day" (5.1.163) to time now full. The law has not been abolished, but it has been softened. The word of God, too, has been filled out. It has expanded from the consonants with points to the complete word.

In the first scene of the play an effective authority in the storm is being sought, a master of the storm. There is a need for the absolute. It is not to be found in the duke of Milan, "Absolute Milan" (1.2.109), or even in Prospero as schoolmaster or magician. In the presence of "mad" men, who would be "as gods," who would take the life of another to gain authority, Shakespeare points to the servanthood of the master who has "chalk'd out the way." In *The Tempest* Shakespeare gives the answer to the tragic vision of fallen man, who rather than "shift[ing] for all the rest" has taken "care for himself" (5.1.256, 257), and assumed "what to come,/ In yours and my discharge" (2.1.248, 249), and thus has fallen onto the wheel of fortune, and lost the eternal dimension.

The real master of *The Tempest* is not found amongst the men in the play who are masters or who pretend to mastery. The real master, although he is figured in the characters and the imagery of the play, is exalted and invisible. Prospero's affirmation answers the question asked in the first scene, "Where's the master?" Prospero, too, needs to submit to a higher power, symbolized early in the play by "a most auspicious star" (1.2.182), whose gentleness is symbolized in a "blossom," and whose body, though once broken, like "a royal, good, and gallant ship" serves to bring souls home. In *The Tempest* Shakespeare gives the answer to the problems of royalty described in the history plays and the griefs and splits in the human family arising from errant behavior in the problem plays and the tragedies. Shakespeare's answer is not in relying on the little folk of nature, elves and demi-puppets, nor in the control of nature by magicians' spells, but in eternal providence, the sword of the spirit and God's spell (the Gospel), subsequent prayer and frequent thought ("every third"—a perfect number) for one's office and earthly responsibilities.

In the comedies, histories, tragedies, problem plays, and early romances some kind of restoration takes place. In *The Tempest* a particular kind of restoration takes place. The "high-day" of freedom for the entire human race is celebrated. It is not, as in Macbeth, achieved through the sword and movement of nature with the coming of Birnam Wood to Dunsinane (5.5.44–45). In *The Tempest* kings and kingdoms are merely objects on a chess board to be moved around at will by the true prince and only Son and his bride, whom the Bible designates as the church, which may be read as the true followers of the Master, since according to this play and historical accounts, various unbelievers and desperate characters could be found in cathedral aisles in Shakespeare's day.

Shakespeare may have been playing the part of Prospero, as some interpreters have conjectured, and this may have been Shakespeare's way of departing as an actor and spell-maker. Chambers found "it impossible to doubt that in the famous address to the 'elves of hills, brooks, standing lakes, and groves,'" when Prospero "finally abjures his rough magic, breaks his staff, and drowns his book, Shakespeare is really making his own farewell to the stage and to the arts by which he has exercised a dominion even more elemental than that of enchanter."[8] Chambers goes as far as associating Milan with Stratford: "And so it is hinted that at the end of the play the insubstantial pageant of the great

Shakespearean drama shall fade for ever. Ariel shall have his freedom, and Prospero shall betake himself to the dukedom of Milan — which is Stratford."[9] But Chambers does not tell us what kind of a dukedom Shakespeare returned to in Stratford.

Chambers is one of those referred to in the Introduction to this study — those who associate Shakespeare's leaving the theatre with Prospero's abandoning his magic and returning to Milan as duke — as having failed to identify Shakespeare's dukedom. All agree that Shakespeare returned to his Milan (Stratford), and that after five years he died and was buried in the chancel of Holy Trinity Church. In his will he commended his "Soule into the handes of god my Creator, hoping & assuredlie beleeving through thonelie merittes of Jesus Christe my Saviour to be made partaker of lyfe everlastinge."[10] The questions persist: With what did he occupy the last five years of his life? Why, as a dramatist, was he buried in the chancel rather than the churchyard of Holy Trinity? The answers are not to be found in print. However, during a visit to Holy Trinity Church, this author was informed that for the last five years of his life, Shakespeare was a lay rector in Holy Trinity Church. This is the highest time in Shakespeare's life, the peak of his career as artist-magician, the weaver of spells. Like Prospero he drowns his book and breaks his rod. After having dramatized a mystery, may he not, like the duke of Milan, have taken his rapier, and wielded it as lay rector in Holy Trinity Church in Stratford-on-Avon? At any rate, as he wished, Shakespeare's dust and bones lie undisturbed in the earth within Holy Trinity Church at the center of the providential cluster of the spheres, where solemn music can be heard and songs about the "blossom that hangs on the bough" are sung.

There is comfort in *The Tempest* and "the best comforter," "a solemn air" (5.1.58). Shakespeare put humanity back at the core, not of a physical system, but of a spiritual plan. Today, with the concept of the universe expanded to include a million galaxies and powerful black holes (distanced enough not to appear as a threat to our security), it is difficult to understand a Copernican threat; but for seventeenth century audiences, who had been threatened by scientific discovery, it must have been consoling to be reminded that they were the focus of an eternal providence.

Shakespeare diminished the earthly threat as well as the celestial. There are earthly masters — a ship's and a commonwealth's — and kings, but the prince, as chess-player, moves the kings of earth around in a limited space, controlling their action. The kings of the earth are mere pieces on a chess board, being moved by a prince who has been resurrected from the "ooze." He is the prince of the peace that ensues, the one who has the power to unite the company that was "split."

On the stage where dramatists were forbidden to use the name of Christ, Shakespeare offered images of the Redeemer. In one last substantiation of his interpretation, the prophet Gonzalo calls for rejoicing using another symbol:

"O rejoice/ Beyond a common joy! and set it down/ With gold on lasting pillars" (5.1.206–208). In Shakespeare's time, "a portable pillar [was] borne as an ensign of dignity of office."[11] It also meant "a whipping-post" and was referred to in 1580 as "the pillar of repentance."[12] But more significant in this interpretation is a reference to the "*pillar of flagellation*, that to which Christ was supposed to have been bound when scourged; hence, 'the pillar' was one of the Symbols of the Passion." The Flagellation is associated with the Passion-Flower.[13] The ensign of office ascribed to by Gonzalo is lasting and is inscribed in gold. It represents a master who took upon himself the form of a servant." The "pillar" is a final reminder of the unseen master who gives a reason for rejoicing in the freedom he brings.

Although the parallels of the "corollary" and the main plot evince providence working in both Greek and Judaic cultures, through Prospero's recognition of the "roughness" of his magic Shakespeare subordinates both traditions, which he also reconciles in a tradition that excels the others. Thus through both Prospero's "abjuration" and Gonzalo's "excelling," Shakespeare orders authority. The elements of nature, magic, destiny, the vengeful law, and the Saturnine golden age have been superseded by Godspell. Shakespeare does not abandon the supernatural, nor does he abandon man to the limitations of scientific reason. Rather he supersedes both white and black magic and the vengeance of the law, and presents a vision of virtue, grace, and eternal providence, which culminates in the mystical sacrifice of love and the resurrection of a Son "bedded in the ooze," so that one who at the outset "swear'st grace o'erboard" now reports "the best news" (4.1.219, 221), the good news of God's spell. At the end of the play Shakespeare leaves Ariel and the audience "*Under the blossom that hangs on the bough*" (5.1.94).

Collier wrote that

> the Corpus Christi drama, imitating the Scriptures, dramatizes the action of God. Its scope is all of time, its setting is the universe of heaven, earth, hell. Its focus is an event which joins time with eternity, the world with heaven, and men with God. Necessarily, then, the audience and its present moment are understood as being as much a part of the action of the plays as are the historical characters and events actually depicted. The drama aims above all at making this understanding explicit. Every aspect of these plays — staging, plotting, characterization, music, and poetry — works to reveal the action of God and to persuade the audience to believe in and conform themselves to that action. The Corpus Christi drama, in bringing man and God together, imitates the Incarnation it also celebrates.[14]

The Tempest, too, can be said to imitate the Scriptures. Its scope is all time and its setting the universe. Its dual focus, like the Corpus Christi drama, is on an event which joins time and eternity, which extends from "the sixth hour" to "now," and on the occupants of the isle — the Globe's aisle and Prospero's isle — who have representatives from varying places on earth (England,

Egypt, the Sinai Plain, Bermoothes, Milan, Naples, Nicaea) and various times (Old Testament, early Christian, and the seventeenth century). If this is Shakespeare's mystery play, its purpose, too, would be "to persuade the audience to believe in and conform themselves to" the action of God.[15] In what more likely place in Stratford could Shakespeare continue serving with that purpose in mind than in Holy Trinity Church as lay rector?

As Coleman wrote, Shakespeare was "a purveyor of heavenly light."[16] We might add heavenly *lights*, lives lighted by heaven. *The Tempest* moves from shadow to light, from a scientific rational cosmos to a providential cosmos, from an outgrown model of the universe to a provisional model, from nature to law, from law to grace, from "a chronicle of day by day" (5.1.163) to full time, from a shipwreck to a "ship —/…tight and yare and bravely rigg'd" (5.1.222, 224), from "no hope" to "a most high miracle," from bondage to freedom, from magic to mystery, from "printless foot" to one bearing the print of the nails, from a magician's spell to Godspell, from woe to comfort, from romance to mystical love, from law and vengeance to mercy and forgiveness, from the letter of the law to the spirit of the law, from roots to the "blossom," from the natural and fantastic to the supranatural, from the follies of fallen men to celebration in and around a "cell," from the hegemonic problems of the histories and their kings to "the Prince of Paradise," from evils of the tragedies (beyond Birnam wood) to "lasting pillars," from a "golden age" to that which is set … down/ With gold" on those pillars (5.1.207, 208), from several Old Testament masters to one New Testament master, from tempest to peace, from "weak masters" to the prince of the kings of earth, from beating minds to harmony, from a baseless fabric to reality.

Margaret Lucy, in her investigation into Shakespeare's use of the supernatural, concludes of *The Tempest*, "This play, perhaps more than most of Shakespeare's, possesses the gift of baffling all inquiry. Its meaning is there, but what? and where? He who read the secrets of the stars, had knowledge which has foiled the deepest searching of generation after generation."[17] Although Shakespeare, like Job, was not there when the Lord "laid the foundations of the earth … [and] the morning stars sang together" (Job 38:4, 7), his "reading" of provision in the stars amounts to a great symphony.

This overall unifying image and interpretation of *The Tempest*, like "anybody's personal view of the play is bound to be less than the play itself."[18] Nevertheless, the author hopes this study has uncovered some of the depths of Shakespeare's knowledge, helped in deciphering some of the "marks" of Shakespeare's "own way of seeing life,"[19] untangled the "enormous skein of interrelated words"[20] that make up the play's fabric, and harmonized some of the resonances intoned by specific notes that are played.

Notes

Introduction

1. Maurice Hunt, *Shakespeare's Labored Art, Stir, Work, and the Late Plays*, vol. 3 of *Studies in Shakespeare*, Robert F. Willson, Jr., general ed. (New York: Peter Lang, 1995), 272.

2. Beverly Warner, ed., *Famous Introductions to Shakespeare's Plays by the Notable Editors of the Eighteenth Century* (New York: Burt Franklin, 1968; reprint of 1906 ed.), 231, 251.

3. S. L. Bethell, *Essays on Literary Criticism and the English Tradition* (London: Dennis Dobson, 1948), 16.

4. S. T. Coleridge, "An Analysis of Act I (1811)," in *Shakespeare: The Tempest: A Casebook*, ed. by D. J. Palmer (London: Macmillan, 1968), 54.

5. John Russell Brown, *Discovering Shakespeare: A New Guide to the Plays* (New York: Columbia University Press, 1981), 3.

6. Warner, xxvii.

7. Bethell, 16.

8. Ann Barton Righter, "Introduction," to *William Shakespeare: "The Tempest"* (Middlesex, England: Penguin, 1968), 14.

9. S. L. Bethell, *Shakespeare and the Popular Dramatic Tradition* (Durham, North Carolina: Duke University Press, 1944), 26.

10. Bethell, *Literary Criticism*, 16.

11. Bethell, *Popular Dramatic Tradition*, 142.

12. Warner, xxii.

13. Richmond Noble, *Shakespeare's Biblical Knowledge and Use of the Book of Common Prayer as Exemplified in the Plays of the First Folio* (Folcroft, Pennsylvania: Folcroft, 1935, reprinted 1969), 249–251.

14. Hamilton Coleman, *Shakespeare and the Bible* (Folcroft, Pennsylvania: Folcroft, 1955, reprinted 1969), vi.

15. Coleman, 1–43.

16. Wilson, 6.

17. William Burgess, *The Bible in Shakespeare: A Study of the Relation of the Works of William Shakespeare to the Bible* (New York: Haskell House, 1968).

18. Northrop Frye, *The Myth of Deliverance: Reflections on Shakespeare's Problem Comedies* (Toronto: University of Toronto Press, 1983), 25.

19. Alan C. Dessen in Edward Pechter, ed., *Textual and Theatrical Shakespeare: Questions of Evidence* (Iowa City: Iowa University Press, 1996), 45.

20. Terence Hawkes, *Meaning of Shakespeare* (London and New York: Routledge, 1992), 3.

21. Hawkes, 3.

22. Dessen, 2.

23. Wilson, 1–2.

24. Jean I. Marsden, *The Re-Imagined Text: Shakespeare, Adaptation, and Eighteenth-Century Literary Theory* (Lexington: University Press of Kentucky, 1995), 154.

25. G. Wilson Knight, *The Wheel of Fire: Essays in Interpretation of Shakespeare's Sombre Tragedies* (Oxford: Oxford University Press, 1930), 3.

26. Stephen Greenblatt, *Shakespearean Negotiations: The Circulation of Social Energy in Renaissance England* (Berkeley: University of California Press, 1988) 4.

27. E. K. Chambers, *Shakespeare: A Survey* (New York: A Dramabook, n.d.), 9.

28. Cumberland Clark, *Shakespeare and the Supernatural* (London: Williams & Norgate, 1931 reprint; Folcroft Library Editions, 1972), 105.

29. Clark, 105.

30. Righter, 15.

Chapter I

1. Francis Griffin Stokes, *A Dictionary of the Characters and Proper Names in the Works of Shakespeare with Notes on the Sources and Dates of the Plays and Poems* (London: George G. Harrap & Co., 1924), 10, 294; J. M. Nosworthy, "The Narrative Sources of *The Tempest*," *Review of English Studies* XXIV (1948): 281–294, esp. 282–283.

2. Stefan Zweig, *Conqueror of the Seas: The Story of Magellan*, trans. by Eden and Cedar Paul, (New York: Viking, 1938), 193–195.

3. Nosworthy, 286; Frank Kermode, in his Introduction to *The Tempest* by William Shakespeare (Arden Shakespeare Series [Cambridge: Harvard University Press, 1958]), xxvi, xxvii.

4. Kermode, in his Appendices to *The Tempest* by William Shakespeare (Arden Shakespeare Series [Cambridge: Harvard University Press, 1958]), 145.

5. Paul Brown, "'This Thing of Darkness I Acknowledge Mine': *The Tempest* and the Discourse of Colonialism," in Jonathan Dollimore and Alan Sinfield, eds., *Political Shakespeare: New Essays in Cultural Materialism*, 2d ed. (Ithaca: Cornell University Press, 1994), 48–71.

6. Peter Brook, quoted in Richard Wilson, and Richard Dutton, eds., *New Historicism and Renaissance Drama* (London: Longman, 1992), 239.

7. Maurice Hunt, *Shakespeare's Labored Art, Stir, Work, and the Late Plays*, vol. 3 of *Studies in Shakespeare*, Robert F. Willson, Jr., general ed. (New York: Peter Lang, 1995), 272.

8. Brook Thomas, *The New Historicism and Other Old-Fashioned Topics* (Princeton, New Jersey: Princeton University Press, 1991), 11.

9. Nosworthy, 282.

10. Curt Breight, "*The Tempest* and the Discourse of Treason," *Shakespeare Quarterly* 41, No. 1 (Spring 1990): 1–28, esp. 1.

11. Breight, 28.

12. Emma Brockway Wagner, *Shakespeare's* The Tempest: *An Allegorical Interpretation*, ed. from mss. and notes by Hugh Robert Orr (Yellow Springs, Ohio: Antioch, 1933), 2.

13. Wagner, 2; see also 2–12.

14. Colin Still, *Shakespeare's Mystery Play: A Study of "The Tempest"* (London: Cecil Palmer, 1921), 207.

15. Still, 206.

16. Still, 205.

17. John W. Draper, *The Humors and Shakespeare's Characters* (Durham, North Carolina: Duke University Press, 1945). Draper pointed out that little effort was made by nineteenth century interpreters to discover Shakespeare's meaning and intention in terms of the Elizabethan Age. He claimed that "the early nineteenth century bowdlerized Shakespeare; the later nineteenth century Victorianized him. It let its own feelings and predispositions be its guide in determining character and theme" (4).

18. Stokes, 267. Trinculo says, "Monster, I do smell all horse-piss, at which my nose is in great indignation" (4.1.198).

19. W. Bang & W. W. Greg, *Ben Jonson's "Every Man in His Humor"* (repr. *The Quarto*, 1601; Louvain: A. Uystpruyst, 1905, Liechtenstein: Kraus Reprint, 1968), 6. Amongst actors listed in the 1968 reprint are Prospero and Stephano. Shakespeare was listed first among the principal actors in the Lord Chamberlain's players when *Every Man in His Humor* was first acted in September 1598. In the Folio version of Jonson's play, Prospero is named Wellbred. See Martin Seymour-Smith, ed., *Every Man in His Humor* (London: Ernest Benn, 1966), xxviii.

20. Nosworthy, 287–292.

21. Nosworthy, 288; C.J. Sisson, "The Magic of Prospero," *Shakespeare Survey* II (1958): 70–77, esp. 76; Horace Howard Furness, ed., *A New Variorum: The Tempest*, 308–315; Sharon L. Smith, "*The Commedia dell'Arte* and Problems Related to Source in *The Tempest*," *The Emporia State Research Studies* XIII (1964): 11–23.

22. David L. Hirst, *The Tempest: Text and Performance* (London: Macmillan, 1984), 20.

23. Kermode, Introduction, xvi.

24. J. de Perott, *The Probable Sources of "The Tempest,"* in Kermode, Introduction, lxv.

25. Nosworthy, 283–285; Carol Gesner, *Shakespeare and the Greek Romance: A Study of Origins* (Lexington: University Press of Kentucky, 1970), 127.

26. Gesner, 127.

27. Gesner, 128.

28. Gesner, 129.

29. Gesner, 138.

30. Gesner, 139.

31. Gesner, 139.

32. Woodman, 44.

33. Woodman, 12–13.

34. Woodman, 73.

35. Kermode, Appendices, 145.

36. Edward A. Armstrong, *Shakespeare's Imagination: A Study of the Psychology of Association and Inspiration* (London: Lindsay Drummond, 1946). Armstrong traced word associations and unlikely links in the plays in his effort to explore Shakespeare's creative mind. He investigated "the associative processes [of Shakespeare's mind] revealed in his imagery" (7, 143).

37. Nosworthy. 294.

38. S. L. Bethell, *Shakespeare and the Popular Dramatic Tradition*, Introduction by T. S. Eliot (Durham: Duke University Press, 1944), 95; Wylie Sypher, *The Ethic of Time: Structures of Experience in Shakespeare* (New York: Seabury, 1976), 195.

39. S.T. Coleridge, "An Analysis of Act I (1811)," in *Shakespeare* The Tempest: *A Casebook*, ed. by D.J. Palmer, (London: Macmillan, 1968), 58.

40. J. Dover Wilson, *The Meaning of "The Tempest"* (The Literary & Philosophical Society of Newcastle Upon Tyne, 1936; reprint, Folcroft Library Editions, 1972), 1–2, 23, 21.

41. G. Wilson Knight, *The Wheel of Fire: Essays in Interpretation of Shakespeare's Sombre Tragedies* (London: Oxford University Press, 1930), 3, 4.

42. Knight, 2.

43. Knight, 2.

44. Northrop Frye, *A Natural Perspective: The Development of Shakespearean Comedy and Romance* (New York: Columbia University Press, 1965), 48.

45. Sypher, 199, 204–205.

46. Wilson, 23; Frye, 48.

47. T.S. Eliot, Introduction to *The Wheel of Fire* by G. Wilson Knight (London: Oxford University Press, 1930), xviii.

48. Mystery Plays and the Corpus Christi play are used interchangeably in this study. The Feast of Corpus Christi took place sixty days after Easter. The English cycles were usually performed on that day. The name "mystery" derived from the French *mystère* and in England from the various trades or "mysteries" which performed them.

Chapter II

1. King James the First, "Daemonologie (1597) Newes from Scotland," in G.B. Harrison, ed., *Elizabethan and Jacobean Quartos* (Edinburgh: Edinburgh University Press, 1966).

2. Jean Howard cites Jonathan Dollimore in "The New Historicism in Renaissance Studies," in Richard Wilson and Richard Dutton, eds. *New Historicism and Renaissance Drama* (London: Longman, 1922), 22.

3. Martin Stevens, *Four Middle English Mystery Cycles: Textual, Contextual, and Critical Interpretations* (Princeton, New Jersey: Princeton University Press, 1987), 18, 260; Marianne G. Briscoe and John C. Coldewey, eds., *Contexts for Early English Drama* (Bloomington: Indiana University Press, 1989), 120.

4. Martial Rose, ed., *The Wakefield Mystery Plays* (London: Evans Brothers, 1961), 28.

5. V. A. Kolve, *The Play Called Corpus Christi* (Stanford, California: Stanford University Press, 1966), 1, 50.

6. R. T. Davies, ed. *The Corpus Christi Play of the English Middle Ages* (New Jersey: Rowman and Littlefield, 1972), 53.

7. Briscoe, 106.

8. See Briscoe, 106–107, for discussion of reasons.

9. Briscoe, 106.

10. Roland Mushat Frye, *Shakespeare's Life and Times: A Pictorial Record* (Princeton, New Jersey: Princeton University Press, 1967), 90.

11. L. W. Cowie and John Selwyn Gummer, *The Christian Calendar* (Springfield, Massachusetts: Merriam, 1974), 5.

12. Davies, "The Shepherds," p. 170, gloss on "Sacramentes": "i.e. of Baptism, the Eucharist, Absolution, Confirmation, Ordination, Marriage and Anointing."

13. R. Chris Hassel, *Renaissance Drama and the English Church Year* (Lincoln: University of Nebraska Press, 1979) 5.

14.˙ Hassel, 2.

15. Hassel, 2.

16. Northrop Frye, in his comments as editor of *The Tempest,* by William Shakespeare (Middlesex, England: Penguin, 1970; first pub. Pelican Shakespeare, 1959; repr. Kingsport, Tennessee: Kingsport, 1970), 23.

17. James Hastings, ed, *Encyclopedia of Religion and Ethics* (Edinburgh: T. & T. Clark; New York: Scribner, 1913), Vol. I: 10.

18. Hastings, Vol. V: 331 Col 2; George M. Gibson, *The Story of the Christian Year* (New York: Abingdon, 1945), 128.

19. Kolve, 69.

20. Hastings, Vol. V: 331 Col 2.

21. Hastings, Vol. V: 331: Col 2.

22. Hastings, Vol. I: 10.

23. Stephen Greenblatt, *Shakespeare Negotiations: The Circulation of Social Energy in Renaissance England* (Berkley: University of California Press, 1988), 4.

24. Greenblatt, 4.

25. Peter Brook, *The Shifting Point ... 1946–1987.* (New York: Harper and Row, 1987), 78.

26. Brook, 84.

27. Brook, 85.

28. Few dramatizations of the Mystery Plays occur today. Those seen by this author have focused on individual plays and have been played in a church. However, the two observed during the preparation of this manuscript have reinforced their relevance in interpreting *The Tempest.*

29. E. K. Chambers, *Medieval Stage,* 1903; Marie Caroline Lyle, *The Original Identity of the York and Towneley Cycles: Studies in Language and Literature,* Vol. VIII, no. 3 (Minneapolis: University Press of Minnesota, 1919).

30. The Rev. J. S. Purvis, *The York Cycle of Mystery Plays, A Complete Version* (London: SPCK, 1957), 7.

31. Purvis, 8.

32. Kolve, 1.

33. Kolve, 1.

34. Kolve, 99, citing Cawley's conclusion which uses a phrase borrowed from E. O. James; A. C. Cawley, *Wakefield Pageants,* xxv (quoting E.O. James, *Christian Myth and Ritual,* 1933).

35. Kolve, 99, quoting Hardin Craig, *English Religious Drama,* 134.

36. Kolve, 99.

37. Kolve, 100.

38. Kolve, 65.

39. Davies, 31.

40. Davies, 31.

41. Davies, 31.

42. Davies, 32. see E. Prosser, *Drama and Religion in the English Mystery Plays* (Stanford, California: Stanford University Press, 1961), 17–18, 23–25.

43. Peter Happé, ed., *English Mystery Plays: A Selection* (Middlesex, England: Penguin, 1975), 9, 11–13.

44. Walter E. Meyers, *A Figure Given: Typology in the Wakefield Plays* (Pittsburgh: Duquesne University Press, 1970), 37–55.

45. Meyers, 18–19.

46. Meyers, 18–19.

47. Mark Rose, *Shakespearean Design* (Cambridge: Harvard University Press, 1972), 40.

48. Rose, 44.

49. Rosemary Woolf, *The English Mystery Plays* (Berkeley: University of California Press, 1972).

50. Happé, 25.

51. Happé, 25.

52. Northrop Frye, *The Myth of Deliverance: Reflections on Shakespeare's Problem Comedies* (Toronto and Buffalo: University of Toronto Press, 1983), 25.

53. Stevens, 11.

54. Stevens, ix.

55. Stevens, ix.

56. Stevens, ix. Stevens wrote, "Two significant events occurred in the period from 1521 to 1532 — the cycle was expanded into a three-day performance, and it was shifted from Corpus Christi Day to Whitsuntide" (260).

57. Stevens, 307.

58. Stevens, 307.

Chapter III

1. J. Dover Wilson, *The Meaning of "The Tempest"* (The Literary & Philosophical Society of Newcastle Upon Tyne, 1936; Folcroft Library Editions, 1972), 13.

2. Wilson, 13.

3. S. T. Coleridge, "An Analysis of Act I (1811)," in *Shakespeare:* The Tempest: *A Casebook,* ed. by D. J. Palmer (London: Macmillan, 1968), 51.

4. Reuben A. Brower, "The Mirror of Analogy," in The Tempest: *A Casebook,* ed. by D. J. Palmer (London: Macmillan, 1968), 161, 155.

5. E.M.W. Tillyard, *Shakespeare's Last Plays* (London: Chatto and Windus, 1964), 50–51.

6. Clifford Davidson, *From Creation to Doom, The York Cycle of Mystery Plays* (New York: AMS P, 1984), 50.

7. E.M.W. Tillyard, *The Elizabethan World Picture* (New York: Vintage, n.d.), 56, 52.

8. Frank Kermode, in his Introduction to *The Tempest* by William Shakespeare (Arden Shakespeare Series [Cambridge: Harvard University Press, 1958]), 8.

9. Rust, Paul R., O.M.I., *The First of the Puritans and the Book of Common Prayer* (Milwaukee: Bruce, 1949), 118.

Chapter IV

1. S. L. Bethell, *Shakespeare and the Popular Dramatic Tradition* (Durham, North Carolina: Duke University Press, 1944), 69.

2. Peter Brook, *The Shifting Point ... 1946–1987* (New York: Harper & Row, 1987), 85.

3. Bethell, *Popular Dramatic Tradition,* 95.

4. Cumberland Clark, *Shakespeare and the Supernatural* (London: Williams and Norgate, 1931; reprint, Folcroft Library Editions, 1972), 109.

5. D. G. James, *Scepticism and Poetry: An Essay on the Poetic Imagination* (London: George Allen and Unwin, 1937) 239.

6. E.M.W. Tillyard, "The Tragic Pattern" (1938), in *Shakespeare:* The Tempest:

A Casebook, ed. by D. J. Palmer (London: Macmillan, 1968), 122–129, esp. 122-123; G. Wilson Knight, "The Shakespearean Superman" (1947), in Palmer, 130; Edward Dowden, "The Serenity of *The Tempest*" (1875), in Palmer, 73; Rose Abdelnour Zimbardo, "Form and Disorder in *The Tempest*"(1963), in Palmer, 234; Frank Kermode, "Introduction to *The Tempest*" (1954), in Palmer, 187; Derek Traversi, *Shakespeare: The Last Phase* (New York: Harcourt Brace, 1956), 194; Clark, *Shakespeare and the Supernatural,* 233; Colin Still, *Shakespeare's Mystery Play: A Study of "The Tempest"* (London: Cecil Palmer, 1921), 202; Emma Brockway Wagner, *Shakespeare's "The Tempest": An Allegorical Interpretation,* ed. from mss and notes by Hugh Robert Orr (Yellow Springs, Ohio: Antioch, 1933), 23, 27.

7. Wagner, 28–33.

8. Richard C. Dales, *The Scientific Achievement of the Middle Ages* (Philadelphia: University of Pennsylvania Press, 1972), 34. Gottschalk, considering available astronomical fragments from Simplicius and Aetius, found "complete agreement" about Heraclides' view of the earth, and "the only thing he [Simplicius] positively attributes to Heraclides is belief in the axial rotation of the earth." H. B. Gottschalk, *Heraclides of Pontus* (Oxford: Clarendon, 1980), 61.

9. R. Chris Hassel, Jr., *Faith and Folly in Shakespeare's Romantic Comedies* (Athens: University of Georgia Press, 1980), 220–222.

10. Bethell, *Popular Dramatic Tradition,* 95.

11. Roland Mushat Frye, *Shakespeare's Life and Times, A Pictorial Record* (New Jersey: Princeton University Press, 1967), 90.

12. Frank Kermode, ed., note to *The Tempest* by William Shakespeare, Arden Shakespeare Series (Cambridge: Harvard University Press, 1958), 20. Kermode describes different interpretations of what is meant when Prospero says "Now I arise." "Some take him to mean simply that he is getting up, in order to resume his robe, which he needs to put Miranda to sleep, and they usually add the Stage Direction *Resumes his mantle.*"

13. Levin L. Schucking, *Character Problems in Shakespeare's Plays: A Guide to the Better Understanding of the Dramatist* (Gloucester, Massachusetts: Peter Smith, 1959), 243.

14. Ira Clark, *Christ Revealed, The History of the Neotypological Lyric in the English Renaissance* (Gainesville: University Press of Florida, 1982), ix, x.

15. Ira Clark, 7.

16. Kolve, 134.

17. Cumberland Clark, 109.

18. Anne Barton Righter, "Introduction," to *William Shakespeare: "The Tempest"* (Middlesex, England: Penguin, 1968), 15.

19. Numerology in the Middle Ages and the Renaissance was considered one means of understanding the nature of man, the universe and God. In writing about creation in *The City of God,* xi xxx, Augustine quoted Wisdom 11: 20: "Thou hast ordered all things in measure and number and weight." Anyone familiar with Scripture can observe the recurrence of certain numbers and their association with times, characters, and events. In this chapter numerics were used to confirm the Prospero-Moses figuring.

Forty represents periods of threat and endurance (the Flood, Israel's wanderings in the wilderness and Christ's temptation). Twelve tribes were called to "bless" the world, and twelve disciples were chosen to "go into all the world to preach the Gospel." The number three was associated with divinity. God is described as Father, Son, and Holy Spirit, a Trinity. Christ rose from the dead on the third day. In the Bible the number seven was associated with time periods. Seven days, seven weeks, seven months, seven years and seven times seven, 49, with the following year Jubilee, a time of restoration of land which had been lost and of celebration. It is not surprising, then, that biblically based dramatists should discern and assign seven ages in the duration of human existence.

Woolf noted that "the measurements and structure of the ark [a type of salvation and as a wooden vessel of the Cross] were replete with symbolical meaning. ...A chapter from the *De arca Noe morali* of Hugh of St. Victor may be taken as typical of the method: the length of three hundred cubits denotes the three periods of history, those of the natural law, the written law and of grace." Rosemary Woolf, *The English Mystery Plays* (Berkeley: University Press of California, 1972), 136, with reference to Hugh of Saint-Victor, *Selected Spiritual Writings* (London, 1962), 64–65.

20. Northrop Frye, ed., *The Tempest* by William Shakespeare (Middlesex, England: Penguin, 1983), 46.

21. David Woodman, *White Magic and English Renaissance Drama* (Rutherford, New Jersey: Fairleigh Dickinson University Press, 1973), 124.

22. Woodman, 64–65.

23. Woodman, 35, 39.

24. J. Dover Wilson, *The Meaning of "The Tempest."* (The Literary & Philosophical Society of Newcastle Upon the Tyne, 1936; reprint, Folcroft Library Editions, 1972), 14.

25. E. M. W. Tillyard, *Shakespeare's Last Plays* (London: Chatto and Windus, 1964), 54.

26. Jeffrey Truby, *The Glories of Salisbury Cathedral* (London: Winchester, 1948), 31.

27. John E. Booty, ed., *The Book of Common Prayer, 1559, The Elizabeth Prayer Book* (Charlottesville: University Press of Virginia, for the Folger Shakespeare Library, 1976), 270.

28. V.A. Kolve, "Principles of Selection," *The Play Called Corpus Christi.* (Stanford, California: Stanford University Press, 1966), 76.

29. Isaiah 27:3, 6; 29:19–24; 35:5–9; 40:4, 11; 41:5, 18–20; 42:3, 16; 60:5; 66:11.

30. Wagner, 38.

31. "In the stained glass of Fairford Church, made in the fifteenth century in the heyday of these plays [Mystery Plays], there are many of the same dramatic episodes that portray the redemption of Man.... But there is a great deal else in addition which never occurs in the plays, and, moreover, the four Old Testament scenes differ from those with which the plays begin. They are chosen because they are 'antitypes' of various aspects of the Incarnation: Eve (who is represented alone with the serpent) is the antitype of Mary, who is the second Eve; the burning bush of Moses and the fleece of Gideon represent Mary who bore Jesus but remained a virgin." R. T. Davies, ed., *The Corpus Christi Play of the English Middle Ages* (New Jersey: Rowman and Littlefield, 1972), 30.

32. *Oxford English Dictionary* Vol X: 213 Col. 3:1d.

33. J. M. Nosworthy, "The Narrative Sources of *The Tempest*," *Review of English Studies* XXIV (1948): 281–294, esp. 287.

34. Wagner, 34, 36.

35. Wagner, 46.

36. Traversi, 207.

37. Wagner, 55; Frank Davidson, *"The Tempest"*: An Interpretation" (1963), in *Shakespeare:* The Tempest, *A Casebook*, ed. by D. J. Palmer (London: MacMillan, 1968), 219; G. Wilson Knight, "The Shakespearean Superman" (1947), in Palmer, 151; Joseph Warton, "Amazing Wildness of Fancy" (1753), in Palmer, 38; William Hazlitt, "Unity and Variety in Shakespeare's Design" (1817), in Palmer, 70; Jan Kott, "Prospero's Staff" (1964), in Palmer, 248, 253–254; E. K. Chambers, *Shakespeare: A Survey* (London: Sidgwick and Jackson, 1925, reprinted 1963), 310.

38. George Arthur Buttrick, ed., *The Interpreter's Dictionary of the Bible: An Illustrated Encyclopedia* (New York: Abingdon, 1962), Vol V: 218, Col. 1.

39. Kott, 252.

40. Walter Clyde Curry, *Shakespeare's Philosophical Patterns* (Gloucester, Massachusetts: Peter Smith, 1968), 198–199.

41. Frank Kermode, ed., note to *The Tempest* by William Shakespeare, Arden Shakespeare Series (Cambridge: Harvard University Press, 1954), 143.

42. Frank Davidson, 217.

43. S.T. Coleridge, "An Analysis of Act I" (1811), Palmer, 56.

44. E. M. W. Tillyard, *The Elizabethan World Picture* (New York: Alfred A. Knopf, n.d.), 34–35.

45. Chambers, 313, 314.

46. David L. Hirst, *The Tempest: Text and Performance* (London: Macmillan, 1984), 17.

47. Chambers, 313.

48. Traversi, 231.

49. Traversi, 212–213.

50. Schucking, 264, 242.

51. See Ira Clark.

52. Bethell, *Popular Dramatic Tradition*, 67–68.

53. Bethell, *Popular Dramatic Tradition*, 131, 130.

Chapter V

1. R. T. Davies, editor, *The Corpus Christi Play of the English Middle Ages* (New Jersey: Rowman and Littlefield, 1972), 68. The text is also available in *Ludus Coventriae* or *The Plaie Called Corpus Christi*, published for the Early English Text Society (London: Oxford UP, 1872).

2. Marianne G. Briscoe and John C. Coldewey, eds., *Contexts for Early English Drama* (Bloomington: Indiana University Press, 1989), 46: Robert Potter claims that only Wakefield and York are "pure" Corpus Christi plays; 121: Lawrence M. Clopper disclaims Lincoln as the *Ludus* locale, 222; Stanley J. Kahrl asserts "there is not a shred of evidence connecting the plays in this manuscript *[Ludus]* to the city of Coventry."

3. Page numbers immediately following quotations in the first part of this chapter refer to the text in R.T. Davies.

4. John Bale, *The Dramatic Writings of John Bale, Bishop of Ossory*, edited by John S. Farmer. Facsimile of the edition published by the Early English Drama Society, London, 1907 (New York: Barnes and Noble, 1966), 85–125.

5. L. A. Hamand, *The Ancient Windows of St. Malvern Priory Church* (St. Albans: Campfield, 1947), 71.

6. H. D. M. Spence, *The White Robe of Churches of the XIth Century, Pages from the Story of Gloucester Cathedral* (London: J. M. Dent, 1899), 181.

7. Page numbers following quotations in the remainder of this chapter refer to John E. Booty, ed., *The Book of Common Prayer, 1559: The Elizabethan Prayer Book* (Charlottesville: University Press of Virginia for the Folger Library, 1976).

8. Booty, the Collects and Scriptures used for all the days of Christmastide are given on 29–30, 83–94.

9. Booty, 27.

10. Northrop Frye, in his comments as editor of *The Tempest* by William Shakespeare (Middlesex, England: Penguin, 1970; first pub. in *Pelican Shakespeare*, 1959; repr. Kingsport, Tennessee: Kingsport, 1970), 23.

11. James Hastings, ed., *Encyclopedia of Religion and Ethics* (Edinburgh: T. and T. Clark; New York: Charles Scribner's Sons, 1913), Vol I:10.

12. Booty, 36, 37.

13. Davies, 45.

14. Davies, 46–47.

Chapter VI

1. Robert Hodge, *Literature as Discourse: Textual Strategies in English and History* (Baltimore: Johns Hopkins University Press, 1990), 37.

2. James C. Fernald, *Historic English*, 2d ed. (New York: Funk and Wagnalls, 1921), 251.

3. S. L. Bethell, *Essays on Literary Criticism and the English Tradition* (London: D. Dobson, 1948), 33, 34.

4. Edward A. Armstrong, *Shakespeare's Imagination: A Study of the Psychology of Association and Inspiration* (London: Lindsay Drummond, 1946).

5. *The Oxford English Dictionary* [hereafter OED], 2d ed. (Oxford: Clarendon Press, 1989) Vol. II: 437, Col. 2:3a.

6. Roland Mushat Frye, *Shakespeare and Christian Doctrine* (Princeton: Princeton University Press, 1963), 149.

7. Roland Mushat Frye, *Shakespeare, The Art of the Dramatist* (London: George Allen and Unwin, 1956), 125.

8. OED Vol. VI: 782, Col. 3:4

9. OED Vol. VI: 782, Col. 2:3a.

10. OED. Vol. VI: 782, Col. 3:3.

11. OED Vol. VI: 783, Col. 1:3b.

12. OED Vol. XIV: 444, Col. 2.

13. OED Vol. XI: 1125, Col. 2:3b.

14. OED Vol. XI: 1125, Col. 3:4a.

15. Armstrong's book in general.

16. OED Vol. XII: 501, Col. 2:BI.1b.

17. OED Vol. XII: 501, Col. 2:BI. 2 *fig*.a.

18. R. T. Davies, ed., *The Corpus Christi Play of the English Middle Ages* (New Jersey: Rowman and Littlefield, 1972), 111.

19. OED Vol. VIII: 974, Col. 2:2a.

20. OED Vol. VIII: 973, Col. 3:I1a.

21. OED Vol. VIII: 974, Col. 3:5.

22. OED Vol. VIII: 975, Col. 2:10a.

23. OED Vol. VIII: 974, Col. 2:4b.

24. OED Vol. VIII: 863, Col. 2:3b; Vol. VIII: 863, Col. 1:I.1a.

25. OED. Vol. VIII: 863, Col. 2:I.1a.

26. OED Vol. VIII: 863, Col.1:I.1a: 1578 Timme *Calvin on Gen 28I*.

27. OED Vol. XI: 332, Col. 2:3.

28. OED Vol. II: 1076, Col. 2:4.

29. OED Vol. II: 1076, Col. 1:3b.

30. OED Vol. II: 1076, Col. 1:4a, 4b.

31. OED Vol. II: 1075, Col. 2:4: 1634 S.R. *Noble Soldier* V. iii. in Bullen O. *Pl.*I.333.

32. OED Vol. II: 1076, Col. 2:4a: 1571 Golding *Calvin on Psalm xviii.44* and 1678 Bunyan *Pilgr.* I.Apol.

33. OED Vol. II: 1076, Col. 1:2b.

34. OED Vol. XVI: 41, Col. 1:II. 9; Col. 2:10a.

35 OED Vol. XVI: 40, Col. 1:2a.

36. OED Vol. XVII: 752, Col. 1:2.

37. OED Vol. XV: 76, Col 2:2 **sete**, obs., and **bos**, an obsolete form of **boss**; Vol II: 424, Col. 2:3.

38. OED Vol. II: 424, Col. 2:3; Vol. II: 423, Col. 3:2a.

Chapter VII

1. James Hastings, ed., *Encyclopedia of Religion and Ethics* (Edinburgh: T. & T. Clark; New York: Charles Scribner' Sons, 1913), Vol. V. 331.

2. OED Vol. I, 287, Col. 3, forms beta 6–8.

3. John E. Booty, ed., *The Book of Common Prayer, 1559, The Elizabethan Prayer Book* (Charlottesville: University Press of Virginia, for the Folger Shakespeare Library, 1976), 270.

4. Booty, 270.

5. W. R. Matthews and W. M. Atkins, *History of St. Paul's Cathedral and the Men Associated with It* (London: Phenix House, 1957), 108–109.

6. Matthews, 109.

7. Matthews, 109.

8. H. D. M. Spence, *The White Robe of Churches of the XIth Century, Pages from the Story of Gloucester Cathedral* (London: J. M. Dent, 1899), 128.

9. Spence, opposite 128.

10. Spence, 128–129.

11. Spence, 129.

12. OED Vol. XIV: 444, Col. 2:1; Col. 3:1b; and Col. 3:2.

13. R. T. Davies, ed. *The Corpus Christi Play of the English Middle Ages* (New Jersey: Rowman and Littlefield, 1972), 68. The text is also available in *Ludus Coventriae or The Plaie called Corpus Christi*, published for the Early English Text Society (London: Oxford University Press, 1872); Davies 135, 157; *Godes sand* (sending, dispensation)

14. Davies, 104.

15. Davies, 107.

16. Booty, 37.

17. **Bass:** OED Vol I: 988, Col. 3:2, **bass:** "Deep-sounding, low in the musical scale"; I:989, Col. 2, "To utter or proclaim with bass voice or sound." **Burden:** OED Vol. II: 664, Col. 1:I, "That which is borne." I.1: "A load"; Col. 1:I.2 *fig.* a, "A load of labour, duty, responsibility, blame, sin, sorrow, etc."; Col. 2 III.8, "Used in the Eng. Bible (like *onus* in the Vulgate) … which … would translate 'lifting up (of the voice), utterance, oracle.' … But it is generally taken in English to mean a 'burdensome or heavy lot or fate.'"

18. See I Corinthians 11:29.

19. Booty, 140.

20. Booty, 257.

21. Booty, 19.

Chapter VIII

1. G. F. Waller, *The Strong Necessity of Time: The Philosophy of Time in Shakespeare and Elizabethan Literature* (Paris: Mouton, 1976), 156, 155.

2. G. Wilson Knight, *The Shakespearean Tempest/With a Chart of Shakespeare's Dramatic Universe* (London: Methuen, 1953), 263.

3. E.M.W. Tillyard, *Shakespeare's Last Plays* (London: Chatto & Windus, 1964), 50.

4. Tillyard, 78.

5. Tillyard, 80.

6. Harry Levin, *Shakespeare and the Revolution of the Times: Perspectives and Commentaries* (New York: Oxford University Press, 1976), 223.

7. Mark Rose, *Shakespearean Design* (Cambridge, Massachusetts: Belknap, 1972), 173, 28, 173.

8. Wylie Sypher, *The Ethic of Time: Structures of Experience in Shakespeare* (New York: Seabury, 1976), 8.

9. Northrop Frye, *A Natural Perspective: The Development of Shakespearean Comedy and Romance* (New York: Columbia University Press, 1965), 9.

10. Tillyard, 79–80.

11. David P. Young, "Shakespeare's Early Comedies, 'A Midsummer Night's Dream': Structure" in *Modern Shakespearean Criticism, Essays on Style Dramaturgy, and the Major Plays,* ed. by Alvin B. Kernan (New York: Harcourt, Brace & World, 1970), 178.

12. Young, 180.

13. Sypher, 8.

14. Derek Traversi, *The Literary Imagination: Studies in Dante, Chaucer, and Shakespeare* (Newark: University of Delaware Press; London and Toronto: Associated University Presses, 1982), 261.

15. D. G. James, *Scepticism and Poetry: An Essay on the Poetic Imagination* (London: George Allen & Unwin, 1937), 239.

16. Jan Kott, "Prospero's Staff," (1964) in *"The Tempest": A Casebook,* ed. by D. J. Palmer (London: Macmillan, 1968), 25l, 246.

17. G. Wilson Knight, *The Wheel of Fire: Essays in Interpretation of Shakespeare's Sombre Tragedies* (London: Oxford University Press, 1930), 3.

18. Knight, *Wheel,* 4.

19. Knight, *Wheel,* 4, 12, 6.

20. Knight, *Wheel,* 12.

21. OED Vol. II; 602, Col. 2:2.

22. Waller, 11–12.

23. OED Vol. III; 950, Cols. 1, 2:4.

24. OED Vol. III; 950, Col. 1:3.

25. Luminasky, R. M. and David Mills, eds. *The Chester Mystery Cycle, Essays and Documents* For Early English Text Society. London: Oxford University Press, 1974, reprinted Chapel Hill: University of North Carolina Press, 1983.

26. Rastall, 114–116.

27. Martial Rose, ed., *The Wakefield Mystery Plays* (London: Evans Brothers, 1961), 44.

28. Rastall, 120–122.

29. Rastall, 123.

30. E. M. W. Tillyard, *The Elizabethan World Picture* (New York: Alfred A. Knopf, n.d.), 34.

31. David L. Hirst, *The Tempest: Text and Performance* (London: Macmillan, 1984), 27, 38.

Chapter IX

1. Reuben A. Brower, "The Mirror of Analogy," in *"The Tempest": A Casebook*, ed. by D. J. Palmer (London: Macmillan, 1968), 164.
2. G. Wilson Knight, *The Shakespearean Tempest/With a Chart of Shakespeare's Dramatic Universe* (London: Methuen, 1953), 263.
3. David L. Hirst, *The Tempest, Text and Performance* (London: Macmillan, 1984), 16.
4. Traversi, Derek, *The Literary Imagination: Studies in Dante, Chaucer, and Shakespeare* (Newark: University of Delaware Press; London and Toronto: Associated University Presses, 1982), 246.
5. Mark Rose, *Shakespearean Design* (Cambridge, Massachusetts: Belknap, 1972), 173.
6. Rose, 172.
7. D. A. Traversi, "The Romances, the Last Plays of Shakespeare," in *Modern Shakespearean Criticism, Essays on Style, Dramaturgy and the Major Plays,* ed. by Alvin B. Kernan (New York: Harcourt, Brace & World, 1970), 445.
8. Edward Dowden, "The Serenity of *The Tempest*" (1875), in Palmer, 74–75.
9. Dowden, 78.
10. Rose, 39.
11. Rose, 16.
12. Roland Mushat Frye, *Shakespeare and Christian Doctrine* (Princeton, New Jersey: Princeton University Press, 1963), 149.
13. Henry Green, *Shakespeare and the Emblem Writers* (New York: Burt Franklin, n.d), 320–21.

Chapter X

1. Wylie Sypher, *The Ethic of Time: Structures of Experience in Shakespeare* (New York: Seabury, 1976), 5, 41.
2. G. F. Waller, *The Strong Necessity of Time: The Philosophy of Time in Shakespeare and Elizbethan Literature* (Paris: Mouton, 1976), 12.
3. Frederick Turner, *Shakespeare and the Nature of Time: Moral and Philosophical Themes in Some Plays and Poems of William Shakespeare* (Oxford: Clarendon, 1971), l73–174.
4. Ricardo J. Quinones, *The Renaissance Discovery of Time* (Cambridge, Massachusetts: Harvard University Press, 1972), 443.
5. Quinones, 441–442.
6. See Exodus 20–32, esp. 31:18 and 32:19.
7. Waller, 162–164.
8. Waller, 165.
9. Plotinus: *The Ethical Treatises Being the Treatises of the First Ennead with Porphyry's Life of Plotinus, and the Preller-Ritter Extracts Forming a Conspectus of the Plotinian System,* trans. by Stephen MacKenna (Boston: Charles T. Branford, 1916), 114.
10. Plotinus, 114.

11. Plotinus, 114.

12. Waller, 17.

13. Waller, 17.

14. Walter E. Meyers, *A Figure Given: Typology in the Wakefield Plays* (Pittsburgh: Duquesne University Press, 1970), 19.

15. William Watts, tr., *St Augustine's Confessions* (London: William Heinemann, New York: G.P. Putnam's Sons, 1925) Vol. II, BK XI, Chap. XX, 253.

16. Watts, Vol. II, BK XI, Chap. XVIII, 247–249.

17. Watts, Vol. II, BK XI, Chap. XI, 231, 233.

18. R. T. Davies. ed. *The Corpus Christi Play of the English Middle Ages* (New Jersey: Rowman and Littlefield, 1972), 73–86.

19. A. C. Cawley, ed. "The Wakefield Pageants in the Towneley Cycle," *Old and Middle English Texts*, ed. by G. L. Brook (Manchester: University of Manchester Press, 1958), 14–28, esp. 19–28.

20. Cawley 23: Play 2, "Processus Noe Cum Filiis," ll, 343–351.

21. The Bible does not specify an apple as the offending fruit. The prohibited tree was the "tree of the knowledge of good and evil."

22. Davies, 92–93.

23. Harry Levin, *The Myth of the Golden Age in the Renaissance* (Bloomington: Indiana University Press, 1969), 21.

24. Levin, xv, 167.

25. Meyers, 19, quoting Williams, *Drama*, 39 note.

26. Emma Brockway Wagner, *Shakespeare's "The Tempest": An Allegorical Interpretation*, ed. from mss. and notes by Hugh Robert Orr (Yellow Springs, Ohio: Antioch Press, 1933), 2–3, 9–11.

27. Wagner, 2–3, 9–11.

28. V. A. Kolve, *The Play Called Corpus Christi* (Stanford, California: Stanford University Press, 1966), 231–232.

29. C. S. Lewis, *The Lion, the Witch and the Wardrobe* (New York: Macmillan, 1970), 153, 160.

30. John E. Booty, ed., *The Book of Common Prayer, 1559, The Elizabethan Prayer Book* (Charlottesville: University Press of Virginia, for the Folger Library, 1976), 37.

31. Davies, 173, 257.

32. Wagner, 23, 27.

33. John Vyvyan, *The Shakespearean Ethic* (London: Chatto and Windus, 1968), 22.

34. Sypher, 4.

Chapter XI

1. Peter Brook, *The Shifting Point: Theatre, Film Opera, 1946–1987*. (New York: Harper and Row, 1987), 76.

2. Beverley Warner, ed., quoting Johnson in *Famous Introductions to Shakespeare's Plays by the Notable Editors of the Eighteenth Century* (New York: Burt Franklin, 1968, reprint of 1906 ed.), xxiii.

3. John Erskine Hankins, *Shakespeare's Derived Imagery* (Lawrence: University of Kansas Press, 1953), 279.

4. S. L. Bethell, *Shakespeare and the Popular Dramatic Tradition*, (Durham, North Carolina: Duke University Press, 1944), 40.

5. Bethell, 40.

6. William J. Rolfe, ed., *Shakespeare's Comedy of "A Midsummer-Night's Dream"* (New York: Harper and Brothers, 1889).

7. OED Vol. XII, 503, Col. 3:2b: "To impress (an image, thought, saying, etc.) upon the heart, mind, or memory; to fix in the mind."

8. E. K. Chambers, *Shakespeare: A Survey* (London: Sidgwick and Jackson, 1963), 309.

9. Chambers, 310.

10. F. E. Halliday, *Shakespeare and His Critics* (London: Gerald Duckworth, 1949, reprinted 1950), 62.

11. OED Vol. XI, 833, Col. 3:5.

12. OED Vol. XI, 833 Col. 1:1b.

13. OED Vol. XI, 833 Col. 1:1a.

14. Richard J. Collier, *Poetry and Drama in the York Corpus Christi Play* (Hamden, Connecticut: Shoe String Press, 1978), 18.

15. Collier, 18.

16. Hamilton Coleman, *Shakespeare and the Bible* (Folcroft, Pennsylvania: Folcroft, 1955, reprinted 1969), 5.

17. Margaret Lucy, *Shakespeare and the Supernatural: A Brief Study of Folklore, Superstition, and Witchcraft, in "Macbeth," "Midsummer Night's Dream" and "The Tempest"* (Liverpool: Shakespeare Press, 1906), 30.

18. Brook, 78.

19. Brook, 75.

20. Brook, 76.

Works Cited

Armstrong, Edward A. *Shakespeare's Imagination: A Study of the Psychology of Association and Inspiration.* London: Lindsay Drummond, 1946.

Augustine. *Saint Augustine's Confessions.* Trans. by William Watts. Vol. II. London: William Heinemann; New York: G.P. Putnam's Sons, 1925.

Bale, John. *The Dramatic Writings of John Bale, Bishop of Ossory.* Edited by John S. Farmer. Facsimile of the edition published by the Early English Drama Society, London, 1907. New York: Barnes and Noble, 1966.

Bethell, S. L. *Essays on Literary Criticism and the English Tradition.* London: D. Dobson, 1948.

_____. *Shakespeare and the Popular Dramatic Tradition.* Durham, North Carolina: Duke University Press, 1944.

Booty, John E., ed. *The Book of Common Prayer, 1559, The Elizabethan Prayer Book.* Charlottesville: University Press of Virginia for the Folger Shakespeare Library, 1976.

Breight, Curt. "*The Tempest* and the Discourse of Treason." *Shakespeare Quarterly,* Spring 1990, 1–28.

Briscoe, Marianne G., and Coldewey, John C., eds. *Contexts for Early English Drama.* Bloomington: Indiana University Press, 1989.

Brook, Peter. *The Shifting Point: Theatre, Film, Opera, 1946-1987.* New York: Harper and Row, 1987.

Brower, Reuben A. "The Mirror of Analogy." In *Shakespeare:* The Tempest, *A Casebook,* edited by D. J. Palmer. London: Macmillan, l968. Pp. 153–175.

Brown, John Russell. *Discovering Shakespeare: A New Guide to the Plays.* New York: Columbia University Press, 1981.

Brown, Paul. "'This Thing of Darkness I Acknowledge Mine': The Tempest *and the Discourse of Colonialism.*" In *Political Shakespeare: New Essays in Cultural Materialism,* edited by Jonathan Dollimore and Alan Sinfield. Ithaca: Cornell University Press, 1985. pp. 48–71.

Burgess, William. *The Bible in Shakespeare: A Study of the Relation of the Works of William Shakespeare to the Bible.* First published 1903; reprinted New York: Haskell House, 1968.

Buttrick, George Arthur, ed. *The Interpreter's Dictionary of the Bible: An Illustrated Encyclopedia.* New York: Abingdon, 1962.

Cawley, A. C., ed. *The Wakefield Pageants in the Towneley Cycle.* Old and Middle English Texts Series, general editor G. L. Brook. Manchester: University of Manchester Press, 1958.

Chambers, E. K. *Medieval Stage*. 1903.
_____. *Shakespeare: A Survey*. London: Sidgwick and Jackson, 1963.
Clark, Cumberland. *Shakespeare and the Supernatural*. London: Williams and Norgate, 1931; reprint, Folcroft Library Editions, 1972.
Clark, Ira. *Christ Revealed: The History of the Neotypological Lyric in the English Renaissance*. Gainesville: University Press of Florida, 1982.
Coleman, Hamilton. *Shakespeare and the Bible*. Folcroft, Pennsylvania: Folcroft, 1955; reprint, 1969.
Coleridge, S. T. "An Analysis of Act I" (1811). In *Shakespeare:* The Tempest, *A Casebook,* edited by D. J. Palmer. London: Macmillan, 1968. Pp. 49–61.
Collier, Richard J. *Poetry and Drama in the York Corpus Christi Play*. Hamden, Connecticut: Shoe String, 1978.
Cowie, L. W., and Gummer, John Selwyn. *The Christian Calendar: A Complete Guide to the Seasons of the Christian Year Telling the Story of Christ and the Saints from Advent to Pentecost*. Springfield, Massachusetts: Merriam, 1974.
Curry, Walter Clyde. *Shakespeare's Philosophical Patterns*. Gloucester, Massachusetts: Peter Smith, 1968.
Dales, Richard C., *The Scientific Achievement of the Middle Ages*. Philadelphia: University of Pennsylvania Press, 1973.
Davidson, Clifford. *From Creation to Doom: The York Cycle of Mystery Plays*. New York: AMS, 1984.
Davidson, Frank. "*The Tempest*: An Interpretation" (1963). In *Shakespeare:* The Tempest, *A Casebook,* edited by D. J. Palmer. London: Macmillan, 1968. 212–231.
Davies, R. T., ed. *The Corpus Christi Play of the English Middle Ages,* (New Jersey: Rowman and Littlefield, 1972).
de Perott, Joseph. "*The Probable Source of the Plot of Shakespeare's* Tempest." Worcester, 1905. In *The Tempest* by William Shakespeare. Arden Shakespeare Series. Cambridge: Harvard University Press, 1958.
Dessen, Alan C. In *Textual and Theatrical Shakespeare, Questions of Evidence,* edited by Edward Pechter. Iowa City: Iowa University Press, 1996.
Dollimore, Jonathan, and Sinfield, Alan, eds. *Political Shakespeare: New Essays in Cultural Materialism*. Ithaca: Cornell University Press, 1985.
Dowden, Edward. "The Serenity of *The Tempest*" (1875). In *Shakespeare:* The Tempest, *A Casebook,* edited by D. J. Palmer. London: Macmillan, 1968. Pp. 72–78.
_____. *Shakespeare: A Critical Study of His Mind and Art*. New York: Harper and Brothers, 1918.
Draper, John W. *Humors and Shakespeare's Characters*. Durham, North Carolina: Duke University Press, 1945.
Eliot, T. S. Introduction to *Wheel of Fire: Essays in Interpretation of Shakespeare's Sombre Tragedies* by G. Wilson Knight. London: Oxford University Press, 1930.
Fernald, James C. *Historic English*. Second Edition. New York: Funk & Wagnalls, 1921.
Frye, Northrop. *The Myth of Deliverance: Reflections on Shakespeare's Problem Comedies*. Toronto and Buffalo: University of Toronto Press, 1983.
_____. *A Natural Perspective: The Development of Shakespearean Comedy and Romance*. New York: Columbia University Press, 1965.
_____. ed. *William Shakespeare, "The Tempest."* Middlesex, England: Penguin, 1959, 1970; reprint, 1983.
Frye, Roland Mushat. *Shakespeare: The Art of the Dramatist*. Boston: Houghton Mifflin, 1970.
_____. *Shakespeare and Christian Doctrine*. Princeton, New Jersey: Princeton University Press, 1963.

_____. *Shakespeare's Life and Times: A Pictorial Record*. Princeton, New Jersey: Princeton University Press, 1967.

Furness, Harold Howard, ed. *A New Variorum Edition of Shakespeare "The Tempest."* New York: American Scholar, 1966.

Gesner, Carol. *Shakespeare and the Greek Romance: A Study of Origins*. Lexington: University Press of Kentucky, 1970.

Gibson, George M. *The Story of the Christian Year*. New York: Abingdon, 1945.

Gottschalk, H. B. *Heraclides of Pontus*. Oxford: Clarendon, 1980.

Green, Henry. *Shakespeare and the Emblem Writers: An Exposition of Their Similarities of Thought and Expression, Preceded by a View of Emblem Literature Down to* AD *1616*. New York: Burt Franklin, n.d.

Greenblatt, Stephen. *Shakespearean Negotiations: The Circulation of Social Energy in Renaissance England*. Berkeley: University of California Press, 1988.

_____, ed. *The Power of Forms in the English Renaissance*. Norman, Oklahoma: Pilgrim, 1982.

Halliday, F. E. *Shakespeare and His Critics*. London: Gerald Duckworth, 1949; reprint, 1950.

Hamand, L. A. *The Ancient Windows of Gt. Malvern Priory Church*. St. Albans: Campfield, 1947.

Hankins, John Erskine. *Shakespeare's Derived Imagery*. Lawrence: University of Kansas Press, 1953.

Happé, Peter, ed. *English Mystery Plays: A Selection*. Middlesex, England: Penguin, 1975.

Harrison, G. B., ed. *Elizabethan and Jacobean Quartos*. Edinburgh: Edinburgh University Press, 1966.

Hassel, R. Chris, Jr. *Faith and Folly in Shakespeare's Romantic Comedies*. Athens: University of Georgia Press, 1980.

_____. *Renaissance Drama and the English Church Year*. Lincoln: University of Nebraska Press, 1979.

Hastings, James, ed. *Encyclopaedia of Religion and Ethics*. Edinburgh: T.&T. Clark; New York: Charles Scribner's Sons, 1913.

Hawkes, Terence. *Meaning by Shakespeare*. London and New York: Routledge, 1992.

Hazlitt, William. "The Unity and Variety of Shakespeare's Design" (1817). In *Shakespeare: The Tempest, A Casebook*, edited by D. J. Palmer. London: Macmillan, 1968. Pp. 67–71.

Hirst, David L. *The Tempest: Text and Performance*. London: Macmillan, 1984.

Hodge, Robert. *Literature as Discourse: Textual Strategies in English and History*. Baltimore: Johns Hopkins University Press, 1990.

Howard, Jean. "The New Historicism in Renaissance Studies." In *New Historicism and Renaissance Drama*. London: Longman, 1992. P. 22. Howard cites Dollimore.

Hunt, Maurice. *Shakespeare's Labored Art, Stir, Work, and the Late Plays*. Studies in Shakespeare, Vol. 3. New York: Peter Lang, 1995.

James, D. G. *The Romantic Comedy*. London: Oxford University Press, 1948.

_____. *Scepticism and Poetry: An Essay on the Poetic Imagination*. London: George Allen and Unwin, 1937.

James the First. King of England. *Daemonologie* (1597); *Newes from Scotland* (1591). Elizabethan and Jacobean Quartos series G. B. Harrison, general editor. Edinburgh: Edinburgh University Press, 1966.

Johnson, Ben. *Every Man in His Humour*. From the Quarto 1601. Edited by W. Bang and W. W. Greg. Louvain: A. Uystpruyst, 1905; reprint, Lichtenstein: Vraus Reprint, 1968.

_____. *Every Man in His Humour*. Edited by G. B. Harrison. Second Edition. London: Methuen, 1949.

Kermode, Frank. "Introduction to *The Tempest*" (1954). In *Shakespeare:* The Tempest, *A Casebook*, edited by D. J. Palmer. London: Macmillan, 1968. 176–195.

Knight, G. Wilson. "The Shakespearean Superman" (1947). In *Shakespeare:* The Tempest, *A Casebook*, edited by D. J. Palmer. London: Macmillan, 1968. 130–152.

_____. *The Shakespearean Tempest/With a Chart of Shakespeare's Dramatic Universe.* London: Oxford University Press, 1932; reprinted Methuen, 1953.

_____. *The Wheel of Fire: Essays in Interpretation of Shakespeare's Sombre Tragedies.* London: Oxford University Press, 1930.

Kolve, V. A. *The Play Called Corpus Christi.* California: Stanford University Press, 1966.

Kott, Jan. "Prospero's Staff" (1964). In *Shakespeare:* The Tempest, *A Casebook*. Edited by D. J. Palmer. London: Macmillan, 1968. Pp. 244–258.

Levin, Harry. *The Myth of the Golden Age in the Renaissance.* Bloomington: Indiana University Press, 1969.

_____. *Shakespeare and the Revolution of the Times: Perspectives and Commentaries.* New York: Oxford University Press, 1976.

Lewis, C. S., *The Lion, the Witch and the Wardrobe.* New York: Macmillan, 1970.

Lucy, Margaret. *Shakespeare and the Supernatural: A Brief Study of Folklore, Superstition, and Witchcraft, in* Macbeth, Midsummer Night's Dream *and* The Tempest. Liverpool: Shakespeare Press, 1906.

Lumiansky, R. M., and Mills, David, eds. *The Chester Mystery Cycle: Essays and Documents.* London: Oxford University Press for the Early English Text Society, 1974. Chapel Hill: University of North Carolina Press, 1983.

Lyle, Marie C. *The Original Identity of the York and Towneley Cycles.* Research Publications of the University of Minnesota, Vol. 8, No. 3. Minneapolis: University of Minnesota Press, June 1919.

Marsden, Jean I. *The Re-Imagined Text: Shakespeare, Adaptation, and Eighteenth-Century Literary Theory.* University Press of Kentucky, 1995.

Matthews, Honor. *Character and Symbol in Shakespeare's Plays: A Study of Certain Christian and Pre-Christian Elements in Their Structure and Imagery.* New York: Schocken, 1969.

Matthews, W. R., and Atkins, W. M., eds. *A History of St. Paul's Cathedral and the Men Associated with It.* London: Phoenix House, 1957.

Meyers, Walter E. *A Figure Given: Typology in the Wakefield Plays.* A Modern Humanities Research Association Monograph, Duquesne Studies Philological Series. Pittsburgh: Duquesne University Press, 1970.

Milton, John. *John Milton: Complete Poems and Major Prose.* Edited by Merritt Y. Hughes. New York: Odyssey, 1957.

Noble, Richmond. *Shakespeare's Biblical Knowledge and Use of the Book of Common Prayer as Exemplified in the Plays of the First Folio.* Folcroft, Pennsylvania: Folcroft, 1935; reprinted 1969.

Nosworthy, J. M. "The Narrative Sources of *The Tempest.*" *Review of English Studies.* 24 (1948), 281–294.

Oxford English Dictionary. Second Edition combined with *A Supplement to the* Oxford English Dictionary. Oxford: Clarendon, 1989; reprinted with corrections, 1991.

Palmer, D. F., ed. *Shakespeare:* The Tempest, *A Casebook.* London: Macmillan, 1968.

Pechter, Edward, ed. *Textual and Theatrical Shakespeare: Questions of Evidence.* University of Iowa Press, 1996.

Peterson, Douglas L. *Time, Tide, and Tempest: A Study of Shakespeare's Romances.* San Marino, California: Huntington Library, 1973.

Plotinus: *The Ethical Treatises Being the Treatises of the First Ennead with Porphyry's Life of Plotinus, and the Preller-Ritter Extracts Forming a Conspectus of the Plotinian System.* Trans. by Stephen MacKenna. Boston: Charles T. Branford, 1916.

Purvis, J. S., ed. *The York Cycle of Mystery Plays, A Complete Version.* London: SPCK, 1957.

Quinones, Ricardo J. *The Renaissance Discovery of Time.* Cambridge, Massachusetts: Harvard University Press, 1972.

Rastall, Richard. "Music in the Cycle." In *The Chester Mystery Cycle, Essays and Documents,* edited by L. M. Lumiansky and David Mills. For Early English Text Society. London: Oxford University Press, 1974. Chapel Hill: University of North Carolina Press, 1983. Pp. 114–164.

Righter, Anne Barton, ed. Introduction to *The Tempest* by William Shakespeare. Middlesex, England: Penguin, 1968, 1984.

Rolfe, William J., ed. *Shakespeare's Comedy of "A Midsummer-Night's Dream."* New York: Harper & Brothers, 1889.

Rose, Mark. *Shakespearean Design.* Cambridge, Massachusetts: Belknap Harvard University Press, 1972.

Rose, Martial, ed. *The Wakefield Mystery Plays.* London: Evans Brothers, 1961.

Rust, Paul R. *The First of the Puritans and the Book of Common Prayer.* Milwaukee: Bruce Publishing, 1949.

Schucking, Levin L. *Character Problems in Shakespeare's Plays: A Guide to the Better Understanding of the Dramatist.* Gloucester, Massachusetts: Peter Smith, 1959.

The Complete Works of William Shakespeare, Edited by W. J. Craig. London: Oxford University Press, n.d.

_____. *The Tempest.* Edited by Frank Kermode. Sixth Edition. Arden Shakespeare series. Cambridge: Harvard University Press, 1958.

_____. *The Tempest: A New Variorum Edition.* Edited by Horace Howard Furness. New York: American Scholar, 1966.

_____. *Troilus and Cressida.* Edited by Alice Walker. In *The Works of Shakespeare,* edited by John D. Wilson. Cambridge: Cambridge University Press, 1969.

Shirley, Frances Ann. *Shakespeare's Use of Off-Stage Sounds.* Lincoln: University of Nebraska Press, 1963.

Sisson, C. J. "The Magic of Prospero." *Shakespeare Survey,* II, (1958).

Smith, Hallett, ed. *Twentieth Century Interpretations of* The Tempest: *A Collection of Critical Essays.* Englewood Cliffs, New Jersey: Prentice Hall, 1969.

Smith, Sharon L. "The Commedia dell'Arte and Problems Related to Source in *The Tempest.*" *The Emporia State Research Studies* 13 (1964), 11–23.

Spector, Stephen, ed. *The N-Town Play, Cotton MS Vespasian D.8.* Vol. I. Oxford: Oxford University Press for the *Early English Text Society,* 1991.

Spence, H. D. M. *The White Robe of Churches of the Eleventh Century: Pages from the Story of Gloucester Cathedral.* London: J.M. Dent, 1899.

Stevens, Martin. *Four Middle English Mystery Cycles: Textual, Contextual, and Critical Interpretations.* Princeton, New Jersey: Princeton University Press, 1987.

Still, Colin. *Shakespeare's Mystery Play: A Study of* The Tempest. London: Cecil Palmer, 1921.

Stokes, Francis Griffin. *A Dictionary of the Characters and Proper Names in the Works of Shakespeare with Notes on the Sources and Dates of the Plays and Poems.* London: George G. Harrap, 1924.

Sypher, Wylie. *The Ethic of Time: Structures of Experience in Shakespeare.* New York: Seabury, 1976.

Thomas, Brook. *The New Historicism and Other Old-Fashioned Topics.* Princeton, New Jersey: Princeton University Press, 1991.

Tillyard, E. M. W. *The Elizabethan World Picture.* New York: Vintage, n.d.

_____. *Shakespeare's Last Plays.* London: Chatto and Windus, 1964.

_____. "The Tragic Pattern" (1938). In *Shakespeare:* The Tempest, *A Casebook,* edited by D. J. Palmer. London: Macmillan, 1968. Pp. 122–129.

Traversi, D. A. "The Romances, The Last Plays of Shakespeare." In *Modern Shakespearean Criticism: Essays on Style, Dramaturgy and the Major Plays*, edited by Alvin B. Kernan. New York: Harcout, Brace and World, 1970. Pp. 427–447.

Traversi, Derek. *The Literary Imagination: Studies in Dante, Chaucer, and Shakespeare.* Newark: University of Delaware Press; London and Toronto: Associated University Press, 1982.

Traversi, Derek A. *Shakespeare: The Last Phase.* New York: Harcourt and Brace, 1956.

Truby, Jeffrey. *The Glories of Salisbury Cathedral.* London: Winchester, 1948.

Turner, Frederick. *Shakespeare and the Nature of Time: Moral and Philosophical Themes in Some Plays and Poems of William Shakespeare.* Oxford: Clarendon, 1971.

Vyvyan, John. *The Shakespearean Ethic.* London: Chatto and Windus, 1968.

Wagner, Emma Brockway. *Shakespeare's* The Tempest: *An Allegorical Interpretation.* Edited from manuscript and notes by Hugh Robert Orr. Yellow Springs, Ohio: Antioch, 1933.

Waller, G. F. *The Strong Necessity of Time: The Philosophy of Time in Shakespeare and Elizabethan Literature.* Paris: Mouton, 1976.

Warner, Beverley, ed. *Famous Introductions to Shakespeare's Plays by the Notable Editors of the Eighteenth Century.* New York: Dodd, Mead, 1906. New York: Burt Franklin, 1968.

_____. *Famous Introductions to Shakespeare's Plays by the Notable Editors of the Eighteenth Century.* New York: Dodd, Mead, 1906.

Warton, Joseph. "'Amazing Wildness of Fancy'" (1753). In *Shakespeare:* The Tempest, *A Casebook*, edited by D. J. Palmer. London: Macmillan, 1968. Pp. 37–41.

Watts, Williams, trans. St. Augustine's Confession. London: William Heinemann; New York: G. P. Putnam's Sons, 1925.

Wilson, J. Dover. *The Meaning of* The Tempest. The Literary and Philosophical Society of Newcastle Upon the Tyne, 1936; reprinted, Folcroft, Pennsylvania: Folcroft Library Editions, 1972.

Wilson, Richard, and Dutton, Richard eds. *New Historicism and Renaissance Drama.* London: Longman, 1992.

Woodman, David. *White Magic and English Renaissance Drama.* Rutherford, New Jersey: Fairleigh Dickinson University Press, 1973.

Woolf, Rosemary. *The English Mystery Plays.* Berkeley: University of California Press, 1972.

Young, David P. "*A Midsummer Night's Dream*: Structure." In *Modern Shakespearean Criticism: Essays on Style, Dramaturgy, and the Major Plays*, edited by Alvin B. Kernan. New York: Harcourt, Brace and World, 1970.

Zimbardo, Rose Abdelnour. "Form and Disorder in *The Tempest*"(1963). In *Shakespeare:* The Tempest, *A Casebook*, edited by D. J. Palmer. London: Macmillan, 1968.

Zweig, Stefan. *Conqueror of the Seas: The Story of Magellan.* Translated by Eden and Cedar Paul. New York: Viking, 1938.

Index

201